# TIN PAN ALLEY
## THE RISE of ELTON JOHN

### KEITH HAYWARD

soundcheck books
the stories behind the sounds

First published in Great Britain in 2013 by
Soundcheck Books LLP
88 Northchurch Road,
London,
N1 3NY
www.soundcheckbooks.co.uk

ISBN: 978-0-9575700-0-9

Book design: Benn Linfield  www.bennlinfield.com
Cover design: David Larkham

www.soundcheckbooks.co.uk

Printed by MPG Printgroup, UK

*For my boys,*
*Mark, Steven, William, Teddy,*
*Daniel and Archie,*
*with love*

# CONTENTS

# ACKNOWLEDGEMENTS

This book is not just about the emergence of one of Britain's most accomplished singer-songwriters. It is a history of the music business in the UK, and London's Denmark Street – or Tin Pan Alley, as it was affectionately known, during the 1960s and 1970s – told through the early career of Elton John. This was a landmark period in British music history and a time that will never again be repeated. Being a fan of that era, I wanted to capture the culture, fashion and fads of those times with this book, and it seemed a logical progression to tell the story through Elton's rise to fame.

Although this book is an oral history, many, many more contributed to it in important and significant ways. First, I wish to express my profound gratitude to Phil and Sue Godsell at Soundcheck Books. Beyond those who helped with the mechanics of turning my manuscript into a book are the people who offered information that made the story live and breathe, all of whom knew Elton John at one time or another. I owe tremendous gratitude and thanks to the following: Geoff Dyson, Len Crawley, Roger Pope, Tony Taupin, Peter O'Flaherty, Simon Platz, Pinner County Grammar School Old Students Association, John Wharton, (Krumlin Festival) and Stuart Epps, for letting me use their personal photographs, most of which have never been published anywhere in the world before now. I would also like to thank them for providing me with endless hours of interview material. I must single out Roger Pope for particular praise, as not only was he one of the most prolific drummers in the history of popular music, but he was also a huge inspiration for me to complete this book during the times when I thought I wouldn't. Aside from the fact I became his manager in 2011, he is also a true and valuable friend, alongside his partner Sue Tressider.

I would also like to thank Freddy Gandy for introducing me to Roger and for the valuable material he allowed me to use about the history of Bluesology. The same goes for Mick Inkpen (a real gem of a guy), Geoff Dyson, Bernie Holland and Pete Gavin Rowney whose contribution to that history was more than any author could wish for. I would also like to thank Gary Osborne for his invaluable contribution, his contacts and taking time out from his day job to introduce me to his friends in the music business, and arrange interviews with some of the best known songwriters and music business executives in the music world, and for the all day breakfasts at the local café in Rustington.

Through Gary, I had the opportunity to speak with and interview people like Tony King, Bill Martin, Muff Winwood and David Hockman, who all gave me such invaluable information about the early career of Elton John and Tin Pan Alley; I am still completely bowled over.

I pay tribute to George Hill for not only giving Elton his first gigs at the Northwood Hills Hotel but also for telling me the story. Sadly, George died during the preparation of this book but his legacy lives on in his son Andy. I was simply thrilled to meet Cyril Gee who is still a music publisher to this day and possibly the last of the great publishers of the fifties and sixties who frequented Denmark Street. He gave me a real insight into Tin Pan Alley publishing and Mills Music. I would also like to thank Eric Hall who took time out from his soccer agency and radio shows to tell me about his career at Mills, EMI and Rocket, and who introduced me to Cyril.

To Tony Hiller, who not only gave me an insight into the *Eurovision Song Contest* but what it was like working with publishers as a songwriter during the Tin Pan Alley heyday; and to Tony Hatch and Larry Page who completed the picture regarding the history of Denmark Street. Stephen James was another who gave a valuable insight into the career of his father, Dick James, who, alongside David Platz, was one of the most successful publishers of the time, and who invested time and money to establish the career of a budding singer-songwriter; and to Russ Regan whom I met in Beverly Hills with Paul Buckmaster. Russ told me the story of Elton's early success in America, and Paul about the making of the landmark *Elton John* album and his contribution with Gus Dudgeon to the 'Elton John sound'.

Thank you to all of the 'backroom staff' at Dick James Music whose invaluable descriptions of working for a music publisher made the research come to life, including Victoria Pope, Chrissie Cremore, Sue Ayton and Geoffrey Ellis, (who had first-hand experience of the rise of not only Elton John but also the Beatles).

To others, I remain grateful for making this book more than a pipe dream. They include Nigel Hunter, Graham Boaden, Helen Piena, Caleb Quaye, Chris Charlesworth, Linda Woodrow, Ray Williams, Ian Duck, Dave Glover, Lionel Conway, Brian Keith, Tony Burrows, Roger Greenaway, Robert Fripp, Tony Brandon, Bernie Calvert, Pete Langford, Danny Hutton, Tony Murray and Kirk Duncan, Terry Carty, Sue Cooke, Del Newman, Skaila Kanga, Phil Greenfield, Barbara Moore, John Stewart and Bill Cameron.

I must also express my eternal gratitude to David Larkham. His enthusiasm for this project was matched only by my own. Not only was he one of the first to provide invaluable information about the early career of Elton and Bernie, but when I asked him to design the book jacket he didn't hesitate in saying he would love to – and what he achieved is nothing short of breathtaking.

Finally, thank you to my lovely wife Kelli for her patience, love and support, and for listening to me tell her about each one of my interviews in the greatest of detail.

# PREFACE

I first ventured along Denmark Street in the late spring of 1954. I had completed my two years of National Service in the Army in January of that year and returned to my job of junior library assistant at Fulham Central Library. It didn't take long for me to realise I could no longer stand the tedium of anti-social shift hours or the prospect of studying for the necessary Library Association qualifications to progress in the profession. A move to correspondence clerk at a postal tuition college in Wimbledon also failed to enthuse me.

I was visiting Tin Pan Alley to see Jack Heath, professional manager at Campbell Connelly. Jack was married to a sister of one of my aunts on my father's side of the family and had promised to help, if possible, find me an entry into the music business. Campbell Connelly was at 10-11 Denmark Street, to where it had moved in 1926 a year after being founded in nearby Tottenham Court Road by songwriting friends Jimmy Campbell and Reg Connelly in frustration because no publisher had shown any interest in their song 'Show Me The Way To Go Home'. My audience with Jack proved unproductive on that occasion but I experienced the Alley for the first time.

It had an air of endearing seediness about it and still does, long after the departure of the music publishing fraternity. This is partly because of the antiquity of its buildings (it was laid out in 1687 – named in honour of Prince George of Denmark, who was married to Queen Anne – and eight of its original Georgian properties survive today) and partly because of the persistent tendency of the public to drop litter where and when they please. Space was always at a premium at most of the music publishers in TPA and at Noel Gay Music and Agency at No.19, for instance, some of the secretaries' desks were located in the corridors in days before Elf'n' Safety rules reigned. Noel Gay, aka Reginald Armitage, wrote the music for *Me And My Girl*, notably 'The Lambeth Walk', and for many interwar revues and films as well as the World War II hit 'Run Rabbit Run'. The Noel Gay music catalogue and that of Campbell Connelly have been subsumed beneath the banner of the Music Sales Group.

I organised my own entry into the music business by obtaining a post in the catalogue section of the Decca Records Publicity Department in 1955, followed by a transfer to the sleeve note office. I began freelancing for *Record Mirror*, writing about Latin music and personalities, and then added the title of Tin Pan Alleygator to my activities, a weekly column about current song titles and records, their composers, performers and publishers. I also began compiling programmes of Latin music for BBC radio after knocking on the door many times and I cannot recall whether it eventually opened because I had begun reviewing Latin records for the monthly *Gramophone* magazine or vice versa.

Meanwhile Jack Heath had left Campbell Connelly to launch Good Music with bandleader Ted Heath (no relation) in New Bond Street, as the UK outpost of the World Music group headquartered in Brussels. Good Music obtained the UK rights to España Music and Tropicana Music, two catalogues of Spanish and Latin American music, and Jack, aware of my interest and involvement in those areas, hired me to work the catalogues. Unfortunately Good Music lost the UK rights within a matter of months and I transferred to plugging its pop catalogue with singer songwriter and hand jive specialist Jimmy Jaques. Inevitably the economics of a small publishing company kicked in and I was let go, which caused some tension *chez* Heath as Mrs Jack maintained I was 'family' and shouldn't be treated in such a fashion.

After Good Music, I opted for full-time music journalism and moved from *Record Mirror* to *Disc* where I inaugurated a weekly column called Along The Alley, similar to the Tin Pan Alleygator. As before, this entailed regular visits to Denmark Street (or use of the telephone if the weather was inclement). I was always made welcome although I seldom made specific appointments and tea and coffee (and sometimes something stronger) were readily offered while I was regaled with the latest song wares and publishing gossip. In the 1950s and 60s the short street was a remarkably friendly place with prominent singers and disc jockeys walking along it and being accosted from upstairs windows and invited in to listen to the new songs and records.

Lawrence Wright is generally accepted as the first music publisher to set up shop in Denmark Street. He began in the basement of No.8 in 1911 and after World War I moved to No.19 which he named Wright House. Lawrie was also a very successful songwriter under the pen name of Horatio Nicholls ('Among My Souvenirs', 'Babette') and a great showman and publicist. He used the Blackpool summer season as a regular showcase for his songs with eye-catching gimmicks ranging from camels to aeroplanes. He also founded *Melody Maker* in 1926 with Edgar Jackson as its first editor. Another famous publication still with us in somewhat different format was also born in Denmark Street (at No.5) in March 1952. Maurice Kinn was its founder and he called it *New Musical Express*, more generally known as the *NME*.

The Alley was as famous for its characters as its songs. One of my favourites was Eddie Rogers, an irrepressible individual with a nasal construction reminiscent of Concorde. Eddie had an inexhaustible fund of jokes and anecdotes and I never heard him tell one twice. At the time I knew him he was plugging for Chappell & Co., the oldest UK popular music publisher founded in 1811 by Samuel Chappell and based in New Bond Street throughout its long life until it was purchased by Warner Communications in 1987 to form Warner Chappell.

Teddy Holmes was Chappell's professional manager through mid-20th century times and a hard taskmaster who expected much from his team of pluggers and no excuses. Eddie made history by impressing Teddy so much with the huge amount of airplay he gained for the Henry Mancini-Johnny Mercer classic 'Moon River' that he took the unprecedented step of rewarding Eddie with a bonus cheque. The actual amount was rumoured to vary between a pony (£25) and a ton (£100) but it had never happened before and never happened again to the best of knowledge. Eddie is credited with coining the memorable slogan: 'Art for art's sake, money for Chrissake'.

Watering holes were essential facilities for the thirsty music business. The Royal George was originally a Victorian boozer on Charing Cross Road opposite the western end of Denmark Street but was demolished and rebuilt in the Goslett Yard cul-de-sac off Charing Cross Road in vaguely hacienda architectural style. At the eastern end of the Alley on St Giles High Street stood another 19th century pub called the Crown which was demolished as part of the Centre Point redevelopment. Its modern successor was named the Conservatory and is now the Intrepid Fox transplanted from Tottenham Court Road. The Tin Pan Alley Club has become Bar at No.7 and is no longer exclusive and members only, as it was when it was the Club. The 142 Club around the corner in Charing Cross Road at that number no longer exists.

My perambulations along the Alley in the late 1950s, 1960s and 1970s witnessed an accelerating change in music publishing. The first half of the 20th century saw sheet music and printed song copies reign supreme as the publisher's highly profitable stock in trade. I was amused every year by the Christmas advertisement in *Melody Maker* by F R Walsh, the printed music distributing firm, which annually claimed to be 'the biggest sheet house in the business'. By mid-century the pendulum swung to recorded music and mechanical royalties flowing from huge record sales. Now the scene has changed radically again as record sales decline steeply with the rise of the internet and digitally downloaded music, much of it accessed without payment by younger generations who believe that music should be free and don't realise, or fail to acknowledge, that most songwriters and composers are not multi-millionaire stars like Sir Elton and Sir Paul.

The rock'n'roll explosion in the early sixties and economic pressures changed the face of publishing with famous companies like Francis, Day & Hunter, Feldman, Robbins and Keith Prowse-Peter Maurice (KPM) joining forces under the name of Affiliated Music Publishers which in turn was absorbed into EMI Music Publishing. The latter has now been swallowed into the empire of Sony/ATV Music. Those once well-known publishing names are now only found occasionally on a corporate wall list. Music men (and women) were superseded by lawyers and accountants and much of the old camaraderie disappeared. Ben Nisbet, a soft-spoken Scotsman at Feldman Music and a Deep Purple champion, was particularly critical of the constantly recurring excuse he was given when trying to reach somebody of influence – I'm sorry, he's in a meeting'. I was in his office once when he slammed the phone down in exasperation, glared at me, and said: 'Good grief, now they're having meetings about having meetings'.

There was an enduring sense of fun throughout the approximately 70 years of music publishing history in Denmark Street and surrounding areas. I remember a reception given by Boosey & Hawkes at their Upper Regent Street offices where Ralph Boosey was working the room and welcoming guests. He halted before my comely blonde reporting equivalent from *Record Retailer* and shook her hand. 'Good evening, my dear,' he said. 'I'm Boosey.' Which elicited the response: 'Yesh, sho am I!'

We owe a debt of gratitude to Keith Hayward. In recounting the early days of young Reg Dwight in Tin Pan Alley at the start of his journey to fame and fortune, he has also preserved the heyday of that short, narrow thoroughfare, the names and the atmosphere of a unique business at the height of its success. Those of us privileged to be around in those days can relive the ambience of the TPA Club, Julie's Café, La Giaconda, the pokey little offices and the cluttered equipment of Regent Sound. Those who weren't there then but who pass along the street now looking at the musical instrument shops will require little imagination on their part to picture it as it was through the pages of this book.

*Nigel Hunter*
Music Industry Journalist

# INTRODUCTION

This book is not just an ordinary biography. It is effectively an oral history using interviews conducted over a two year period with just about every musician, producer, sound engineer, manager and key figure that worked with Reg Dwight, before and when he was Elton John, both in Britain and America, up to 1970. It is their story, about how they contributed to the success of Sir Elton during that time, and how Denmark Street in London – Britain's Tin Pan Alley – also played an unwitting part in his rise to fame.

Although it is my name that appears on the cover, it is really their collection of stories that makes this book possible. They were the people who were there, observing what was going on and, in some cases, in close proximity to Sir Elton. It is really is the story of those who still see him as an acquaintance or as a friend. To my knowledge, it is the first time some of them have spoken out about their years working and sharing Sir Elton's life.

This is primarily a book about the man's music, so you won't find too much in the way of gossip of the 'sex and drugs and rock'n'roll' school, unless it is relevant to the making of the music. A quick search on the internet reveals enough tittle-tattle on Sir Elton (some true, some not), to satisfy those with a taste for the sensational and I see little merit in repeating it here.

My own affinity with Elton John goes back as far as some of those of my contributors. I had just turned 11 when Elton released his first album and single. Like all of Britain, I sat transfixed in front of my radio the first time I heard it on Radio Luxembourg, which for most teenagers was listened to under a blanket at night. But when I heard 'Rocket Man' a couple of years later, I was astonished by what I heard because it was such a unique sound. Since that time, and since persuading my younger sister to swap her copy of the record for my 45rpm single of George Harrison's 'My Sweet Lord', I have wanted to know everything there was to know about the man and his music for the period that this book covers. Eventually, my fascination set me on a path to find out more, talk to the people who were involved in helping to create such an impact on my appreciation for music and write about it. The result is this book.

My greatest wish for this book is that Elton's fans will enjoy delving into this full account of what really happened, how, when and where. Certainly it shows a very revealing side to the story of his early life and career in far greater detail than has ever been published previously. But I also hope it will be seen as a definitive account that uncovers the history of 1960s pop music, cultures, fads and fashions, which, in turn, will hopefully appeal to all those who still work in the business, and of course, for those, interested in its history.

Like the 1950s, the 1960s was a unique decade in the world of popular music. My hope is that this book will be a reminder of that time through the words, thoughts and commentary of my collaborators.

*Keith Hayward*
West Sussex

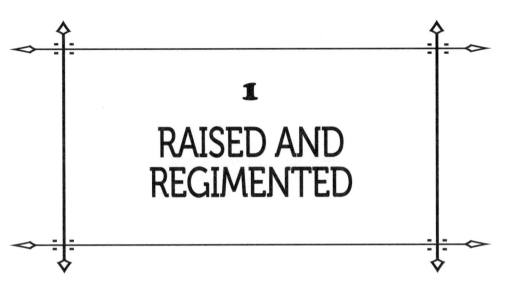

# 1

# RAISED AND REGIMENTED

It's a Monday morning in April 1962 around 7a.m. and normally getting ready for school is nothing more than a tedious chore to be suffered for this teenager. Usually he buries himself beneath the blankets pretending that school doesn't exist until he is more or less prised out of bed, like a limpet from a rock, by one of his parents. But today is different. He literally leaps out of bed and into his uniform.

Reg Dwight has every reason to be excited. The new long playing record by Ray Charles, *Modern Sounds In Country And Western Music*, a studio album of R&B-style covers of country and western songs with Charles' unique take, was released just three days ago and Reg is going to hear it today after school.

His best school friend's sister, Rosalie Boaden, picked up a copy of the album after finishing her Saturday job. Now, on his way home from school, Reg can make a detour and join his other mates, Barry, Tub, Keith and Rick at Rosalie and brother Graham's house to listen to the album before catching the bus back home.

Home was a first floor, two bedroom maisonette situated at Frome Court in Northwood Hills near Pinner, a quiet London suburb. If anything, it was a rather humble place in which to live, accessed by a steep internal single flight of narrow stairs from a front door on the ground floor. The outside resembled a conventional 1930s style semi-detached house and blended well with nearby homes. Even the small parking apron to the front was concealed by a low privet hedge.

Inside the Dwight home there were two bedrooms, both neatly kept by Reg's mother Sheila, each one typically wall-papered and painted in neutral colours by Fred Farebrother, Reg's stepfather, a painter and decorator by trade. Reg's room was equipped with bunk beds and a large storage unit for his constantly growing record collection, which stretched along two walls and almost to the ceiling, at least four albums high. To most, the general impression would be one of an extremely neat, clean and tidily-kept room.

Frome Court wasn't handy for Reg to get to school and the bus ride he had to make every day was, as far as he was concerned, always a long and tedious journey, recalls Graham. 'He would walk to Pinner to catch the 209 bus and then pick up a second bus to where the school was, about half a mile walk from the bus stop.' Graham's house was better situated, being right next to the bus stop and thus ideal for Reg and his mates to have their regular hop off to wait for the bus. It was where they would swap the outside wait for the next bus for a more comfortable wait inside Graham's home.

And what could be a better way to pass the time than to be able to listen to the latest album and single releases of the day? To this day, Graham's sister can remember when Reg came to the house to listen to the Ray Charles album, just a few days after its release. 'I would make tea and coffee for all of them. They used to crowd into the front room, where the gramophone was.' Not that Reg made a daily habit of it, recalls Graham. 'He came in sometimes on the way home, but was always polite and was welcomed.'

What was startling to Graham was Reg's eclectic taste in music. 'He would listen with interest to anything that was put onto the turntable.' Mostly, he was drawn to the pianists like Russ Conway and Winifred Atwell but, according to his mother Sheila, he loved all kinds of music. Today she says, 'I recall lots of Elvis, Bill Haley and Lonnie Donegan, and Little Richard was a big favourite.' But Gary Osborne, one of Reg's later collaborators when he had become Elton John, remembers, 'He also had an almost anorak-like knowledge and appreciation of all facets of the pre-rock British musical landscape of his childhood. Throw a name at him, like Lita Roza, Michael Holliday, Mantovani, Dickie Valentine, Geraldo, Ruby Murray, the Beverley Sisters, the Mudlarks, and he would be able to give you some biographical detail, an opinion and the titles of a couple of numbers made famous by that artist. It was quite amazing for a lad of his age to carry such infinite detail around in his head and then give it out at will.'

To finance his record collecting, Reg did what most kids of his age did in the 1960s to get extra pocket money, which was to work in his free time. For Reg, the ideal weekend job was helping out at the local record store, both on a Saturday and, whenever he could manage it, some weekdays after school.

There was a local school behind his mother's maisonette at Northwood Hills, which Reg might have been expected to grace with his presence; after all, it was only a short walk and two of his pals, Geoff Dyson and Stewart Brown, attended the school. But no, instead of making life simple, he was made to take a six mile hike on two buses to Pinner County Grammar School. But for good reason.

Like most mothers, especially those of an only child, Sheila wanted the best for her son. Besides, he had already passed his 11-plus exams, and so it is understandable that she wanted him to get the finest education possible, which just happened to be at a school six miles away. To many, Pinner County Grammar was regarded as the best in the area. Graham Boaden certainly thought so. 'Most children that joined the school from other schools always said it was the best they had been to.' But there was something far more important to Reg than 'the chore and necessary evil of attending school day in, day out', as he put it, and that was music.

Some of the lessons were held in post-World War II prefabricated units, continues Boaden. 'There were six of them in all, and they were used due to the lack of accommodation in the main school complex, and an all-too familiar lack of money available to warrant the need for any possible extension to the main building. But then again, it was a typically old public school, laid out in a square shape, central quadrangle, corridor with classrooms around it.'

Due to lack of space and the ever-expanding intake of students, they all had to take turns in experiencing the prefab units during lessons. The school was, however, according to those who studied there, a happy place to attend, as long as they kept their noses to the grindstone. As Boaden points out, 'If anyone did misbehave or abuse school rules, they would certainly have faced the wrath of our firm but fair headmaster, Mr Westgate-Smith.'

In other areas of the school, classrooms were surrounded by playing fields, two rugby pitches and a hockey pitch. In those days, rugby was a pivotal part of school life, but not for Reg, who favoured football. Overall, Reg says he had some very happy school years at Pinner and it does seem to have been a remarkably pleasant and stable environment in which to learn.

Reg doesn't seem to have been picked on, bullied or ostracised by his classmates. He sported big horned rimmed glasses in tribute to Buddy Holly, but was generally a quiet, shy boy, who rarely put up his fists in anger. In class he was not known for his academic prowess, either by the teaching staff or other students. If anything, he was always very quiet, sat at the back of the room, and never raised his voice. The occasional tantrums that would later be exhibited as a musician certainly weren't evident in the schoolboy. Nonetheless, he was extremely determined, especially at sports.

'He was never quite good enough to take it further, though,' recalls Boaden. 'Although rugby was the main school sport, he was never that enthusiastic about it.' And even though he did his best whenever he took part it didn't really appeal to him. Football, on the other hand, was one of his favourite pastimes during school breaks, and what he lacked in skill he certainly made up for with his drive, grit and determination. These traits would later serve him well throughout his musical career.

Football was his passion. It would not be unusual for him to travel with his mates to the local club, Wealdstone Town, for whom he had a strong affinity, and, on special occasions, usually when his real father was on leave from his postings in the Air Force, they would go together to watch the local big club, Watford FC. Like most fathers and sons, they would often stand on the terrace come rain or shine (and pay the princely sum of 6p, for the privilege) and, when it did rain, they would grin and bear it. Reg would simply shelter himself under his father's coat, just like any other dad and lad who share a mutual interest.

But Reg's love of football also stemmed from his cousin Roy, whose significant success as a professional player probably inspired him the most. After all, how cool is it to have a famous relation who plays the game for a living? Reg must have been the envy of his mates.

And Roy wasn't just any old run of the mill player either. He scored the first goal in a 2-1 win for Nottingham Forest in the 1959 FA Cup Final against Luton Town at Wembley Stadium, before breaking his leg in the same match. Roy watched the end of the match on TV from a bed in the local hospital. Roy was described as one of the fastest and most tricky wingers in the game, but although his broken leg healed, he was never the same player again.

Although football was Reg's first love, he also played a mean game of tennis. Graham Boaden recounts, 'Most kids could have tennis lessons, especially in the fourth, fifth and sixth years but he was always on the court. He was actually very good at it, and a sport that he still plays to this day as part of his charitable fundraising exploits for the Elton John AIDS Foundation.' And there were many times, Boaden remembers, that they played against each other. 'Once I hit the ball so hard over the net I was surprised he managed to hit it back. He shouted with a satisfied smile, "That was a bit of a cannon ball!" but he got it back and made the point. He was a very good player.'

Even though Reg was totally passionate about football and tennis, it never seemed to match his enthusiasm for the lessons he attended with music teacher, Mr Stoupe, who would eventually introduce him to the Royal Academy of Music.

At that time, London schools could nominate pupils for a Scholarship to the Royal Academy of Music through the London County Council, (LCC), which ran the schools. Luckily for Reg, Pinner School was an LCC School and, according to Stoupe, he had a raw and rare talent. Whenever he would play the piano, Stoupe was in no doubt about his latent talent. The Headmaster also knew about Reg's musical ability and, along with Stoupe, knew that the Scholarships for the Royal Academy of Music would be ideal for Reg to develop his gift further. Indeed neither headmaster nor music teacher had any hesitation in recommending Reg. With recommendation and paperwork completed, Reg was invited to audition.

This must be an ordeal for any 11-year-old, but after showing what he was capable of when it came to playing the piano, plus an oral test, and convincing his auditioners that he had an ear for music, Reg was accepted into the Academy and, as far as he was concerned, he was now on the first rung of the ladder to becoming a professional musician.

Helen Piena, his piano tutor at the Academy, recalls that he was offered a Junior Exhibitionist Scholarship even though he couldn't read music, not even a note. He was chosen, says Piena, because he had such a good ear. She taught him the rudiments of playing the piano but not composition. 'I didn't teach him for composition. He had lessons with a composer for that, but I don't know how he was doing in his other classes at the time. I know his compositions were, and still are, classically based, and that was due to his education at the Academy; he learned a lot about music structure whilst he was there.'

As well as practising the piano, he was also in Harmony classes in Room 114. 'I came to the Royal Academy as a junior Saturday morning student in the early sixties,' recalls Skaila Kanga, a fellow student, and later a principal harp player on Elton's second album. 'He used to always sit at the back, out of the way. We were keen and eager, sitting at the front and swotting, but Reg wasn't like that, he was shy and hid away in this very big room, by the window. He remembers me in that class but I don't have a huge amount of recollection of him because he was so very shy. It was quite a tussle for him. He had such a different way of listening to music, and was playing piano mostly by ear, which was, and still is, his incredible skill, but which the Academy didn't really engender in those days. It was a much more classical training, and for those students who wanted to go down the classical path, it was invaluable.'

Certainly, he didn't seem to be comfortable doing Mozart and Haydn, continues Kanga. 'And so, therefore, the stricture and all the classes that we had were hard for him.' What he could do, however, was play and improvise on what he could remember, which is a phenomenal thing to do, and vital for the route into rock'n'roll music.

'But that,' says Piena today, 'wasn't really what we were learning at the Academy. It wasn't plain sailing for him. I remember on Saturday mornings, he and other very talented children were given scholarships to learn music from the basics upwards. They were given a three quarters of an hour lesson with their principal study, and in Reg's case, this was the piano, and half an hour lesson with a second study. They also had choir practice, orchestra appreciation and oral training, which included reading music and anything else that they wanted to do in music. The young people on the courses would be the only ones to attend the Academy on a Saturday morning, so they took over.'

One thing Boaden remembers was how Reg went to the Academy every Saturday morning, and even during school times, to do exams, but didn't make a fuss about it at all. Nor could he remember Reg ever talking about the Academy or even that he played piano at school. But when he did play the piano at his home in Frome Court, 'It was as if he had a gift. He could play anything he heard with almost perfect reproduction.'

Indeed, Reg was so keen about music, that he would drag himself out of bed at 5.30a.m. on a Saturday morning, no doubt with the assistance of his doting mother Sheila, get dressed in what seemed like a record time, before taking the fifteen minute walk to Northwood Hills tube station to catch the underground train to Baker Street and the hallowed halls of the Royal Academy of Music. There were other occasions when his stepfather would be up early enough to take him in his builders van to the Academy and then hang around until he had finished his lessons. One can only imagine what it must have been like to be in the same place and on the same seat with the same learning process that many famous and professional classical musicians before him had followed.

Helen Piena had only just been appointed at the Academy when Reg was accepted. Her mentor and Head of Department was Margaret Baddington, who had lectured Helen as a student and was, she says, a marvellous role model. As Helen explains, 'In those days, learning music at school was singing songs and learning songs by rote.' Helen had completed the GRSM (Graduate of the Royal Schools of Music) course while Margaret was teaching there and she asked Helen to join her staff at the Royal Academy, 'I couldn't accept because I had a small family, so she said she would wait for me. It just happened that I was ready to join when Reginald Kenneth Dwight was about to start as well.'

It seemed that Helen had finally found what she wanted to do with her life, and that was to dedicate herself to nurturing the talent of young budding musicians like Reg. Like others at the Academy, Helen describes Reg as a talented child and very committed. 'Being an 11-year-old, and getting up early on a cold morning, and always arriving on time was just one of the many commitments he took on in his self-discipline of determination.' Indeed, Helen was very quickly drawn to Reg's commitment, and soon found him to be someone she could work with.

If you asked Elton today about Helen, he would probably agree with that summation, and indeed how fond he was of her. One thing she noticed about Reg was how easy it was to rub along with him. 'If you have someone sitting on a piano stool very close to you for half an hour every week you become very close. I was fond of him from the beginning; he was so obviously committed and good to look at. I remember him as a very loving little boy. When he went on his holidays, for instance, he would always send me postcards full of kisses, and he always used to bring me a present.' The habit of sending postcards would continue into adulthood. It was the same story when he joined DJM Records; he would regularly send postcards to the office girls from wherever he was.

It was during his first lesson that Helen discovered he couldn't read music. Not that she was worried. 'He had this marvellous ear and some time later during his time at RAM, I played some Handel to him, which was four pages long. He played it back to me just like a gramophone record.' With another, more senior, student to take Reg through each lesson, under Helen's instruction, he would learn exactly what she wanted him to do. As Helen says, 'He was a very good pupil, and by the next lesson, he had learnt everything perfectly.'

Reg confided in Helen that his parents' marriage had broken down, and that lack of money was quite an issue in the Dwight household since his father had left. In 1960, Reg's father, Stanley Dwight, who was in the RAF, had received a posting to Harrogate, Yorkshire, but was not accompanied by wife or son – a sign surely that all was not well with the marriage. Whilst there he received a devastating message from Reg's mother that she had met someone else, and wanted a divorce. At first, his father refused to give Sheila the divorce she wanted after she met, and fell for, Fred Farebrother, but relented in 1962. Stanley too found love in the form of Edna, whom he was later to marry and have four children with.

Before the marriage had broken down, Reg had lived in a two up, two down detached house with his parents at 111 Potter Street. If you had visited the Dwight home at that time, you would have found rock'n'roll records by such names as Elvis Presley and Bill Haley, and an old family piano that both his musician father and Reg would practise on as well as playing it regularly at family functions. But directly after the divorce it was different. Reg and his mother went to live with his maternal grandmother at 55 Pinner Hill Road, the place where he was born on 25 March 1947, and where there was no piano. Helen was, excuse the pun, instrumental in getting Reg the much-needed piano on which to practice. Helen wrote to his father who eventually splashed out on one from Hodges and Johnson.

Helen needed to teach Reg to read music. She had no opposition from Reg, as it was something he wanted to do. Although he could easily pass an exam by playing back what he heard, it was no way to teach, or for the youngster to learn. She would give him homework on sight reading music, his weakest area. 'Pupils like Reg were very difficult to teach because they were already so talented, but you just had to go with them really. In Reg, I noticed he could not read [music] so that is what I concentrated on,' Helen remembers.

Throughout the time Reg made the journey to the Academy he never once missed a single lesson. If he had, Helen confirms, he would have been thrown out; there were no second chances at the Academy. The powers that be didn't want the sort of wannabe musicians who could not be bothered to turn up. In fact, Reg was so keen, and Helen so committed to honing his talent, that she used to take him for practice during the school holidays. 'He used to catch a long bus ride to my house where he played the piano in the front room. He played classical piano all the time when he was with me.'

Reg was only a Grade Six when he left the Academy, which according to Helen, wasn't very good. 'There were pupils *starting* at the Academy with a Grade Six at aged 11, and he was 16 when he achieved that grade, and then he left.' On his examination report, the examiner made a negative comment on his scales. Helen wrote a letter of explanation about it to the examiner, which was not something she did for any other student. When the examiner replied, he said, 'Thank you for bringing this (the scales), to my notice. He would be a good pianist if he could practice his scales.' Indeed, when he did leave, Helen recalls how he felt ashamed of his results because, as, far as he was concerned, he felt he had let her down. 'He was a typical teenager,' she affirms. 'What he was playing at the Academy was not what he really wanted to play.'

Reg, of course, could have continued and completed his studies. Normally students who wanted to become professional musicians would stay on at the Academy and move into the senior category, much the same as Skaila Kanga did. 'He didn't want to do this and he left when he was 16 to work in a music publishers,' recalls Skaila.

Helen believes that he would have been good enough to progress to become a senior. 'I was always worried that his talent was so obviously rare, but I couldn't draw it out and one of the things I pride myself with was drawing out talent, but I couldn't do this with Reg. One day, I remember him sitting next to me on the piano stool for a forty-five minute lesson and I was trying to make him say he would go to university but he wouldn't.' He told Helen that, 'None of my family have ever been to university, so I'm not going either.'

Helen was only too aware that from the age of 14, 'Reg had his own group, and had started playing in a pub, where he was playing the music he liked and enjoyed. Academy students are now, and were then, classically minded and, only recently, has the Academy introduced a jazz course, but there was nothing like that back in Reg's time. Jazz was frowned upon and if the Academy had known that he was playing in a band that was jazz-blues based, then he would have likely been kicked out.'

As far as Helen was concerned, classical music was not right for Reg then – and never would be. 'What we were trying to teach him were the foundations of writing, reading and playing music, which he really wanted to do, but the kind of music he was learning was wrong for him, and that was why he left and I can understand that now. When I have a student that is losing interest, as they sometimes do in their teenage years, it becomes too much for them as they need to work harder but, with all the school work they have to do as well, they give up. I tried to give them all the music I loved first: Mozart, Handel, Bach, etc, but this was not the music he liked. In the end Reg didn't do very much study, and this was why he was only put in for his Grade Six, just so he would do some work. It was a very tough exam as it turned out. I don't know how he passed, but I don't think I taught anyone who just received a classic pass, so I think he might have got a merit but not a distinction.'

When Helen met up with Reg, after he had become Elton John, in a moment of reminiscence he told her that she was wrong to teach him Mozart as he couldn't get his fingers around the keys. She replied that she gave him Mozart to practice because he wasn't doing any practice at all and she wanted to interest him. Even though he was a big star by then, she couldn't resist giving him some further advice: 'I told him to learn how to manage your hands, it doesn't matter if you have a big stretch or not, you can still be a world class pianist. And then, when I saw him on television, I was so proud of the way he was sitting at the piano – like the piano and he was one and I had taught him that, together with the art of peddling.'

As she herself admits, 'In classical music the student has to play it as it is written, but the training doesn't enable them to find their own compositions; in fact what it does do is train them to interpret other people's compositions, which is not what Reg was about. To get into the style of Beethoven or Mozart was what the Academy was trying to teach its young students but Reg wanted Elton John's style and personality and that was something, in the future, he would have to fight hard to develop, not only in the Royal Academy but generally.

'It's very easy to be channelled into a set path but much harder to do what Reg set out to achieve. The music business was not about passing exams, there were some students at the Academy who have gone onto to get 90% in their final degree exams but haven't got a job. In the world of popular music it's about finding your own niche and identity; and Reg was on the hunt to find his.'

And, of course, she was right. Most evenings Reg could be found at the local youth club in the church hall, about 500 yards from his front door. It was an ideal place for him to play the piano and meet other musicians. Like most youth clubs of the period, the church hall was a cavernous place with three table tennis tables and a piano, but little else. It was also perfect for meeting other like minded musicians and to have the opportunity to play together. And for Reg, that was far more important than playing classical music.

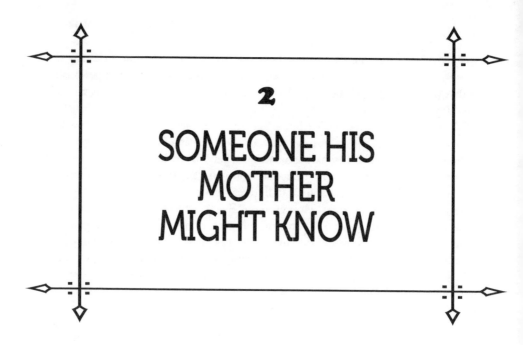

# 2

# SOMEONE HIS
# MOTHER
# MIGHT KNOW

The first time Reg met Mick Inkpen was at the local church hall in Pinner in about 1962. Like Stanley Dwight, Inkpen's father was also a musician, an accomplished violinist, so it wasn't surprising that Mick grew up committed to the idea that he would follow in his father's footsteps, though on a different instrument. It was only when he decided that he would become a drummer that he found himself in much the same position as most other drummers starting out, looking for a snare drum and a cymbal. He would eventually find both at a local thrift shop that sold second-hand musical instruments.

With some practice behind him, the next step was to try and find gigs. His own recollection of how he got things going was to turn up and ask any likely bands-to-be whether they needed a drummer. He got to play with one or two guys, building a reputation locally as a drummer, and ended up playing in most of the local youth clubs in Reg's manor.

'I was always making a nuisance of myself on the drums, and Reg was doing the same with his piano playing, so the pair of us would usually be relegated to the back room where we could thump the most out-of-tune and disreputable piano ever seen. Even so we still went in there and played whatever we could find, be that a piano or some other beaten up old instrument.' Reg, he remembers, would play a bit of Beethoven and then go into Winifred Atwell, and imitate other pianists of the day: 'There was a lot of fooling around.'

Whether fooling around or not, it wasn't long before Inkpen had become friendly with the lead singer of the Phantoms, a local band who had quite a following. They were the first band to generously allow Inkpen and his two pals to play during the interval at some of their gigs. 'We had half an hour to do our stuff and it was scary, especially when you are 14 years old and you don't know what you're doing, but that was the way you started in those days. There's no point in playing in some tiny back room, hiding and not being heard, you have to go out and perform live in front of an audience.

In time, however, Inkpen soon came to the conclusion that the other guys in his band weren't much cop. The only one who stood out, he remembers, was 'Rex Bishop, a tall, good looking bass player who seemed to know exactly what he was doing. He had a nice sound and he learned quickly, and he became a pretty accomplished player.' It also helped that Bishop liked what Inkpen was doing, which is pretty vital for a rhythm section. 'The band wasn't going anywhere, they spent all of their time just rehearsing and there is only so much rehearsing you can do. You have to get out there and play a gig every now and again, or it all just falls apart.'

In the same period that Inkpen and Bishop were pulling their hair out over not going anywhere fast, Reg had formed an alliance with two pals, Geoff Dyson and Stewart Brown, who went to Northwood School, and whose playing fields backed onto Reg's maisonette. They had been pals from the age of 12 onwards, and were both in the same year at school, and had a shared interest in the same type of music. Brown had been learning to play guitar since he was 12 and clearly had a natural aptitude. He involved Dyson in his enthusiasm for music by teaching him chords and the rudiments of guitar playing. They formed a band, just a normal school combo, made up of Brown, Dyson and two other boys from the school, one of whom would play an extremely important part in what was to happen next. As well as being a drummer, his father owned The Gate pub at the bottom of Mount Vernon Hill in Northwood, where the band rehearsed. And although the bar was equipped with a piano, the boys had no-one to play it.

They had pretty much everything else necessary; even a name for themselves. They would call themselves the Corvettes, the name of which was taken from the popular *Route 66* television series. It followed the exploits of a couple of guys driving around the American countryside in a Corvette, which Dyson and Brown thought was a really cool idea. In the early days of getting his band together, Dyson was still learning the guitar and was also the vocalist for the band, whilst Brown did his own thing on guitar.

But, as Dyson remembers, 'We were a very amateurish setup, and not surprising really as the members of the band were no more than 14 years old at the time. We did some rehearsing at the Northwood School with Mr Blake, a forward-thinking music teacher who encouraged us no end. He was a great fan of jazz, and Duke Ellington in particular, and he encouraged us to play that style of music. He would teach us the difference between good and bad music and, yes, he was the driving force for both me and Stuart. But due to my lack of vocal ability, I was introduced to this bespectacled piano player who turned up at The Gate and was introduced to us by Stuart. It was obvious that he could play the piano, but even better, he could also hit the notes vocally that I couldn't get to.'

Brown had previously been introduced to Reg by his female cousin, who was going steady with Brown at the time. Brown had told her that he was forming a band and needed a piano player and she told him about Reg. 'I personally couldn't believe my ears that this young guy could play the "grown up" style of piano that he was playing; it was strident, rock'n'roll piano and he had a real personality that came over in his performance.' One of the songs Reg played was 'Great Balls Of Fire', the 1957 Jerry Lee Lewis hit from the film, *Jamboree*, and it completely blew the rest of the band away.

One of the downsides though was Reg's image. The others in the band thought he was a rather straight looking guy, and didn't really fit in with the cool look of the rest of them – or at least in their opinion. He had round glasses, a short haircut and grey flannel trousers, but he really knew his piano chops and when he did play a remarkable transformation took place, remembers Dyson. 'He really did change when he was playing piano; he was not boring at all. When he got down on a piano and started to sing and play rock'n'roll, he was quite remarkably transformed into someone else.'

From that moment onwards, Dyson took over on guitar, and Reg got the vocal duties. Knowing that Brown was a much better guitarist than he was, Dyson saw his opportunity to establish his own niche in the band by buying a Vox bass guitar for twenty pounds from a school chum who had lost all interest in the instrument. By the time the newly formed Corvettes had progressed from the rehearsal room in the pub to the school music room, the band were able to use a proper-sounding piano and take advantage of music teacher Blake in the background, who was always on hand to offer advice and encouragement.

The band members were young and pretty naive when it came to playing live music and Reg was the most experienced amongst them. 'We all looked up to him as being much more accomplished in his art than we were,' recalls Dyson. And certainly he was right. To start with, Dyson was still learning the bass guitar from Brown, who would teach him to play the instrument in his bedroom, or in Dyson's family home. 'We used to practice together and that worked quite well, but neither of us had a piano, so we had to wait until we could get to the school music room or where we rehearsed at the pub.'

Compared to Reg and Brown, Dyson's early playing, as he freely admits, was not that accomplished. It was, he says, basic two-note bass. All the same, they used to meet up twice a week for rehearsals, and would soon start to play gigs in school halls and youth clubs at least once a fortnight, if they could get the bookings. In fact, it was during their rehearsal periods, in the comfort of the Northwood School Music Room, under the guidance of Mr Blake, that they were introduced to rock'n'roll, the most popular of the musical genres at that time.

But there was a problem. Considering the boys' relative inexperience, it was never going to be rock'n'roll in anything other than in its rawest form. They selected songs from the catalogues of such artists as Little Richard, Jerry Lee Lewis and Cliff Richard. 'Move It' was one of their favourites, simply because Brown could play the now-famous guitar intro, which many musicians still can't manage to this day. It was probably the only British rock'n'roll record that they included in their act as most tunes they were performing had originated from places like Memphis and Nashville in America.

Perhaps what is incredible to look back on now, is how Reggie, as he was then known to the rest of the band, performed the piano pieces almost note for note. Well, almost, according to music teacher Blake, who would usually be seated at the back of the music room during their rehearsals, listening and watching their performance.

As far as the gigs themselves went, they were few and far between, perhaps two a month, if they were lucky; usually at youth clubs either in Pinner or Northwood. The very first gig they played was at a church hall in Northwood Hills, when the nascent showman in Reg came to the fore. 'That was the first time that Reggie stood up and kicked the piano stool away during "Great Balls Of Fire" and played standing up for the first time, which he had never done in rehearsals. It was like watching Jerry Lee Lewis and, yes, it shocked us to the core, but it gave great credence to our band,' remembers Dyson.

Getting the gigs though, was another story entirely. Usually, Brown would simply call up an organiser and ask for a booking. From this rather basic method of putting the band up for hire, they ended up playing end of term school concerts, usually at Northwood Secondary School but, strangely enough, never at Reg's school in Pinner. As Dyson points out, the gigs were not always that easy to find, even if they were just youth clubs, church halls and schools. 'We always had to try and find gigs that had a piano, and more often than not, even if we did find a venue that had one, it was usually pretty battered and out of tune, mainly because it had been moved around the stage so much and the keys were rickety, missing or stuck.'

'On top of that,' continues Dyson, 'we didn't really make any money out of playing live either. If we made £5, we were pretty pleased with ourselves, but usually it was for a cola each. The most embarrassing thing about the Corvettes live gigs was that most of the pianos were out of tune in the places we played. It must have sounded pretty awful, but the kids liked it because it was live music and there just wasn't so much around back then. I think it also helped that we could play the music that the kids were listening to.'

In the early days of the band, it was Brown, remembers Dyson, who chose the set list, but as they progressed, and because Reg was such an accomplished pianist and vocalist, he subconsciously swayed the band into playing more of the heavy rock'n'roll material that was doing the rounds at the time. For whatever reason, the Corvettes didn't stay together for very long and eighteen months after they had started, they disbanded. 'We were about 15 and during those eighteen months we must have played between eight and fifteen gigs. We were just learning our instruments really, and having fun, getting together and fooling around with music. We sort of fizzled out, probably because we all left school, and we were not seeing each other on a regular basis anymore,' says Dyson.

After the break up of the Corvettes, Reg still kept up his musical interests and landed himself a regular gig at the Northwood Hills pub, a 1930s style hotel, opposite Northwood Hills tube station. It was where he would become the resident piano player bashing out honky tonk hits and songs from his Winifred Atwell songbook. He would play the old standard upright piano in the public bar, as the saloon bar had a more refined clientele. 'It had remnants of furniture rather than the full thing, probably due to the regular fighting on a Saturday night,' smiles Mick Inkpen. Not the most auspicious place in the world but it paid Reg enough money to continue adding to his record collection.

'The customers' reaction in the pub was like most live music in pubs in those days, mostly positive to Reg playing the piano. If he played anything that they knew, they would sing along to it, especially towards the end of the evening when they'd had a few drinks. It was a fairly jovial affair,' reflects Dyson.

Reg played every Saturday and Sunday evening and, of course, the odd scrap broke out. Not that he was particularly worried, having already built up a quite a fan club in the guise of a family of gypsies who befriended him. He played their type of songs and they accepted him as one of their own. On several occasions, according to legend, the gypsies stopped Reg from coming to harm when fights had broken out. On one occasion, they took him through the window with his equipment to shepherd him from trouble. 'We were also under age so we kept our heads down and did not really get too involved,' laughs Dyson. 'But the trouble, luckily, didn't happen very often.'

Although they weren't playing music together, Reg still kept in touch with Inkpen, Brown and Dyson, who remembers meeting up at the Northwood Hills pub on a regular basis. 'I would go up there with friends and sit at the table next to the piano. He [Reg] would play all sorts of stuff but mainly it was honky tonk pub piano music. He made a lot of friends during the gigs. There was, I remember, a very nice looking gypsy girl who came to a couple of gigs with Bluesology. No one was ever sure what sort of relationship it was though, and it eventually fizzled out.'

Not that George Hill, the landlord of the Northwood Hills, remembers Reg being an instant hit: far from it. Even though, he had been responsible for booking Reg for his first live gigs, he has quite a different recollection of Reg's exploits.

By the time Reg started playing at the pub, Hill had cleaned it up quite considerably and it was considered a respectable place to go. 'I can recall the occasional fight when I first took over, but I dealt with those pretty promptly, so by the time Reg arrived, the clientele were not the fighting type.' As far as Hill was concerned, the stories of Reg being scrambled out through a window with his gear to keep him out of trouble, have become part of the mythology. Likewise, Hill couldn't recall any Gypsies coming into the pub. 'It was not the type of clientele I wanted to encourage, however I do recall that Gypsies were always on the Green, near the pub, so maybe that is where the stories came from.'

Reg also continued to rehearse inside the pub on a Sunday, firstly by himself, and then with Bluesology. When the band first started, 'He was writing songs,' said Hill. 'And then, he started to write and rehearse in the public bar on the upright piano when the cleaner was around. He used to tape the songs and give them to the cleaner to take home to listen to, he even wrote a song about my wife.'

Before going to the Northwood Hills, Hill was the landlord of The Hare in Stanmore, North London, where he engaged a blind albino pianist nicknamed Albino Bob. 'He was a fantastic pianist. He just turned up one day with his white stick and started playing the honky-tonk style piano.' Bob stayed with Hill at The Hare for about five years until Hill moved to the Northwood Hills, with his family, in 1963. 'When I moved to the Hills, Bob just followed me there. Everyone just loved him, but the travelling got too much, so he said he had to pack it in.'

Soon after Albino Bob had jumped ship, Reg, or his parents, must have heard about his departure, and decided to visit the pub one evening, to see if there was an opening for their young son, who desperately wanted to play the piano in front of a live audience. 'Reg turned up with his stepfather and mother and she asked if he could play,' said Hill. 'They weren't regulars in the pub but they must have heard that Albino Bob was no longer playing there'.

Despite giving him a chance, Hill wasn't that impressed with the young schoolboy at first, and didn't think he was as good as Albino Bob. However, his wife persuaded him otherwise, and Reg ended up with three sessions a week, on a Wednesday, Thursday and Saturday, earning the princely sum of £1.10s per session. On top of that, he was also allowed to practice in the pub on a Sunday, provided he didn't disturb Hill who took the opportunity, like the Good Lord, to have a nap on the Sabbath.

Even with practice, it took some time before the regulars accepted Reg and his style of playing piano. And when you consider it was mainly a middle-aged crowd who were set in their ways, it's not surprising that many considered Reg a poor substitute for their favourite pianist. 'Albino Bob was a hard act to follow and Reg was not received very well at first and must have felt quite intimidated by all the negative response,' continues Hill. One regular, in particular, a guy called Charlie Furnish, a gardener, who held sway over the others regulars, persuaded them not to be impressed with the new kid tickling the ivories. 'My wife insisted that he was good, and eventually Charlie and the crowd came round and started to enjoy his playing.' Once Reg had got them all involved in sing-alongs to pub standards, the bar soon started to get packed again.

In addition to the piano, Hill also provided Reg with a microphone and speakers, so that he could be heard over the din of the bar. At the end of the evening, Mary Whitmarsh and Toby Barry used to take a tin tray around to all the customers and get him some tips. During the couple of years that Reg played at the pub, his mother and stepfather dutifully sat in the corner having a drink watching their son playing and seeing that he came to no harm. They would normally help him to set up the equipment and then dismantle it at the end, before embarking on their short journey back to Frome Court in Fred's van.

At the time, Reg was saving up to buy an electric piano but his impatience was getting the better of him. 'He asked me if he could borrow £200,' recalls Hill. 'I couldn't afford to give it to him, so I refused.' Although it would have been hard going, Reg, of course, did eventually save enough money to buy himself the Hohner Pianette that he was so desperate for. If anything, it was a crude instrument that sounded like a piano which, in the end, replaced the piano that was in the pub. It seems incredible to look back on now but, at age 17, Reg had left school after deciding that 'A' level music was not necessary to further his career in the music business. With the headmaster's permission, Reg left just before he completed his exams and headed off to join the hustle and bustle of the real music business in London's Tin Pan Alley, renowned as the place to be if you wanted to be part of the record industry in Britain. Reg, it seemed, was on the way to finding his spiritual home.

# 3
# FROM PINNER TO TIN PAN ALLEY

Mills Music was an American music publishing company, owned by song publishers, Jack and Irving Mills. They set up offices in 1954 in London, just off Charing Cross Road in the West End, at 20 Denmark Street, or Tin Pan Alley, as it was affectionately nicknamed after its American counterpart on Manhattan. Jack and Irving had a long affinity with music. Irving was the showman of the pair, having been responsible for the careers of musicians like Duke Ellington and Fats Waller, whilst Jack had the business head.

With their HQ in New York ensuring visiting musical talent was often flying in and out of the British capital, it was an ideal place for Reg to cut his teeth. Not only would he have the opportunity to meet both American and British songwriters and recording artists coming in and out, but it placed him firmly at the centre of the music business in Britain. It also helped that he was rubbing shoulders, albeit briefly, with the same artists and songwriters whose music he adored and collected.

Paul Simon was one of those, and a frequent visitor to London. On one occasion, he had been hawking two songs around every music publisher up and down Denmark Street. One was 'The Sound Of Silence' and the other was 'Homeward Bound.' Not that he would have any success in flogging them. Most publishers, including Mills, turned his songs down, saying they were not commercial enough, and sent him packing back to the States. As Simon quickly discovered to his cost, much the same as Reg would over the next few years, songwriters working out of Tin Pan Alley, were, more often than not, writing material for established artists, shows and musicals. In 1964, strangely enough, the business didn't accommodate new, young and fresh songwriters like Simon, even though it was only one year way from Simon having the last laugh and taking both songs to the top of the charts with his partner Art Garfunkel.

In the same year that Simon had his songs turned down, Reg landed a job working in the Trade Department of Mills Music for a weekly salary of £5. One of his main duties was to deliver sheet music to publishers, distributors and sellers. He had been hired by Cyril Gee, then the managing director of Mills Music, who had started his career in music publishing at Ascherberg, Hopwood & Crew. They were based in Mortimer Street in London, and had become well known for publishing 'The Skaters Waltz', coincidentally one of the songs Reg first cut his teeth on.

But it all started by accident, explains Gee:

At the end of 1941, our school got bombed and we were told that they would let us know when they could put another school together. This was made worse by a lot of the teachers being called up to serve in the war. My father said to me, if you think you are going to hang around doing nothing, then you must think again. I was 14 years of age and able to leave school, so on 14 January 1942, my father took me to the West End of London to find me a job. We went up during that week and we walked up Wells Street off Oxford Street and there was nothing available, so my father said 'We will walk back to Bloomsbury and catch the trolley bus back home from Bloomsbury Square.' As we were walking back, there was this shop which had a couple of pieces of music in the window but we couldn't see much else as it was all boarded up because of the war. On the window was a sign saying 'Boy Wanted' so my father said 'Go on then' and I went in and spoke to the manager, and he gave me the job to start the following Monday on 21 January. And that chance opportunity was how I started a career that spanned the next 70 years, and still continues to this day.

Gee was employed as an office boy working in the Trade Department, which involved putting together orders for sheet music during the war, much the same as Reg would do over twenty years later. 'The guy who was running the Trade Department was called up for service,' continues Gee. 'There were two older people working there as well, a woman called Emily and a man called Bill. The MD asked them if they could keep the whole thing going, but both said no. He then called me into his office and said "Cyril, do you think you could help us out?" I gladly agreed, so I was running the Trade Department at 14 years of age.' He stayed for another ten years and enjoyed a fantastic relationship with the MD Walter Eastman, who told him that he would make him a publisher. 'He took me into the accounts department, copyright, royalties and I even went out on the road doing promotions and selling sheet music.'

And then, in 1952, he was offered a job with Campbell Connelly and entered the world of Denmark Street at number ten. 'I stayed there for about two years until 1954, when I decided I wasn't happy. I went into the office one Friday and said I was handing in my notice. I didn't have another job, but I didn't want to stay somewhere where I wasn't happy.' It just so happened that Mills Music had just set up shop in Denmark Street at number twenty.

'A guy called Ben Nisbet, who eventually took over the running of Francis, Day & Hunter, asked me what I was doing. I told him I had given in my notice and I hadn't got a job. I said I was fed up with working for someone who I didn't get on with, I want to go freelance.' By this time, Gee had learned most aspects of the publishing world and had developed into a good seller of sheet music. Nisbet suggested that he give Mills Music a try.

'He told me they were just moving in and they may want somebody, so I went across and told them that I wanted to be freelance in sales, and we came to an agreement on salary and commission and what they wanted me to do and, so, I became a salesman for Mills Music. I did promotion and sales work mainly in the north of England and that's where I got to know Joe Loss very well, who was playing in Glasgow and in Blackpool at the Tower Ballroom,' Gee recalls.

He eventually took over as general manager, and then as managing director at Mills in 1958 on £35 a week, which gave him a good living wage from which he was able to buy a house and marry his wife Ruth, who also worked at Mills Music in the accounts, copyright and royalties office. 'Walter Eastman helped me get the job as managing director. When Jack Mills found out I had worked for him, he said to me "If Walter Eastman thinks highly of you, then that's O.K. by me." It was only later that I found out that Jack had worked with Eastman and thought very highly of him.'

Although there have been numerous different versions over the years as to how Reg landed the job at Mills, the true version has never been told which, in many ways, was literally down to a series of circumstances. A young man called Eric Hall had been given the job as office boy at the age of 15 having been introduced to Mills Music by his uncle, Tony Hiller. When Eric was sacked, due to a misdemeanour over an incident involving Gee's bowler hat, he was replaced by Reg.

As Hall himself explains, things went wrong for him the day Gee spotted him with a pile of 78rpm records and a bowler hat, and told him to pack them well, and then take them to the post office immediately as the parcel needed to be back with Jack Mills in America as soon as possible. Hall got the wrong end of the stick and packed the hat in with the records.

'I was never a very good packer, but I packed this parcel and took it to the post office as instructed and went back to Mills. Cyril's secretary, Jo Wright, asked me whether Cyril had left his bowler hat in the trade department earlier in the day. I denied seeing it which was the wrong thing to do because a few days later the parcel came back with the bowler hat in it. What made things worse was that all the records were smashed and the bowler hat was in tatters. With that, Fred Hartnell, the head of the Trade Department, sacked me. Not for the damage to the records or the bowler hat, but because I had lied to Jo Wright. If I had told the truth, no, Cyril probably wouldn't have been happy about it, but he would have laughed and called me a stupid boy. I was sacked on the Friday, and Reg started the following Monday.'

But it wasn't Hartnell who hired Reg, explains Gee. 'My professional manager was Pat Sherlock, who I had known since his days at Leeds Music. He said to me that there was a kid who was wandering around Denmark Street knocking on doors looking for a job, and had we got anything for him. Fred had just sacked Eric and had an opening in the Trade Department so I said O.K., we could do with someone, a youngster, in the Trade Department and that was to become Reggie Dwight. I believe Pat already knew Reggie's father from his love of football, and so it was his father who recommended Reg to Pat as someone who really wanted to work in the music business.'

After his dismissal from Mills, it didn't take Hall long to find another job, especially since his uncle knew a lot of people in the business. 'After Reg took my job, I got one in the Trade Department next door at 21 Denmark Street at Lawrence Wright Music. I used to pack parcels, take the tea urn to Julie's café and fill it up, get sandwiches for the staff, much the same as Reg was doing next door at Mills. My ambition was just to work in the music business but Reg wanted to be a star, and he would talk about it all the time and always wanted to play the piano.

'I remember in the reception of Lawrence Wright Music there was a receptionist who worked an old telephone exchange and opposite her was an upright piano. I used to meet Reg once or twice a week for lunch and he would come and meet me and sit at the piano and play. My boss, Sid Richardson, in the Trade Department used to hate it, and say to me, "Get him out of here, he can't play the piano," and I used to tell him what a good player he was, and that he should allow him to play, but in the end, Reg got banned from coming to Lawrence Wright Music.'

According to Hall, Reg would often be getting the teas for the office staff and guests from Julie's café, and was a good packer of sheet music. But it wasn't all work, work, work. In their lunch hours, they would hang out with other soon-to-be famous names who were also working for music publishers in Denmark Street. People like Davie Jones, who later became David Bowie, and Steve Marriott, who eventually found fame as the lead vocalist with the Small Faces and later Humble Pie. 'Yeah, we were all similar ages, so we would always meet up and go to the Giaconda café or up to Julie's café for some spaghetti, egg, chips and beans,' says Hall.

Even though Gee had sacked Eric Hall, he always tried to be thoughtful towards the staff and make sure it was a fun place to work, and that, he reflects, 'Served me well for 70 years in the business. They worked hard and I made sure they did their work and didn't take advantage of me or the company, but they were a happy crowd. I believe that people work harder if they enjoy their work and so that is what I tried to create at Mills even though we still had to make money for the owners. I like to think I helped people to establish careers in music publishing. Reg was a pushy little kid, but I always treated him well and he thanked me for that. He did anything that he was asked from packing up sheet music to running errands and taking the jug across to Julie's café in Denmark Street to fetch the tea.'

When Pat Sherlock left Mills, Cyril Gee decided to give Eric Hall's uncle, Tony Hiller, his job and so, in effect, he became Reg's new boss and the head of the Trade Department. 'He became the promotions guy and he got to know everyone as that was the sort of guy he was. Interestingly enough, he used to be a taxi cab driver in London and used to pick up Walter Eastman of Ascherberg's every day at 4p.m., and now he was working for me as a songwriter and later as the Promotion guy at Mills Music. Publishing in those days was such a small world.'

Hiller agrees. And certainly about Reg. 'The orders for sheet music would come in from Cyril, and Reg would run up and down to his office to collect the orders, and then make them up ready to take to the other publishers in the area. Usually it would be thirty songs at a time. All he really did was deliver sheet music.'

In those days, sheet music was bigger than records. 'It was big business at the time,' says Hiller today. But Reg was a good worker and did his job diligently. 'What he enjoyed most, though, being an ardent soccer fan, were the times when the Chelsea Football Club players used to visit me at Mills Music virtually every day at lunch time. He loved football, and was always knocked out when he met players like Terry Venables, John Hollins and Peter Osgood. This was one of the highlights of his day. He would always scurry off and make me and all the players a cup of tea. He was a talented boy and a great impressionist. He was always laughing and was a lovely kid.'

Overall though, one of the main roles that Mills Music played in Denmark Street was to construct the sheet music arrangements for bands' broadcasting light music, explains Gee. 'We did a lot of light music and we published for all of Leroy Anderson's piano music and so, of course, there were a lot of the light orchestras playing Leroy Anderson piano music, like 'Belle Of The Ball', 'Blue Tango' and 'Serenata'. Also songwriters came in with a manuscript and demonstrated the song by playing it on the piano, but I also used the arrangers who would take the music down if they couldn't write themselves. We had three staff arrangers, Jones, Baker and Williams who all had pianos in their offices. But no one quite as pushy as Reg.' He can still remember the day when Reg approached him to ask a favour.

'My office door was open always unless I had an important call to Jack in America or had a visitor. To get to my door you had to go through my secretary's office. As soon as I had finished, I opened my door and if my secretary's door was open I had time to talk to the staff. Reg came to me one day and said would it be possible for him, when the arrangers were out at lunch, to practice piano? I said as long as you get permission from the particular arranger whose office you are going in and do not touch anything that they were working on, then it was fine. That was the first thing that indicated to me that he could play music.'

Someone else who agrees with all that is said about Reg was Caleb Quaye. Like Reg, he also had aspirations to become a professional musician as a teenager, so they immediately had something in common. It also helped that they were both working in the music business; Quaye at Paxtons, and Reg at Mills. They first met in the winter months of 1964 during one of Quaye's rounds delivering sheet music. 'I was introduced to him by a guy who showed me the rounds called Nigel, who worked for Paxtons, and he took me to Mills to deliver some sheet music. The first thing Reg said to me was "Do you want a cup of tea?" which I thought was very nice of him and, from there, we just hit it off.' To this day, Quaye remembers him as a very funny guy, one whom he always made a point of meeting up with during his rounds of delivering sheet music. If nothing else, he knew he could always stop off at Mills and get a cuppa off Reg.

Unlike most of their school mates, they were doing something that other school leavers could only dream of: they were soaking up the atmosphere of the music business, talking about music and always swapping opinions about what the other one was listening to. 'We were right in the middle of the music industry by default. Even though we were both doing menial work, we knew about the latest stuff coming out,' recalls Quaye. Sometimes they would use their lunch hours to meet up and go to Francis, Day & Hunter which was just around the corner from Denmark Street in Charing Cross Road, opposite the Astoria Theatre.

The record department at Francis, Day & Hunter probably carried the biggest stock of vinyl in London at that time. Not only that, but they also had listening booths where you could ask for records to be played without any intention of buying them until the staff got irritated and chucked you out. It seemed as if the entire shop floor had been taken up by racks of record sleeves on one side of the ground floor, and sheet music on the other. The albums covered every genre of music imaginable, from original soundtracks and cast albums of films and musicals to the latest pop, blues and jazz releases, the stuff that Reg and Caleb were interested in. It was the sort of place where you could get hooked on the smell of the vinyl and the clarifoil laminate of the record sleeves. It was like going into a guitar shop and immediately being hit by the aroma of the wood and varnish of having so many instruments in one place, all made out of the same materials.

'We were on top of all the latest records, singles and albums that were coming out,' remembers Quaye but, as he explains, 'We were very lucky as I had an old school friend who worked at the store. He would share all the latest music biz news with me, and even divulged what was coming out, and when it would be in stock, so we could go and listen to it as soon as it was released. American Rhythm 'n' Blues was the latest thing in the States, but in the UK, it was very much the underground music, even though its influence was huge. We were probably among the first to hear it before it got out to the mainstream record collectors.'

For Reg, working in the trade department of a music publisher wasn't like any other job. It wasn't like being trapped in an office for eight hours each day, or stuck in a factory or a shop. His average day would have probably have started around ten in the morning and finished about six in the evening. And where else could you turn up to work and head off to the café next door for a bacon sandwich and coffee, minutes after you had clocked in, and before you had done any work?

It was much the same during the afternoon, when returning from their rounds of delivering sheet music to shops and distributors in the heart of Soho, beyond the strip joints, most of the post boys and packers from Denmark Street would grab an extra tea break at the Giaconda café. Not surprising really, as it was then the most popular hangout for musicians, bands and talent spotters. But the post boys had to be careful not to be spotted skiving by their bosses.

On the same side of the street as the Giaconda, and opposite most of the publishers, was Regent Sound, where the Rolling Stones would cut their first album in 1964, and where there was always a steady flow of staff from the publishers popping in and out to have tapes cut onto acetate discs, which were usually needed for demo or evaluation purposes. Was the song good enough for recording or publishing? And was it good enough for an A side of a single, a B side or an album track?

After a few months, Quaye left Paxtons and went to work for Dick James Music. Although the DJM office and studio was just around the corner from Denmark Street in New Oxford Street, it meant that Reg and Caleb wouldn't see so much of each other. Soon after Caleb had left Paxtons, Reg left Mills to join Bluesology, so it became even less likely they would bump into each other. But they did, by chance, quite unexpectedly one morning in Denmark Street, just before Reg went on the road with his new band, as Caleb recalled:

> As we hadn't seen each other for a while, we were pleased to meet and asked each other what the other was doing. He said he had formed a new band. As I was interested to hear more, I asked him what the band was called, and he said Bluesology. I just laughed. He was offended when I did that, but to me it sounded pretentious. I knew a tune by Django Reinhardt called 'Bluesology' which was a cool tune, so I thought 'What are you doing calling yourselves Bluesology after a tune like that?' It didn't make sense to me and so I laughed, but he didn't like that.

In many ways, what Reg and Caleb left behind in Tin Pan Alley was, first and foremost, a family atmosphere. Whether you worked at a music publisher, in a recording studio, café or guitar shop, everyone knew everyone else and would share the ups and downs of the business together.

'It was like a village in itself,' says Cyril Gee. 'A crowd of us used to meet in Julie's café, which was on the same side as Mills Music but towards St Giles; you'd sit at any table you like, as there were no reservations but you couldn't talk privately. There were so many people who came down to Denmark Street: people selling songs and artists wanting to buy songs; they would all come into the cafés and we all knew each other. We were competitors but we were all friends. There were three or four of us in particular that used to meet especially on a Thursday morning after Maurice Kinn, editor and owner of the *New Musical Express*, had put the paper to bed and finished it. There were three of us, including Dick James, who would meet up and would talk about anything and everything, whether it was the state of the music business or the latest political issue.'

'Yes, it was very much like that, like a family,' agrees Hiller. 'Although we would celebrate the sale of a song together, we would also compete against each other to sell one.'

Tony Hatch was introduced to the music business and worked in Tin Pan Alley for three years from 1955 onwards. Not that he had any plans to end up there when he was younger. 'I went to choir school at the age of 10. My mum was so anxious that I should sing in a choir that she had me audition for St Paul's, Westminster Abbey, Salisbury and Winchester Cathedral schools, but I wasn't quite a good enough singer. However, I was always very good at the theory of music and was reading music by the age of 8.'

With his mother's persistence, Hatch was finally accepted to a choir school in Kent, where he spent the next four years. His enthusiasm and dedication for his singing led him to the dizzy heights of the school head chorister, in which capacity he was used for radio shows, plays and to augment the choirs at St Paul's Cathedral. 'I used to work hard and sing a lot to develop my music skills,' he continues. 'I was learning to play the organ but lost the interest to play at the age of 14, when I suddenly started to become interested in popular music. My grades were getting worse having started off with Distinctions, and I was just scraping a Pass so I knew that I would have difficulty getting in to the Royal Academy of Music. Also my parents had spent quite a bit of money on my education, so I thought I would really like to get into the music business.'

The problem was that he was pretty naive about it. 'All I knew about the business in 1955 was what I had seen on song copies, with publishers' names on the bottom. I knew I could write music very well and was good enough to read copy, so I decided that I could probably get a job as a copyist which, in those days, was one job up from the post room in a music publishing company. I looked at all the song copies that I had collected, and made a list of the publishers and quickly discovered that they were pretty much all based in the same place, so I decided I would do some cold calling and knock on some doors and off I went to Denmark Street.'

Although Hatch was clearly talented, he quickly discovered that his idea to become a copyist was going to be no easy task. At the time, most of the larger music publishers had their own arranging departments, where copyists would take songs and put arrangements together, by hand, for the BBC, and also for songs they were promoting at the time. 'I remember going to see Stan Butcher at Campbell Connelly. He looked at my music writing, and said it was O.K., but he had an arranging department already. Not even the smaller publishers were interested as they couldn't afford to have their own copyists, so they farmed the work out to the larger ones. I made several visits to publishers in this way, carrying around this piece of manuscript paper over several days. On about the fourth day, I went into Francis, Day & Hunter and found out they were looking for an errand boy in the general office of one of the associated companies located at the back of the building, called Mellin Music. Mellin was an American company, with a subsidiary in the UK, owned by Robert Mellin, who was a songwriter. It was the tiniest of offices at 6 Denmark Place.'

Hatch was introduced to Mellin's two colleagues, who would be his main influences during the first eighteen months of his life in the music business: Len Edwards, the office manager, and his secretary, Pat Williams. 'Although they said they were looking for someone to run errands, do the filing, make the tea and be a general dogsbody, it wasn't what I really wanted to do, but after hunting for four days, I thought it was at least my way into the business.'

Edwards took a shine to Hatch, and having found out that he could play the piano and sing, he asked him to demonstrate his skills. 'He gave me a pro copy of a song, [the same as a published copy but without a picture on the front], and he told me to play it through, which I did easily. Then he asked me to transpose it and play in four notes higher all the way through. As I could memorise the notes very well, I was able to play it as he wanted.'

Edwards was impressed with Hatch and he used him, when he could, to demonstrate songs. Every music publishing establishment had a piano on the premises; it was the stock way of demonstrating songs. 'Artists and record producers used to come in and I would play them a song that was either a new song or one from America that Mellin had the publishing rights for and was looking for a UK recording deal,' Hatch remembers. 'Occasionally, these people would record the song on reel to reel tape recorders or we made a demo at Regent Sound in Denmark Street; either way if an artist came into the office to find a song, you played it for them. No two artists would sing the song in the same way so, as a pianist, you had to find the right key to play in for each singer. That sealed my early career for me, and I enjoyed it. Sometimes I was the only person in the office and I would deal with people on my own even though I was only 16.'

Certainly, says Hatch, Denmark Street was an exciting place to work, with music playing from every building. 'Everyone who was around at the time remembers Johnny Wise, who used to play music as loud as he could, and open all the windows so people could hear the songs. The music publishers all had their own trade departments, mailing sections, accountants, professional offices. It was such a great buzz and everyone was in friendly competition with each other. Songwriters would come into the offices to play the piano and sing their songs and, if their song was rejected, they went away to the Suffolk Dairy, a café opposite Regent Sound, to rewrite parts of the song; usually the words because they were often the problem, and then they would go back to the same publisher, about an hour and half later with the song, which still sounded the same, but with different words, and that's how it worked.'

He continues, 'A lot of the good songwriters like Tommy O'Connor would hang around the cafés and music publishers and, I can remember, they wrote lots of songs, but of course, not all of them were published. The songwriters didn't have permanent contracts with a publisher, except for the odd one like Paddy Roberts, who sold a lot of his work to Essex Music, but they didn't get signed up and get big advances for songs back then.'

Hatch had been writing his own songs from about the age of 14, using his experience as a chorister to write hymns and anthems. 'I knew about the construction of melodies and how to make them sound good. I was doing a bit of writing with a friend of mine and because I was working for a music publisher, I wasn't going to take them anywhere else to sell. We did some adaptations of some American folk songs and had them recorded, but the real break came when I arrived at the office one day; it was just after ten in the morning and standing in the street waiting for his 10a.m. appointment was Dick Rowe from Decca Records, who became known for turning down the Beatles.

'I invited him upstairs and offered him a drink. I couldn't find Len but I knew what songs he wanted played to Dick because he had told me the day before. He had some American songs that we were pushing that had been released in the States, but hadn't been scheduled for release in Britain, so we were looking for someone to cover them in the UK. It worked well for artists like Sandie Shaw and Cilla Black, who had her first hit with a Bacharach and David song.'

The American publishing companies eventually got wise to this practice in Britain, and companies like Liberty Records set up its own UK subsidiary, (managed by Ray Williams), to stop it happening. 'I prepared the stuff for Dick to take away and then I told him, I was a songwriter, and played him a song called "Crazy Bells". It was a catchy song, but had dreadful lyrics, but he liked it all the same. He thought he could do something with it, so he took it away and the next thing I knew was, at the age of 17, we had a record out by Gerry Dorsey, who later became better known as Engelbert Humperdinck. It was his first record for Decca [in 1959].'

Rowe was impressed by Hatch, and so when he was invited by Top Rank, which was setting up a record division, to run its artists and repertoire function, he called Len Edwards and said he needed an assistant and asked if he would release Tony Hatch. 'Len gave him permission to take me with his good blessing and said it would be best for me and my career and a golden opportunity. Tin Pan Alley was a great place to get the experience of the music business, everything happened there. All you needed was the talent to match the experience and you were made.'

Hatch progressed quickly to being a songwriter and in-house record producer, but still made his way back to Tin Pan Alley when he could, to find songs for artists such as Petula Clark. 'As an in-house producer, I was told what to record, although I did get the opportunity sometimes to produce what I wanted to record. One day I would be asked to do some stage music for Bruce Forsyth, so I was down at the theatre putting the arrangements together with the producers, and the next I was looking for bands like the Searchers, and then find songs or write songs for artists like Petula Clark. There were times when I almost lived in the recording studio. I didn't get out to Tin Pan Alley as much as I would have liked, but music publishers knew me, and would come and see me, or they would send me things. I used to go and see Dick James a lot but he was still singing at the time and only just getting into publishing.

'Even as a songwriter, I needed my piano as that was the only way I could sell my songs,' explains Hatch. 'Very rarely did I do demo records although there were occasions when it was more convenient. Some especially, when I was in the studio working with an artist and at the end of the session, I would use the studio time left to demo one of my songs with the artist. Sometimes I would just demo it myself with the piano and the studio engineer. All of the songs I wrote for Petula Clark were not in demo form. She made her own cassette recording of my interpretation and then she would go away and do her own version, and then play it to me. The invention of the cassette recorder was an amazing breakthrough when it first came out.'

Hatch reached the height of his song writing career when the composition he had originally penned with the Drifters in mind was eventually recorded by Petula Clark. 'Downtown' became his first number one song in America when it hit the top spot in January 1965. 'I had a song that reached number two in Britain called "Sugar And Spice" by the Searchers, but to reach number one in America and sell three million records was an exciting experience.'

Explaining the inspiration for the song, Hatch doesn't remember where it came from. 'I was in New York when I wrote it. I arrived late in the afternoon and was booked into a hotel on Central Park. I decided that I must walk down Broadway to Times Square and during the trip, and in my naivety, I thought the walk was taking me downtown. But every city refers to a downtown area so the song had its connection with everybody.'

When Hatch returned to Britain having written the song, nothing really happened for a couple of months. In October 1964, Hatch decided that he wanted to record the song but at the time Petula Clark was the last person he thought of to do so:

When I first heard her version, I thought it sounded too English and even now I listen to it, I still think that. But that is probably what has made it successful. If she had sung it with an American accent it would have sounded awful, and if someone else had recorded it they would have not got the magic and inspiration that she felt when she sang it. She loved the song from the beginning and she insisted that she recorded it even if it didn't do well. When I played the resultant song by Petula to the record people they didn't know what to make of it. What eventually prompted its release was a comment from record executives at Warner Brothers, who were visiting Pye Records in Marble Arch, following an agreement with Warners to release their albums. I was asked to bring the Petula Clark version of 'Downtown' to the meeting at the ATV building in Cumberland Place, where Pye were based, and when the executives heard it, they wanted it released straight away, before Christmas.

Equally exciting, for different reasons, was how Denmark Street was full of music publishers, such as Mills Music, Campbell Connelly, Peter Maurice, Leeds and Southern Music, all of whom had staff like Tony Hiller, and all of whom were always on the lookout for new songs suitable for publishing and recording. Many engaged their own songwriters, but it was people like Hiller, would-be composers and song pluggers, that played the major roles in Tin Pan Alley. It was vital to plug the songs they wrote, as he said: 'As a plugger, my first job was to plug my own songs and get an artist to record them. It was very competitive, but all the writers were mates, so it was great to see one of your friends sell a song.'

One place to sell songs was the Giaconda café. It was where songwriters mixed with publishers and musicians. They were all looking for the same thing, an elusive song that would give them a hit and turn their career from scratching a living into earning a few decent bucks. 'There was a real buzz and excitement in the Giaconda when someone sold a song,' says Hiller today. 'It was also a fun place to go. I used to meet Dick James in there nearly every morning for coffee, yes, it was very exciting, but there was also a fear in the air as well, very nerve-wracking, so it was quite easy to walk away with nothing but disappointment.'

Most songwriters had no problems composing their own songs, because most of them were musicians to start with. But for those who weren't, they usually knew someone who was and would do it for them. Certainly most would have wanted to cut a demo record of their song if they could. After all, it was the best way to sell it to a publisher, a plugger or a recording artist. 'We would go to Regent Sound,' continues Hiller, 'and would get the song down onto a tape or disc and then we would take it to the promotions department of a publisher and play it to them, so they could decide whether it was for them or not.'

In most cases, if the record label liked a song, they would front the costs for a studio, musicians, producer and arranger. They took all the responsibility for everything after a song had been accepted. Indeed, when Hiller was recording a song on behalf of Mills Music, he would book the rhythm section in the morning, the brass section in the afternoon, and then add the strings at some point during the same day. Unlike today, a song would be completed in a single day. Ironically, when Reg left Bluesology, he became a session musician and worked for Hiller in that capacity. 'If I knew that little Reg could play and write songs when he first started at Mills, I would have snapped him up.'

When Hiller and his songwriting partners were in need of inspiration for a new song, they would always descend on the churchyard at St Giles' Church at the end of Denmark Street, which is still there to this day. It had an amazing churchyard, Hiller remembers, 'We would base songs on some of the things we found written on the gravestones. And then we would try to sell those songs, and we weren't the only ones trying out ideas like that.'

As Hiller continues to explain, 'Denmark Street was also probably one of the few places in London, at that time, where you would encounter every star of the period.

They were all looking for songs. It was really quite exciting getting a song published, getting a few quid for it, and then having it recorded by a star of the day.' As Hiller points out, 'And of course, prior to the Beatles, it was rare for an artist to write their own songs so, they used to rely on people like me and others in Denmark Street to write for them. And once the Beatles arrived, it changed, because they could write their own material and they had their own publisher.'

Another songwriter in Denmark Street at the time was Bill Martin. He first came to London as Wylie MacPherson, had previously worked on the docks, and held a huge aspiration to be in the music business. 'My mother gave me some money and a deadline of two weeks to make a name for myself, or else I had to go back home and back to the docks,' explains Martin. Not that he expected his first trip to London to be so short-lived. 'I had to go back as I couldn't find Tin Pan Alley. I didn't know it was called Denmark Street. I did, however, find Chappell Music in Bond Street on the last day of my two week deadline, but they were a very sophisticated music publisher who had songs by the likes of Cole Porter and Irving Berlin, and were not part of the Tin Pan Alley I was interested in. And certainly they were not my scene, so I went back to Scotland.'

After a short spell back in Scotland, and still with a burning desire to work in the music business, Martin returned to London, and this time located Tin Pan Alley, having discovered through some diligent research and detective work that it was, in fact, Denmark Street. Once back in the West End, and in Denmark Street, and having already decided that he wanted to try his luck at songwriting, he called in on every music publisher he could find.

'The first thing they told me to do was change my name,' chuckles Martin. He was told that Wylie MacPherson was too Scottish. Cyril Gee at Mills Music suggested he call himself Bill Martin, because according to Gee, to have a name with ten letters was lucky in songwriting. Cole Porter, Lionel Bart and Chuck Berry all had names with ten letters. Martin did not argue. 'It was only after I had written "Puppet On A String" and "Congratulations" that I realised Oscar Hammerstein and Irving Berlin were among others that had more than ten letters in their names, but of course, by then, it didn't matter.'

Martin spent most days visiting the music publishers in Denmark Street including, most notably, Mills Music, where Reg Dwight was still soaking up the atmosphere of music publishing in Tin Pan Alley. 'I used to hang around the offices, and always in the reception of each one. That is how I met everyone,' recalls Martin. 'Cyril Gee, who was a Jewish music publisher (as were most music publishers at that time in TPA), was the managing director of Mills, and I always used to hustle him for ten pounds on a Friday night, in return for a song.'

The worst he ever received for a song was five pounds. 'Publishers were essentially business people who didn't necessarily know what a good song sounded like. They were just looking for a song that would sell sheet music. Jimmy Phillips knew all about good songs. He ran Peter Maurice Music, also in Denmark Street, and was responsible for discovering Tommy Steele, who he then introduced to Lionel Bart.'

A publisher who apparently couldn't recognise a good song if it was served up on a silver platter, according to Martin, was Cyril Simons. He was the managing director of Leeds Music, who had a massive hit with 'This Is My Song' in 1967, written by Charlie Chaplin for his film, *Countess From Hong Kong*, which was recorded by Petula Clark as a single and ended up selling 500,000 copies. But, as Martin explains, 'He usually didn't know a good song even if he heard one, but Cyril Shane knew. He was a manager who worked at Mills and eventually went on to start his own music publishing set up in the Marylebone Road in the early 1970s. Like Dick James, he started his career singing in big bands.'

Another was David Platz, continues Martin. 'He was sort of in-between the other two.' He ran Essex Music and was one of Tony Visconti's bosses. In fact he introduced Visconti to David Bowie and was therefore indirectly responsible for Bowie becoming a star. 'There were times when he clearly knew a song but others where he clearly didn't, but he would sign anyone, and the only people he didn't sign were the Beatles. He signed the Rolling Stones, the Moody Blues, you name it, he signed it. Platz just never let you out of the office until you signed, but I am not sure he knew what he was signing. Both he and Dick James were the hot young publishers at the time. Eddie Kassner was another who knew a good song, but he would also give you a tenner if you gave him a laugh. He owned Kassner Music and he had "Rock Around The Clock" and ended up with the Kinks.'

But, looking back today, it was when Hiller introduced Bill Martin to Reg Dwight that he could not have foreseen what he would become in the future. 'He and another guy called Eric Hall were both post boys and packing sheet music.' As Martin recalls, 'I remember going to Mills Music, feeling miserable because my first song with Tommy Quickly was not selling well, and I remember little Reg being there. He was always very cheerful. I used to think that he was a poor little guy with nothing going for him. He had glasses and he wore bib overalls all the time. I hated overalls because I came from the shipyards and I swore when I got out of the shipyards I would never wear overalls again. I used to hear him playing the piano but to me he was not Tin Pan Alley. He was always very polite and opened the doors for you or anybody else. He was well liked by everyone.'

Like Martin, Roger Greenaway was another young songwriter, who with his writing partner, Roger Cook, was also involved with Mills Music. The pair would later become very important influences in Reg's early years at DJM. Greenaway had started his career singing alongside Tony Burrows in a band called the Kestrels, initially playing clubs around Bristol whilst they were still semi-professional.

In fact, they had teamed up together as singing partners and friends from the age of 15. 'We both worked for a company called E. S & A Robinson in Bristol having both left school at the age of 16,' says Burrows. Having decided that music was a career ambition, they started rehearsing in the basement of E. S & A Robinson, and very soon recruited singer and guitar player, Roger Maggs, who was introduced to Burrows by Greenaway. 'Roger was working with us at Robinson's and joined us in the basement to rehearse. We organised local gigs which went down very well, so we decided to get another voice, so we recruited Geoff Williams who was a chorister.'

Having built up confidence from the local gigs and the rehearsals in the basement of Robinson, they decided to audition for the *Carroll Levis Discovery Show* at the Hippodrome in Bristol. The show was essentially a talent show, and probably is best described as the forerunner to the shows we have running today, such as *Britain's Got Talent*.

'Carroll Levis used to go round the theatres doing auditions for his shows,' Burrows continues. 'We entered as the Kestrels but we also entered as a skiffle group because skiffle was the craze then.' But by the time they won their audition, skiffle had more or less faded into obscurity. All the same, they were given what they considered was a once-in-a-lifetime opportunity to make a name for themselves – on ATV television, which they promptly did by winning the show for six consecutive weeks by public vote. At the time, the boys were 18 and, not unexpectedly, were called up for their National Service in the army, which temporarily put the mockers on their musical ambitions.

'National Service was a pain because we couldn't get out and play music,' remembers Burrows. 'We were all put in the same military unit and we were given days off as leave to go and play gigs. Our manager, somehow, managed to get us all together in the one regiment and Greenaway was transferred to where we were stationed as he had joined earlier, being six months older than the rest of us.'

The Kestrels did two years entertaining in the Officer's Mess and were invited onto a television show called *Youth Makes The Show* in Cardiff. 'We were the resident group on the show, and we were given leave to go to do the show for the day. We also did a show called *Cool For Cats*, because we had recorded a single by then called "Chapel In The Moonlight", which didn't quite make it, but this was all we could do during National Service.'

On their release from the Army, the boys went back to E. S & A Robinson. They spoke openly with Mr Robinson about their musical ambitions. 'We told him that we wanted to try and make it in the music business because we had some small success already. He told us he would give us six months, and if we couldn't make it by then, then we could have our jobs back. It was a perfect arrangement, so we went to London, but didn't do much at first until we met Johnny Keating who arranged for us to do some session work. During this time we also met Lonnie Donegan and he put us on television doing backups for shows like the *Six Five Special* and other similar types of things, where either the Kestrels or the Dallas Boys were used as the regular backing vocalists.'

Donegan was so taken by the talents of the Kestrels that he took them on a 26-week summer season with the likes of Des O'Connor and the Clark Brothers, which gave them exposure to the cabaret scene. From those early shows, the Kestrels became more popular than they could have dreamed of and, because of that, they were soon invited to join the Helen Shapiro Show, which was touring the UK between February and March 1963. During the tour, Brian Epstein suggested that his new band called the Beatles could join the tour to close the first half before the interval, which everyone seemed to be pretty happy with ... at least to start with. 'It lasted for about two days and then they were closing the show with Helen closing the first half, even though it was her show and her tour. It was so apparent from the reaction of females in the first few rows of each theatre we played in, that it was going to be one continuous scream. And true to our thoughts, it was. They never stopped,' recalls Burrows.

The Kestrels were paid extra to go on immediately before the Beatles and they literally used to talk amongst themselves. No one could hear anything because of the screaming, and that applied to the Beatles set as well. 'We did the two one nighters and then went to Ireland with them, so we got to know them quite well. They didn't know too much about anything at the time. We all used to travel together on the coach, with another coach following behind carrying the gear.

'Kenny Lynch was on the same tour and during one bus ride he told the Beatles that he wanted to write songs with them as he thought they needed another songwriter to help them. The Beatles were quite taken with the idea as Kenny was a well known artist and writer. "Love Me Do" was already a hit and they were just starting to write "Please, Please Me", but when they played it to Kenny, he thought it was absolute nonsense and told them so. He decided that it was so bad, that he wasn't going to write with them after all, and disappeared across to the other side of the bus.'

The Beatles were all reasonably naive apart from John Lennon, who knew he was going to be a star, much the same as Reg Dwight did during his early days with Bluesology. The Kestrels stayed together until 1966 having introduced Roger Cook to the line-up, who was also a singer from Bristol. 'We ended up doing cabaret on the cabaret circuit and after a while we decided that it wasn't going anywhere. By the time we quit the cabaret thing, Roger Greenaway had written a song with Roger Cook, and so the band split up.'

'That,' affirms Greenaway 'was the very first song we wrote, which was during the final tour of the Kestrels. It was called "You've Got Your Troubles", by which time, we had made a demo of it and had met Tony Hiller, who signed us both up to Mills. When the tour finished, we went back up to London to see Tony who played a record of our song to us. It was by a group called the Fortunes, who we hadn't heard of at the time but, yes, they had recorded our song, which they subsequently released as a single and it became a hit.'

That was the start of a long musical journey for Greenaway and Cook which would soon set them on a course for DJM, where they would reacquaint themselves with one of the young lads they had often visited in the Mills basement. 'When we first met him [Reg Dwight], he was a very shy guy and no one knew that he was a singer and a piano player at the time.'

In fact, it was about the same time that Reg got his job at Mills that Cook and Greenaway were signed by Cyril Gee. 'And it was,' Gee remembers 'at my house later on in their career that they got the call from Coca Cola to do the song "I'd Like to Teach the World to Sing" [a hit for the New Seekers in 1971]. In those days we had to do demo records. Gone were the days when you could go over to a publisher and play the piano, all of a sudden the era of demo records came in and I used to pay Reg extra to play the piano on demo records over at Regent Sound Studios which is where we used to go to cut the demos because it was handy and it was cheap to use. He made demos of many of the pop songs of the day and he could have even played on the demo for "You've Got Your Troubles", "Kaiser Bill's Batman" and many other Mills Music published songs.'

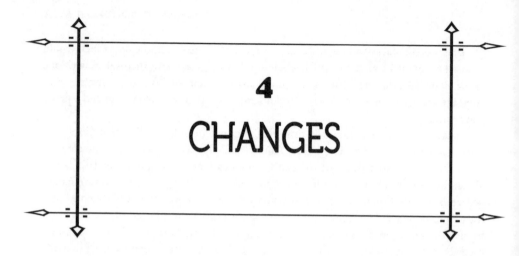

# 4

# CHANGES

In the week leading up to Christmas, there were plenty of parties to go to in Denmark Street, and the one at Mills each year was *de rigueur*. Cyril Gee always insisted in making the most of the yearly celebrations but others, like Jimmy Phillips, preferred to be away from it all, down in Brighton.

The Mills Christmas Party was usually organised by Pat Sheridan, one of the departmental managers. According to most, he was rarely seen sober during the evening of the party; who could blame him? With the Chelsea football club players always in attendance, there was plenty of reason to party. Reg, of course, was always hanging about, because Hiller's mates from Chelsea always attended.

'One Christmas,' remembers Bill Martin, 'Reg asked to play the piano, but I told him to piss off because I didn't think he could play the typical pub standards. I had only seen him play block chords. I remember he was very emotional and upset that he could not play, and he got very angry with me because of it. At the time, I thought he was a little nerd jazz musician because he knew everything that was happening in Tin Pan Alley, and just seemed to be more of a music fan than he was a songwriter or a budding pop star.'

The year before Reg landed his job at Mills, Martin's first published song, 'Kiss Me Now' had been recorded and released by Tommy Quickly, and Dick James was the publisher. It was 1963 and, as far as Martin was concerned, it was probably Brian Epstein's only failure not to recognise a hit. 'I originally wrote that for Gerry And The Pacemakers, under the original working title of "Do It Now".'

Mitch Murray had composed the previous two songs for Gerry, 'How Do You Do It?' and 'I Like It'. It was around the period that Gerry Marsden wanted to do Rodgers and Hammerstein's 'You'll Never Walk Alone', which became a massive hit, and the anthem of Liverpool Football Club. It was one of the reasons that Martin's song didn't get used by Marsden. Dick James and Brian Epstein liked it, but changed the title to 'Kiss Me Now', and gave it to Tommy Quickly instead. Although Martin had now had his first song published as sheet music, and released on record, his elation, he recalls, was short lived.

Martin remembers how: 'I had my first song out in the business, and I just wanted to know how it was doing and that's all that mattered to me. When it first came out, I felt like Jack the Lad and I remember Brian Epstein phoning through to Dick at the start of 1964, and saying that the Beatles had broken the States with "I Want To Hold Your Hand".

'He then started asking Dick about the record sales in Britain for his other artists as well as the Beatles. Dick had an open office so I could go in and see him whenever I wanted to. It was easy to hear any conversation, and I could hear this one with Brian very clearly. Dick was saying that Billy J. Kramer had three million sales, Cilla Black had 2.8 million, and the Beatles had three million. But Brian kept asking him about Tommy Quickly, after telling him about the sales of others, and Brian, persevering about Tommy, finally got his answer; Dick told him the sales of "Kiss Me Now" were 125 copies. I felt deflated. I think my mother had bought most of those.'

Not all publishers were as accessible as Dick James, Martin recalls. 'James would always be in the Giaconda every day for a coffee and he was always very approachable for any songwriter or publisher who wanted to buy a song from him. Even when the Beatles were happening, James was no different.'

It was something that Martin's writing partner, Phil Coulter, agreed with. They used to write about six songs a day, which was the average for Tin Pan Alley songwriters: it was the only way to survive. 'We were professional songwriters,' says Martin. 'And we also knew that whether it was an A side hit or just a B side, the money would still be the same. We wrote "Back Home" for the England Football team prior to the 1970 World Cup. It sold over a million records, and we also wrote the B side, "Cinnamon Stick", which earned us the same money as the A side.' Nice work if you can get it.

Even though Martin was trained to look for melodies to put his lyrics to, it wasn't always that simple. Much later, during his years in Denmark Street, he went to meet Claude François. He had failed to get a melody that François had given to another publisher, which Paul Anka eventually wrote the words for and turned it into 'My Way'. 'I knew Claude had another melody, so I flew to his windmill home just outside Paris. He played me a melody which I liked, and that became "My Boy" which was eventually recorded by Elvis Presley, and gave him a top five hit in November 1974.'

The great thing about Tin Pan Alley, was that it offered the perfect grounding for songwriters because the publishers would be honest about whether a song was good or bad, unlike today. The sole aim, back then, was to find a good song to sell to a publisher, with the songwriter attempting to sell it anywhere they could for as much money as they could get for it.

'There were two guys called Elton Box and Desmond 'Sonny' Cox, who had a big hit with 'I've Got A Lovely Bunch Of Coconuts", published by their own Box and

Cox Publishing, which they were always trying to emulate. They had an office in Tin Pan Alley with a big desk where they sat, either side of it. And they had a piano. You would be invited to play them your song, and then afterwards, one of them would say, "What do you think Mr Box?" and the reply would be "I'm not sure Mr Cox" They then asked if you had a song like "A Lovely Bunch Of Coconuts". They would do things for a laugh, and give you money,' chuckles Martin.

If the rumours are to be believed, they liked a tipple most lunch times. 'It was quite funny,' laughs Martin, 'but they would usually go back to their office in quite a drunken state for the afternoon. And that was the time when songwriters would try and sell them songs. I would go in with a song and they would ask what the title of the song was and, on one occasion, I told them I had a song called "I'll Lay Down My Tweezers Till My Eyebrows Meet Again" and Cox would say "I quite like that Mr Box" and Box would say "So do I Mr Cox" and I got a fiver for it.' Needless to say, the song never made the record charts and probably never left their desks.

Even though the likes of Bill Martin, Phil Coulter, Tony Hiller and Barry Mason, were the exciting young bloods of Tin Pan Alley in the early 1960s, they were still up against the more established names of Denmark Street, such as Michael Carr, Jimmy Kennedy and Bob Halfin. As Martin recounts:

One of my memories of the old school songwriters was about Michael Carr from the songwriting team, Kennedy and Carr. Michael was always skint. He went in to Mills one day with his face all white and he started writhing on the floor. There was this big songwriter who had written these huge songs writhing on the floor. He kept telling everyone that he was dying and to fetch Jimmy Phillips quickly (Jimmy was the big music publisher at the time and looked just like Winston Churchill).

He [Carr] didn't realise he was in the wrong publishers, so I told him he was in Cyril Gee's office at Mills Music, and having made some expletives and picking himself up from the floor, he ran out and went next door. So I followed him to see what he was doing and he went into Jimmy Phillips' office and repeated this farce.

'Tell Jimmy I'm dying,' he shouted from his position on the floor. So someone went into Jimmy's office and told him and Jimmy, knowing all about this common scam, asked this unsuspecting office employee what Michael wanted. After this went on for a while, Jimmy Phillips went down to see Michael himself, and he asked Michael what was wrong with him and Michael said, in his dramatic style, 'I'm dying and I want to say my last wish is just to say goodbye to you.' Jimmy, knowing exactly what was happening, asked Michael whether a £50 advance was enough for the weekend and, making a miraculous recovery, he got up and took the money with thanks. Jimmy then told Michael to go and get himself cleaned up and get rid of the flour he'd put on his face. And all this, was just to get an advance for the weekend. That is what it was like. Friday night you really tried to sell a song, and if not, you tried to get an advance.

Martin continues to explain that there was an interesting mix of old guard and new blood songwriters in Denmark Street. Martin used to hang out with great names such as Ross Parker and Hughie Charles, writers of 'We'll Meet Again' and 'There'll Always Be An England' and Ian Grant, who wrote the lyrics to 'Let There Be Love'. 'To see all the old songwriters hustling together to get and sell a song was an amazing thing to witness. And what was intriguing is that most of them would be on one side of Tin Pan Alley – the drinkers' side of the road – and the new songwriters, like me and Phil would be on the opposite side. The older ones would be reminiscing about the good old days, whereas we were the younger guys on the other side hustling for the new charts. We wrote the new pop songs, but the old school thought that all the new pop groups were rubbish. You could see the old brigade dying and the new guys coming up.'

Martin also remembers that: 'We were asked whether we were going to write another song for *Eurovision* after "Puppet On A String". We said we would, and wrote a song that is now lost in time, but it was called "My Magic Music Box", and it was written for Cliff Richard, who had been chosen to sing Britain's entry in 1968 ["Congratulations"].

'The Publisher had a lovely way of putting you down if he didn't like your song. He would get up from behind his desk and say "You boys… what an incredible song," he would then give us a big hug and say "I am sure you've got something better in you." So that was really how you had a song rejected in Tin Pan Alley.'

Not that it put Martin off. After being told that his song was more or less not good enough, he headed off to the pub to drown his sorrows whilst Phil Coulter went to the piano in the office to write a song. 'I never saw him the next day,' says Martin. 'He eventually came in the following day and he had managed the first line of a new song, which was "I think I love you, I think I love you, I think the world is fine if you will say you're mine." He said, "What do you think?" and I said it was bollocks. Who goes up to someone and says "I think I love you", so I looked at the five syllables of the title and made "Congratulations" and that sold it.'

Once Martin and Coulter had written 'Congratulations', it was up to the songwriters to find a publisher to sell it. So they took it to Regent Sound to cut a demo for hawking around publishers. 'It was a magic place, at Regent Sound, because you could see all sorts of session musicians getting paid for playing on demos. I used to regularly use Clem Cattini as the drummer, (who has played on more number ones that any other musician), a bass player called John Paul Jones, and the guitarist was Jimmy Page [who later became half of Led Zeppelin, of course] . I used to give them £9 for a session, and they all played on the demos for "Congratulations" and "Puppet On A String".' Songwriters didn't pay much attention to the musicians' recording demos, because almost all songwriters could play an instrument of some kind. It was just a means to an end, to get a song to a publisher and end up selling it for publishing purposes.

'We used musicians to play the songs to sell them and we used only those musicians who could portray our song in the way we wanted it so, like most songwriters, we had our favourite musicians for sessions on our songs. It was much the same for the musicians. They were far more interested in their £9 per session fee than in the song they were playing.'

But, according to Martin, writing a song and getting a demo cut wasn't always plain sailing:

> I was in Regent Sound when we were all looking for a song for Sandie Shaw to sing in the *Eurovision Song Contest*. We all had three hour slots at the studio, and when we were not waiting outside, we would all be in the Giaconda having a cup of tea. You could hear what was going on in the studio because the walls were so thin. On one occasion, I remember Gordon [Mills, Tom Jones' manager and a songwriter in his own right] was in the studio demo-ing a song with Tom [Jones], and there was a lot of shouting which culminated in Tom threatening to punch Gordon, and Gordon retaliating. Anyway, they eventually recorded the demo of the song that Gordon wanted Sandie to consider. She declined on the basis that she felt that Tom could sing it much better than she could. And that song was 'It's Not Unusual', which would give Tom his first major hit record [in 1965].

By the time Coulter and Martin started to get known in the business as two names to be reckoned with, they were snapped up as one of the last songwriting teams to be signed to Keith Prowse Music – the publisher who had signed Jimmy Kennedy and Michael Carr, and Lionel Bart and Tommy Steele. Almost overnight, it seemed as if the hustling days to sell a song to pay the rent on a Friday night to the likes of Cyril Gee at Mills Music were not so important, or at least they weren't to Bill Martin. 'I gave up taking the cash from Mills at that point,' recalls Martin looking back at that time. 'We were the last of the old style Tin Pan Alley breeds: Bill Martin and Phil Coulter, Tony Hiller, Greenway and Cook, Les Reed and Barry Mason, we were the young bucks on the street but we were the last ones.'

By the mid-sixties, the so-called new style bands were starting to emerge onto the music scene and threatening the future of solo artists like Elvis and Cliff who had dominated the charts since they began in the 1950s. The Rolling Stones were one of the most outrageous, which is why they became such a huge hit with teenagers. They were just one of many bands that were based in Tin Pan Alley and used Regent Sound at least once a week.

Their management and publishing company, Essex Music, headed by David Platz, had offices based above the studio. Indeed it was Platz, an Auschwitz survivor, who helped the Rolling Stones' manager, Andrew Loog Oldham, turn the band into one of the most successful in British pop music history. And what could be better than to own all the Stones songs between them? Most of their early singles and albums were, in fact, recorded at Regent Sound in Denmark Street, owned by Oldham and published by Platz. It was the perfect arrangement. The difference though, between the Stones and the songwriters in Tin Pan Alley at that time, was that, like Lennon and McCartney, Mick Jagger and Keith Richards wrote their own songs solely and exclusively for their own use (though other people did cover them, of course).

Suddenly, there was little need for the old style of songwriting that had kept Tin Pan Alley at the centre of the British music scene. With bands like the Rolling Stones and the Beatles, and with songwriters like Lennon and McCartney, Jagger and Richards, the magic of Denmark Street began to fall apart. As Martin explains, 'All these groups contributed to finally hitting the Tin Pan Alley formula of songwriting on the head, because they could all write their own songs, but in a totally different style to the way it had always been done before the Beatles and the Stones'. They really changed the way bands thought and did things, as Martin further elaborates:

> The idea of writing your own material, if you were in a band, suddenly became the way to do things. From that point onwards, there was little need for the old traditional songwriters. They either disappeared from the scene or became producers for their own songs. And, of course, it also changed other things like the way in which songs were found for the *Eurovision Song Contest* so, in a way, Britain's role in the *Eurovision* also got a hammering.
>
> This trend was to continue to grow to the present day, where the *Eurovision Song Contest* plays a very small part in the overall UK music industry. Both Tim Rice and Andrew Lloyd Webber entered *Eurovision* and failed, and so did Don Black, as well as Elton and Bernie. They all failed. It was huge back then; and if you think about it, some of the biggest bands in the world have come out of *Eurovision*. Abba was probably the biggest, or went on to be the biggest, after they won the contest in April 1974 with 'Waterloo' at the Dome in Brighton. It is incredible to think that they went on to become one of the most commercially successful acts in the history of pop music, topping the charts worldwide from that time to the early 1980s. It's also incredible to think that they have sold over two hundred million records worldwide, and still sell millions of records each year. And of course, the biggest interval act, Riverdance, made three people billionaires. And if you think of *Eurovision* in those terms, it was seen as a huge stepping stone for the many up-and-coming artists like Reg.

**▐▌▐▌▌**

In addition to the songwriting and publishing companies there were, of course, the record companies who signed the artists to record the songs written in Tin Pan Alley. It was on this side of the scene that Reg's friend, Tony King, first found his niche. He had started in the music business in 1958 at Decca as a progress chaser working in the sleeve department, where they manufactured the album covers.

'I would chase up the printers to make sure they had everything they needed,' he recalls. 'After Decca, I moved to the London American record label, where I was assistant label manager, and handled artists like Jerry Lee Lewis, Phil Spector, Little Richard, Benny King, and all the others American artists that had records released through the label.' But it was when he was introduced to Tony Hall and became Hall's promotions guru, working out of the Decca Records office in London's Hanover Square, that his first direct contact with artists began.

At the time, the main artists were all American but the British had some major names too, such as Cliff Richard. 'I first worked with Brenda Lee, Del Shannon, and Neil Sedaka and part of my role would be to collect them from the airport on their arrival and basically look after them for the week that they would usually be in Britain.'

As there were no promotions and marketing staff as such, King would take care of it all. 'I did all the press, radio, TV, and was the social person who made sure the artists enjoyed their stay in Britain.' Through that job, King came to see a lot of new artists coming up in England as well as in America, such as the Beatles and the Rolling Stones.

'The Beatles came along and I met them during the first week they were in London. Then the Rolling Stones came along. I remember how Andrew Oldham used to visit me quite regularly during the Stones period. I got to know him very well. Like Colonel Tom Parker had once told Elvis, he said to me, he was going to make the Stones massive. He was only 18 years old at the time, and I rather stupidly thought "You're not going to do that, you are only 18". But he went ahead all the same and, of course, he did it because he had a lot of nerve and spark and, as we know, the Stones ended up very big names. I believe a lot of their early reputation was down to Andrew, and the way he manipulated the press to pitch them as the bad boys of rock against the good boy Beatles.'

Not only did Oldham manage the Stones, but he also launched his own record label, Immediate Records, in 1965. Oldham's right-hand man at the time was Terry Carty. Oldham's offices were right next door to Dick James Music in New Oxford Street, where American record giants Warner Bros would eventually move into.

The main artist roster at Immediate included such names as the Faces, Chris Farlowe, PP Arnold, the Nice and Amen Corner. Although they were all very successful in the charts, the label itself says Carty, lacked control. 'Oldham was good with the ideas and letting the bands have studio time, but he didn't have much of a handle on money, so they were always bordering on cashflow problems. On the publishing side of things, however, he had Sea of Tunes Music from the Beach Boys, which he had quite bizarrely secured by simply placing an advert in the *Melody Maker* welcoming the Beach Boys to England during their first tour here.'

Like most others who worked in music publishing at that time, Carty could always be found in Denmark Street. One of his jobs for Oldham was to arrange disc cutting for demos that Oldham wanted to send out to publishers. 'We always used Regent

Sound. I remember the cutting room was upstairs with egg boxes on the ceilings and carpet on the walls. It's hard to believe that the Rolling Stones recorded downstairs in the studio, which also had egg boxes on the ceiling, and carpets on the wall, as well, with a little two-track tape machine. The cutting room had an ancient mono disc cutting machine but it worked. So they were used for disc cutting along with another company called the London Disc Cutting Centre above HMV in Oxford Street.'

**♩♩ ♩♩♩**

It was during the same period that Tony King's career in promotions also started to develop. The one thing he noticed most about that time was the huge camaraderie between artists. Most of them would hang out together and frequent the same clubs and establishments. 'Donovan, Dusty Springfield, the Beatles, the Stones, all used to be out and about together all the time. They were really just a bunch of young people running around London having a good time.' It is most probably what inspired so many other lesser known artists to try and follow in their footsteps and capture the same kind of spirit and success.

'For me, it was where the music publishers used to hang out,' King recalls. 'When I was first starting out, the music publishers were a major force. People like Cyril Simons, Dick James, all these people were very powerful and successful. And the songwriters were just as powerful at that time as well. Names like Barry Mason, Don Black and Bill Martin, were all in demand to come up with songs for artists so that the publishers they were signed to, in Denmark Street, could publish songs.

'The songwriters were always interested in working with producers to get their songs recorded by the most popular artists of the day, such as Dusty Springfield. Once the swinging sixties swung into action, the world of Tin Pan Alley started to spread out because the Beatles and Epstein were not Tin Pan Alley, and nor were the Stones really, even though they recorded there and had their publisher neatly placed above the studio where they laid down their first album.

'It was an important place to be,' continues King, 'because the music business was still relying on songs and songwriters and publishers. There were still some artists like Cliff Richard, Dusty Springfield and Petula Clark who relied on Tin Pan Alley songwriters, but when the Beatles and the Stones came along and they wrote their own material it changed a great deal. I think it was during this period of the 1960s that there were those who started to realise how much money there was in songwriting, and so they did it themselves. Songwriters like Mike Hazlewood, who wrote songs for artists like the Hollies and Dave Berry, and penned "The Air That I Breathe" and "Little Arrows" [both written with Albert Hammond], among other hits and artists, made a lot of money from selling these songs, and yet he could still remain anonymous.'

On top of that, the songs that were coming out of Tin Pan Alley were constantly being covered by many other recording stars of the day and so songwriters would be raking in the royalties. 'Although the buildings each side of Denmark Street weren't the latest big office complexes, it still had a lot of glamour attached to it. After all, it was the centre of the music business for publishers, songwriters, artists, producers, artist management, guitar shops, recording studios and great coffee places to hang out in. Yes, it was pretty glamorous in an odd sort of way.'

Martin concludes, 'I went to see *Billy Elliot* and we had tickets in front of Elton and his mother. They came in together, and I gave Elton a hug, and his mother a kiss, and then his mother said to Elton "Look at Bill's hair, it looks fantastic and he writes terrific songs, "Puppet On A String" and "Congratulations". Elton just smiled. His mother is from my era, but I would give anything now to write a song like Elton and Bernie. How times have changed.'

# 5
# PUBS AND CLUBS

After a year of playing live music in pubs, Reg decided he wanted to broaden his horizons and play to more than just a bar audience. Even though he was already exposed to the music scene through his job at Mills Music, and was still working for Tony Hiller, Mick Inkpen says he didn't really like it that much. What he really wanted to be was a musician and a songwriter, not a gofer for a music publisher, and not a honky-tonk pianist in a pub.

Bluesology, a band that had been put together by Stewart Brown and Geoff Dyson, seemed to be the ideal vehicle for Reg's ambitions. In many ways, it was no more than the Corvettes reuniting with a few changes. It probably helped that both teenagers were now heavily influenced by a different kind of music. In fact, it was probably Dyson's friend Stuart Baird (now a successful film editor, producer and director), who introduced them to the ever increasing popularity of jazz and Chicago blues.

One of their major influences, though not American, was Britain's Georgie Fame And The Blue Flames, who were at that time playing in the style of Mose Allison (an American jazz-blues pianist and singer, who had followed Jimmy Witherspoon's example of introducing brass into his recordings). It was something that was to win Fame and his band chart popularity.

'We thought that we needed to expand on the Corvettes, and if we were going to form a new band, we needed something more versatile rather than just doing covers of Beatles and Hollies numbers. Stewart and I used to sit round a record player and listen to things like "Times Are Getting Tougher Than Tough" and "Corrina Corrina", and it was songs like those that led to the formation of the early Bluesology sound,' states Dyson.

Although they had kicked around some other possible band names, it was only when Stewart played them one of his father's long players, an album by Django Reinhardt called *Djangology*, which Dyson and Brown came up with the name for their new band as a back-handed tribute. However, there is a song called 'Bluesology' by the Modern Jazz Quartet from 1956, which may also have been the inspiration.

They always had Reg down as their first choice for piano player, as they knew what he was capable of. It also helped that they were all on the same page when it came to the kind of music they wanted to play. It wasn't long before Mick Inkpen got wind of the new band. He had heard through the grapevine that Reg Dwight, the piano player he had first come across at a youth club, and another guy named Stewart Brown were trying to form a band and so Inkpen took the bull by the horns and promptly got in touch with Reg. 'I phoned him and then went round to his house one afternoon; we had a chat, and that was it. We had a couple of rehearsals and that was really the start of Bluesology. It was really just a question of being in the right place at the right time, I suppose.'

It probably helped that Inkpen had been a frequent visitor to the New Fender Club in Kenton. It was ideally located for anyone who lived in the Harrow area of London. Basically, it was a Conservative Club hall with a small stage, but the guy who ran it seemed to have the knack of attracting some of the most popular name acts of the day. Names like Cliff Bennett And The Rebel Rousers, Georgie Fame, and the Graham Bond Organisation with Ginger Baker on drums. Although Baker won the cigar for his flamboyance, showmanship and the pioneer use of two bass drums, Fame had George Seaman, who was Inkpen's inspiration.

In fact, it was mainly the American acts such as Sonny Terry and Brownie McGhee, Muddy Waters and Howlin' Wolf who were performing the type of music that Inkpen now adored. He became exposed to them from listening to records and watching them in person every time they came over to Britain to play live gigs. It was also the kind of music he wanted to play himself; much the same as Brown and Reg did. It is probably what led them to the Bluesology sound even though they knew it had a limited appeal. Not that it mattered. They knew they were never going to get rich or famous by playing it, but it was what they wanted to play. As Inkpen explains, 'nobody said we are going to do this and we are going to play here and there, we were just content to drift along to see how it would pan out.'

But it wasn't without its difficulties. Like any other new young band starting out. Bluesology had to find a place to rehearse, and if you had no money, it was the hardest thing in the world to persuade someone to surrender a room or hall for free.

'It was a pretty hopeless situation,' recalls Inkpen. 'If you ended up in somebody's house, the neighbours would usually complain about the noise, and so we had to move on to a church hall or something similar. We eventually found a friendly vicar who let us play in a room at the back of the hall, but overall, we had to beg, steal or borrow any place we could find to rehearse. We used St Edmunds Church Hall for a while, but that was before bands got commercially successful, and started hiring halls to rehearse in. And that's when it got expensive, but we did it all on the cheap. Rehearsal and practice was the key, because the secret of a polished band was to learn the songs and get out and perform them. Rehearsing and finding gigs was the route to everything.'

Another route for what they wanted to do was to replicate the sound of the jazz records they had all been listening to, but to do that, they quickly realised, they needed someone who could play saxophone, and the best way to find someone who fitted the bill was to place an ad in *Melody Maker*. They pooled all their money together and hired a hall in Harrow, and kept their fingers crossed that some hopefuls would show up in response to the ad. In the end, about half a dozen saxophonists turned up, remembers Dyson. 'They were all pretty good but there was one guy who just outshone everyone else. He just dropped into the style that we wanted to play at the time.'

It wasn't long after the auditions that they put together a set list for a gig they played at the Last Chance Club in London's Soho, not far from Denmark Street. It was the first London gig they had played, and now with a brass player in the band, Bluesology were finally starting to achieve the sound they wanted. Sax made all the difference to the songs they had picked to play that were heavily influenced by Reg and Brown. They were the ones that chose the material in general, but it wasn't original stuff as the band didn't have a songwriter, or at least, they didn't think they did.

But all that changed the day Reg turned up to a rehearsal and announced to the rest of the band that he had written a song that he thought they should try. It was called 'Come Back Baby'. 'He just came in during rehearsals and said he had got this song and we said, "Well, come on, let's hear it," and he started playing it,' Dyson recalls. 'It was very classically influenced, a lot of big, rising scale chords that he had put together, and to us, it sounded really great, so we thought maybe we should actually try and record it, which we eventually did.

'We were very excited about it because it really was the first song we could call a Bluesology song, and we knew it would be a positive move away from the covers we were playing at the time. I remember we were all very proud of it, and Reg, and because we considered it such a strong number, we played it a couple times at gigs, just to get a reaction from the audience. Overall, the crowds were very positive about it, and that was enough for us to decide to go ahead and try to make a record of it.'

But the first time his old school friend, Graham Boaden heard the song, he was not that knocked out by it. Along with some of his friends, 'we all piled into Reg's bedroom at Frome Court because he wanted to play us a song he had composed. His bedroom was amazing. It was lined wall to wall with LP records, racked like a record shop. We were still at school and just wondered how on earth he could afford all these records? He then played us this song called "Come Back Baby" on his piano, but I was not fabulously impressed with the song, but it was a good first attempt, when you consider how young he was.'

By now, of course, 'Come Back Baby' wasn't the only song Reg had written. In fact he was secretly building quite a songbook of his own material. Certainly, he was the most capable band member at song composition. And although he could deliver a good vocal, he wasn't the lead singer anymore as that was left to Stewart Brown. It wasn't that Reg couldn't sing or didn't have a good voice, far from it. He just didn't have the charisma that Brown had. Stewart was young, dark haired and slim, and he looked the business, and Reg didn't in those days. It was as simple as that. According to the other band members, Reg was quite content to sit at the back of the band playing his Hohner Pianette. But, as Mick Inkpen confirms, when he did sing, he was pretty good.

Even though Graham Boaden was not that impressed, 'Come Back Baby' was a welcome departure from the usual songs the band were playing at that time, and it was also an opportunity to feature original material, which was something the band very much wanted to do. Like any band from that period, playing covers of other artist's hits was never going to get you noticed, so the introduction of 'Come Back Baby' to Bluesology's set list was a huge step in the right direction.

It also helped when the song became a record in 1965, Bluesology's first single, and Reg's first step into the world of recording. Indeed, it was soon after the brass player joined the band that Brown and Dyson headed out to Rickmansworth to book the recording session at a studio they had both heard about for budding new bands. By now, the group had decided to invest in a recording of Reg's work, both with a plan to release it as a single, and to use it to promote the band with the aim of trying to secure a recording contract so they could get more gigs.

The studio was owned by Jack Jackson, who was to become affectionately known as the 'Daddy Of All Disc Jockeys' during his brief spell on Radio 1 from 1967 to 1968. Jackson, formerly a dance band leader and trumpeter, played regularly at London's Dorchester Hotel. As Dyson recalls, 'I remember his radio show very well, because he played a lot of American stuff. He was also a band leader in the '40s and '50s, and his two sons, Malcolm and John, ran the studio.'

Brown and Dyson took the train and then, due to lack of funds for a bus or taxi, walked the rest of the way to the studio, and ended up booking a session for a couple of weeks later. Once booked, they left the studio, but were completely surprised when one of the Jackson brothers offered them a lift back to the railway station. Even more surprising, was what they were given a lift in: it was a white XJ150 Jaguar. The boys were literally blown away. 'I don't know who sat on who's lap, but he drove us back to the station in this Jag and we thought "Yeah! this is showbiz. This is what we want."'

Two weeks later, they would head back to the studio with the rest of the band to lay down the tracks for the first Bluesology single. The Jackson brothers had set up their own 'hut' – a prefab building in grounds just outside Rickmansworth. It was done up in the same traditional style of other recording studios of the day. It had what looked like egg boxes on the walls to isolate acoustic diffusion and absorption, old scraps of carpet on the floor, a combination of microphone stands and a 4-track mixing desk. Because they were working with 4-track recording, they had to do everything by reduction, which meant recording the backing tracks first and then mixing them all down to one channel, and then recording the vocals and treating them the same way.

The backing track was recorded first, and then they overdubbed their vocals on top of the backing track, much the same way as a lot of bands and recording artists who worked with those limitations did in those days. The session lasted for about four hours as it was all the boys could afford, so they had to make sure they would leave the studio knowing that they had laid down two good songs for an A and B side. Two songs they thought were better than one to tout around the major record labels.

And it seemed they had. After the sessions, the boys were offered acetates of the songs they had recorded from the master tape. 'I do remember the acetates,' notes Dyson. 'They were about £6 each but we could only afford to order three. We had just splashed out for the cost of the recording session, so we were restricted to how many acetates we could order.' And they weren't like normal vinyl discs. They were made for demonstration and evaluation purposes only, and were created by using a recording lathe to cut a sound-modulated groove into the surface of a special lacquer-coated blank disc, and required a real-time operation on expensive, delicate equipment by someone who had enough expert skill to end up with a good sounding result. Although they could be played on any record player, they would often wear out much more quickly than vinyl. Today some acetates are highly prized for their rarity, especially when they contain unpublished material.

All the same, when the acetates arrived by post a week later, the boys couldn't believe how good it was to have a two-sided disc of their recordings that looked and felt like the real thing. Dyson remembers how exciting it was. 'There was nothing quite like it, when we took one of them out of its plain white paper sleeve and put it on the record player, it looked and sounded amazing. To think that was us on that piece of plastic was just a fantastic feeling, and would be even better if we could get it released.'

They immediately started to hawk the discs around various recording studios and labels, but without a great deal of success, until Reg and Brown eventually met with Jack Baverstock at Fontana. He was impressed with the song and appointed a representative to work with the band at the Philips Studios. 'He took it, and said, "O.K. we'll do this" and put it out on Fontana, a subsidiary label of Philips,' recalled Inkpen.

At the Philips studio, which was located in the basement area of Stanhope House in the West End of London, close to Marble Arch, the band did three or four takes of 'Come Back Baby' and then they discussed a flip side. Although they had recorded 'Corrina Corrina' as the flip at the Jackson studio, and although it was a song that was considered to be one of Brown's best vocal performances, the powers-that-be at Philips decided they wanted another number for the B side, so they came up with a song called 'Times Are Getting Tougher Than Tough'. The only trouble was that this had not been recorded during the 'Come Back Baby' sessions, so the band had to record it at Fontana's own studios.

By this time, Dyson had left the band and joined the Mockingbirds, a more blues-based band that suited Dyson's musical taste more than Bluesology did. So Rex Bishop, Mick Inkpen's friend and former bass player was invited to join Bluesology on bass for the eventual B side. As Dyson notes, 'In the end, despite recording some other takes, Fontana released the original "Come Back Baby" as it was recorded for the demo, with Reg's vocal. They didn't touch it, edit or re-record it, so both sides of the single featured two different line-ups of Bluesology'.

In the end though, 'Come Back Baby', was not the song to propel the boys into the promised land. 'I can't imagine why,' complained Inkpen. 'Dusty Springfield used to record in the same studio, but we just didn't sound right there, it might have been because we were nervous. It was a different scenario to what we were used to, but at least we now had a recording contract and had gained valuable experience in the studio.' The first radio airplay of 'Come Back Baby' was on the *Jack Jackson Sunday Night Record Programme*, probably because of his son's involvement. Dyson can still remember to this day how he called the others up and told them that they had just played their record. The band were all very encouraged. 'It was quite a strong sound at the time, with Reg's rising power piano chords. In many ways, it was a bit like Sounds Incorporated with the same powerful sound.'

The song made the airwaves a few more times, sold even fewer copies, and then sank without trace. 'We heard it on the radio a few times, which pleased my mum,' laughs Inkpen. 'We were all very excited when we first heard it on the radio, it was a big deal, but we lacked a genre. To be successful, you need the right material and, more importantly, be around at the right time so it had to fit together and I don't think the first effort was it. It was not quite right for the time. I do recall we had an old Thames van at the time and we heard it in the van on one of those hand-held transistor radios that were all the rage at the time.'

Sometime later, when Graham Boaden asked Reg what had happened to the song, he told him that he had sold it for £500 to Mills Music, which thrilled Reg's boss, Tony Hiller, but amazed Cyril Gee. 'He came to me one day and told me that he may be getting a recording contract with Fontana Records and he was currently working in Fontana studios with Jack Baverstock recording a song called "Come Back Baby" and did I want to publish it. I said I would see what I could do and so I printed up some copies. It sold in somewhere like Timbuktu and he earned some money from it. I went home and said to my wife Ruth, "You wouldn't believe this but even the office boy is writing songs." What is perhaps amazing is how much money Reg made from the song, during a time when most songwriters were earning a tenner a week. It seemed he had made his mark with one song that had earned him more than most of his contemporaries were making in a year.

Although Dyson had left the band with the boys' consent, he still continued his relationship with them as manager to bide his time whilst the Mockingbirds were in rehearsal. His main role in managing them was to get them some gigs; no mean feat. What he would do was just call up the venue bookers and give them a lot of spiel about the band. It helped, of course, that they had a single out at the time, and Dyson always used this and the fact that they had a recording deal with Fontana, as a lever to persuade bookers to book them.

'Our first manager would have been Geoff Dyson,' confirms Inkpen. 'He was not much older than we were, but he helped us enormously to get some gigs, but you need someone in charge and tell us where we need to be and when, and Geoff was too inexperienced at organising those kind of things.' Some of the gigs that Dyson secured for them were somewhat risky to say the least. One of those was when they played a gig in South Harrow to a group of bikers who expected a rock'n'roll band, which Bluesology couldn't claim to be. It was totally inappropriate for a crowd of rockers, who reacted badly.

'The audience migrated to the back of the hall,' remembers Inkpen. 'That is always a bit worrying, and then someone in the car park decides to ride his motorcycle up to the front door of the hall. I am not sure whether they were seriously going to invade the hall with a motorcycle but it certainly looked like it from the stage and there was a lot of bikes revving up outside. But we carried on regardless. Looking back on it today, it was all part and parcel of learning from experience, whether good or bad.'

Soon after 'Come Back Baby' had been released, Dyson contacted an old friend, Howard, whom he knew had a robust attitude towards getting into places and never taking no for an answer. He went into the studios of ATV where they did *Ready Steady Go!* and got to meet with someone senior at Associated Television. He put the record in front of them. And they said 'that's fine, sounds O.K., we will try and fit them in, in a month or so.'

While all this was going on, it was quickly becoming evident that although the band members were grateful to Dyson for his efforts, they wanted more. 'Sometime before we got really under way, we decided to part company with Geoff as our manager,' remembers Inkpen. 'The work was a bit patchy and Geoff didn't really have the contacts in the music scene that we needed, so we made the decision to take up an offer from a guy called Arnold Tendler, who I was working for as an apprentice. What we liked about him was his charming manner and how he appeared not to get ruffled about anything. He was well known for smoothing everything down if there was ever a problem, so we thought he was perfect, especially when we heard what he was offering us.'

It was soon after Tendler was invited to hear the band, and had told them that he thought they were good enough to be professional. 'So we told him,' continues Inkpen, 'about all the things we lacked, like stage clothes, equipment and management. Arnold told us he could fix all that and buy us what we needed if we would like him to be our manager. We agreed and all said yes.' On top of that, he also agreed to put some money into the band which meant they could have better equipment.

For his part, and for the efforts he would put into promoting the band and getting them gigs, Tendler in return wanted a share of the income. Again, the band agreed. In fact, they thought his offer was more than fair as he was prepared not to take any cut from the gigs the boys had already got booked up in advance. What was quite staggering to them was how Tendler still invested even though for those first two months he was not taking a penny from the gigs that Dyson had organised. He bought

Stewart Brown a new Gretsch guitar, along with some amplification and stage gear. They had a uniform, which was the style of the time, (if you consider the Beatles look during the sixties), and Bluesology now looked the part in their dark blue slacks, blue and white striped jackets and red sports shirts, which they bought under Tendler's patronage from Lord John in Carnaby Street.

Until Tendler came along, the instruments were all bought and paid for by the individual members of the band. 'We had to save up to buy cheap copies of guitars, and the drums were pieced together by the efforts of my mum,' recalls Inkpen. 'She got a job addressing cards that *Reader's Digest* used to send out; cartons of address cards and sheets of addresses, and she would sit there, for hours on end, with her typewriter earning about 50p per hundred, but she saved up the money she earned from that to buy me bits for my drum kit. I bought a tom-tom, and then I paid for the bass drum, and then my mum bought some further tom-toms for me.'

Reg, of course, still had his Hohner Pianette, which was pretty portable and easy to lug about, but for the rest of the band, it wasn't so easy. They were all grateful to Reg that his stepfather would lend them his van to transport their equipment from gig to gig. 'We threw our instruments into the back of the van with Fred's paint pots and the dust sheets whenever we went to a gig,' continues Inkpen. 'And before any of us could drive, he used to ferry us about whenever he was available to do so. And when he wasn't, we had to rely on another friend, Stephen Hutchings, who would borrow his father's camper van which was all done out with a sink and beds in the back. We still put our equipment in the back and we must have just about destroyed the camper. We did knock up a lot of mileage in those days, but Fred and Steve's father were brilliant in helping us out, and thank God they were.'

But then again, so was Tendler. He was the one that got them on the local Battle Of The Bands in Kilburn, where Reg would show off his brand new Vox Continental Organ, which he had just bought to replace his beloved Hohner Pianette. His new Vox was the business, as far as he was concerned. It was a transistor-based combo organ that was introduced in 1962. Known for its thin, bright, breathy sound, the 'Connie' was designed to be used by touring musicians. It was also very striking to look at, and had features not often found in keyboard instruments, the most obvious of which was its reverse-coloured keys (black naturals and white sharps) similar to a harpsichord. With a chrome Z-shaped stand and bright vermilion top, it looked very distinctive and handsome, and suited Reg right down to the ground.

The Battle Of The Bands was one of the first gigs that Bluesology had played since 'Come Back Baby' had been released. And it proved to be a good move for them. To play on a large stage with an equally large audience was what every band dreamed of. 'There must have been about two or three hundred people, at least,' Inkpen explains. 'It was good for us because we hadn't played to those kind of numbers before. But, it was a difficult one, because we were playing in front our peers and other bands, so it was a fairly critical gig. I remember feeling nervous, usually it didn't worry me at all, I couldn't wait to get on stage and get on with it because I was normally playing in front of people who couldn't play as well as I could, but this time I was much more nervous because we were playing in front of other musicians. Reg, however, was not fazed by it at all, or even by the other bands.'

Even more intriguing was how he changed what he did on stage, just for that one gig. He didn't stand up or kick over his piano stool like he usually did, simply because he didn't want to take the risk of damaging his new Vox organ. But as Inkpen explains, 'He wasn't the outstanding member of the band whose on-stage performance would attract hordes of onlookers. His playing was wonderful, yes, but he was no front man, not like Stewart was. In fact, he would just sit at the back of the band, quite unnoticeable and play his piano in the style of Jerry Lee Lewis. I guess there was a certain amount of unspoken friction between him and Stewart, but it never really led to any obvious conflict.'

Like any band went through in those days, travelling in a transit van was an experience in itself. 'We would all travel with the kit in the back with very little room for any of us to sit, so obviously it was going to cause friction from time to time. We all cursed my drums as they took up most of the room, but it was still great fun. When Reg was in his better moods, he would break into the Goons or some other mimicry with me and we would do a good show type thing in the back of the van. Despite the odd setback, it was generally a very happy band at the time.'

They didn't win the Battle Of The Bands contest, but they did pick up some kudos from it, which became apparent when they started getting gigs, playing more places in London and earning more money – usually a hundred pounds per gig.

Although Tendler continued to search around for gigs for the band, it was getting more difficult for him as time marched on, simply because he had no grounding in the music business. 'He was a good salesman and didn't lack the gift of the gab, so he did pick us up some work, but he soon realised his limitations, and eventually realising he was no Brian Epstein or Colonel Tom Parker, suggested that we sign with the Roy Tempest Agency to take care of the [main] gigs, which we did, and that was really the start of the professional Bluesology. There was no going back after that because there was so much work coming our way that we had to be a professional working band, and we had to take the decision to go full time, and so we did,' says Inkpen. It was enough to persuade Reg to ditch his job at Mills Music and hit the road with Bluesology.

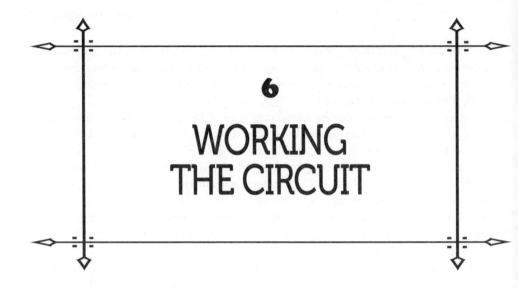

# 6

# WORKING
# THE CIRCUIT

Roy Tempest launched the Roy Tempest Organisation with the idea of bringing some American acts into Britain, whose careers were in the doldrums in the States. Normally, he would set up a 14 day tour for most of the acts he bought in, and then hire Bluesology to back them. Suddenly they found themselves backing such artists as Major Lance, Doris Troy, Patti LaBelle, Edwin Starr and Billy Stewart. Tempest, an ex-boxer, was said to be as shrewd as Colonel Tom Parker was in his handling of Elvis Presley, and never failed to amaze the visiting acts with the sheer number of gigs that he would set up: British tours were no rest cure with Roy around.

'It turned out that for two weeks they were working nonstop every night, and in some cases, more than once a night. So yeah, it was a surprise to most of them,' says Mick Inkpen. 'We didn't know any better. We were teenagers, we knew we were getting paid, and that was really all that mattered.' All the same, remembers Inkpen, 'it was hard graft with the number of gigs we were playing.'

It didn't help matters that they had, by this time, lost their original saxophonist who played on the 'Come Back Baby' session, and decided to up the ante by finding two new brass players to join the band. It was something that was deemed necessary if they were going to keep up the pace and stay together as a professional working band.

These new brass players, Pat Hicks and Dave Murphy, joined the group just before the Roy Tempest arrangement came into play. They were deemed to be the answer for Bluesology to be able to compete with other bands, all of whom were featuring brass arrangements in much of their material. Bands such as Cliff Bennett And The Rebel Rousers and the Graham Bond Organisation were probably amongst the first to introduce and popularise the saxophone and other brass instruments into their line-ups. The only problem was that good experienced brass players were costly and not that easy to come by.

'We would have gone for people of our own age but they would have been beginners like us, learning the trade,' reasons Inkpen. 'We wanted to push the band forward, so we needed guys who were experienced, so we advertised for musicians in the *Melody Maker*. Once again, we rented a hall for the auditions. We had to tell them what we wanted so they could work it out, and then we just busked and improvised, all very ad hoc. The ones we were drawn to were the ones who had more experience, so we recruited Hicks and Murphy, but for some reason we ended up with a trumpet and tenor sax, which I don't think was quite the plan to start with. All we really wanted was two sax players.'

Now regarded as professional musicians, Bluesology would be paid like most bands were, with the proceeds divvied out amongst its members. There were certain expenses that needed to be deducted first, such as van and petrol costs, but the rest was shared out equally and, again like most bands, the money was 'dished out' in the back of the van. It was where most arguments could have ensued. But not, it seems for Bluesology. 'Who gets what, who came the furthest, and who has the most expensive kit to look after,' but Inkpen doesn't recall any major 'band splitting rows like that. We were just given a wad of notes and we shared it out.'

It was from the proceeds of his share that Reg had traded in his Hohner for a Vox Continental; however it proved not to be a wise investment. 'That Vox became increasingly unreliable,' Inkpen remembers. 'Reg used it a lot for a long time and it was a flimsy thing and suffered because it had been thrown around and been given a battering. Reg didn't like the organ though because he was not really an organist, he was a pianist. The Vox was a curious instrument which had a habit of sticking on notes, especially during its latter years. One night, I remember being at the Scotch of St James and one note got stuck on the Vox, which was very embarrassing when you had a room full of showbiz people watching you. So there we were with the Continental humming away to itself.'

In the end, they were helped out by Alan Price who had previously been with the Animals but now had his own band, the eponymously named Alan Price Set. 'We had done some gigs with him already,' continues Inkpen, 'so he knew who we were, and we knew him, and he came over to Reg and tapped him on the shoulder and said, in a broad Geordie accent, "Have you got a problem with your keyboard?" and he just put his fist underneath it, and gave it such a hard thump that he lifted it off the ground. But it cured it. I have never seen Reg look so shocked. He didn't even get the chance to say yes or no, but it pleased the audience no end.'

In between working for Roy Tempest, Bluesology still maintained a heavy gigging schedule of their own. And although they didn't normally do private functions like weddings, birthdays and Bar mitzvahs, there was one occasion when they broke their own cardinal rule and agreed to take on an Irish wedding in Neasden.

According to Inkpen, 'We said yes because we had nothing else to do and we needed the money, but we were completely unsuitable for it. As always, Reg turned up to the gig with the stack of music he took to every gig, it was all kept in a satchel that never let his side, ever. And on this occasion, it was just as well. About halfway through the gig, it was obvious things weren't going well when a fight broke out at the back of the hall with tables and chairs flying everywhere. So, Reg came up with an idea to play some of Winifred Atwell's greatest hits, which he had the music for in his satchel. He picked out a stack of sheet music, opened one of his books at page one, and started to play. We just followed him, and it went down very well with everyone. And in the end, it stopped the fighting.'

Reg showed little sign of changing and, by his own admission, was not one to follow fashion in the way he dressed. Normally it was pretty conventional, unlike most of his band mates. Even so, he did have a wonderful sense of humour. And he could always be relied upon to say something outrageously funny just at the right moment, which would have the rest of the band collapsing in fits of laughter. Luckily, a lot of what he said wasn't heard by the punters.

'We were on stage and he would make some comment about someone in the audience who we all had been looking at, and what he said was bang on target and so we would be helpless with laughter,' chuckles Inkpen. 'He used to imitate the Goons a lot who had a radio show at the time. We could both do the voices of Peter Sellers, Spike Milligan, Harry Secombe and Michael Bentine in their Goon characters, and so it became part of our regular fooling around at the back of the stage.'

Not that there would be time for horseplay when they auditioned to be the backing band for soul legend Wilson Pickett for his tour of Britain. Inkpen recalls: 'He thought he was getting a session band, but instead he was offered us. We were cheaper than a session band, but Pickett knew what he was doing and wasn't about to take any risks. He sent across a Musical Director, and this guy turned up to audition us but wasn't at all happy, so we didn't get that gig, unfortunately. We weren't really ready for it and, certainly, we weren't really capable of learning the songs that quickly. We hadn't learnt all the material, and what material we did know we didn't know properly or how to deliver it for Pickett, so the first gig we ended up doing successfully, under our contract with Roy Tempest, was backing Major Lance.

Lance decided he wanted to do a British tour and Roy Tempest accommodated him as Mick Inkpen remembers:

I remember we were billed to do a gig in a place called Count Suckle's Cue Club in Praed Street, Paddington, in London in the basement of a Victorian House. It was a West Indian club that all the stars used to go to because it was open all weekend. The party started on Friday night and was still going strong Monday morning, so you could go there anytime and there was music going on all the time. It was a nice, friendly atmosphere and we felt safe there, as did the audience. But when we were ready and waiting to play, Lance was late turning up, and the gig was due to start at three in the morning. We had already played a gig somewhere else that night and this was the last one. We got our stuff set up on stage and Lance's Musical Director, Robin, was there, who usually opened the act with a number that he did on his own as a singer. He would do his number and then introduce the maestro who would come on after. Well, Robin was there with us and he said 'Major Lance is late so I will just come on and play with you guys; play your normal set.'

As he had been watching us throughout the tour, he knew all the numbers. He came on stage and did a few numbers of his own, which included one particular number that involved a spectacular guitar solo, some of which he used to play with his teeth and behind his head, like Jimi Hendrix, but this was well before Hendrix.

So Robin was doing all of this and it's all going very well and the audience is in uproar, they are dancing and the place is filling up. What we didn't know, was that Major Lance had arrived and was waiting to enter the stage, but Robin had captured the audience so much that after he had finished his spectacular guitar solo, there were cries for more, and so he decided he would give them more. He continued by playing the guitar between his teeth now and he's not coming off the stage. The upshot of it all was that Major Lance did not like that very much, and there was a lot of finger drumming and glaring, and after the gig, Robin was fired. It was the last gig before he went home. But we loved him, he was marvellous.

Although the boys would normally learn the songs of the American artists they had to back from Reg's enormous collection of records – he seemingly had everything that everyone had recorded in the last twenty years – they also learnt the bones of it from the sheet music they were given. 'In some cases we didn't learn it at all, and just got the hang of it from a brief rehearsal. With Major Lance we had an afternoon to learn his entire act, but with Patti Labelle we were given a whole day.'

The day after LaBelle and the Bluebelles rolled into Britain, they spent the day rehearsing with Bluesology at the Marquee Club in Wardour Street, London, when the club was closed. At the end of the day, at about 5p.m., the band packed up, and the following night they opened at the Scotch of St James.

Almost everyone who was anyone in show business was there. People like the Beatles, some members of the Who, the Animals, the Rolling Stones, film director Dick Lester, and many others. Whether from the world of music or film, they had all crammed into the club to see what LaBelle and her girls could do. 'I don't know how we got through it, but we did, and it was a nightmare really,' recalls Inkpen. 'Due to poor stage management there were no lights on stage, so we were working in very dimmed lighting. We had no music stands, not that we used sheet music, but we had things like set lists, notes and reminders as to what we were doing, but with the poor lighting we couldn't see or read a thing. There was a big stagecoach at the side of the stage taking up most of the room for some reason, possibly for the DJ, so there was not much of a stage for us to sit or stand on. And we had drums, two or three amps, the Vox Continental at one end of the stage, and with all six of us, plus Patti Labelle and her girls in the front, there was not much room for comfort.'

Even though the boys didn't really have time to socialise with the artists, Inkpen remembers how Stewart Brown became quite friendly with Cindy Birdsong, who later went on to join the Supremes. 'According to Stu, she was a delightful girl, sweet and good fun, but they were all heavily chaperoned. I did ask him about his friendship with her, and, apparently, it was all very above board, or so he said. Patti was very professional, she knew what she wanted, and to this day, I am not sure whether we came up to what she expected for a backing band, but I hope we did.'

In between gigging, the band would use any spare time to prepare for recording. Their second session for Fontana was to lay down a newly-penned song by Reg titled 'Mr Frantic'. Mick Inkpen had heard the song for the first time when Reg sang it at his house and told him that it was going to be the new single.

'There were a couple of others that Reg had written that were in the frame, but we needed another strong song to record. We rehearsed "Mr Frantic", which was the one we all liked, so on this occasion we didn't have to make any demos, we just went up to Philips and recorded it. But it was not an entirely successful session. We had the same trouble with the recording and sound that we had at Fontana with "Come Back Baby", and especially "Times Are Getting Tougher Than Tough". With "Come Back Baby", the producer just cleaned up the demo and released it, but it was not quite right. With "Mr Frantic", there was something wrong with it from the start. They took the strange step of double-tracking the drums, which they said would give it some depth, which I couldn't understand as it just made the drum-track confused. I knew what I was doing and was capable of doing it louder or quicker, but they insisted on double-tracking it.'

'I think Reg was reasonably pleased with the final release though,' says Inkpen. '"Mr Frantic" was recorded soon after "Come Back Baby", but the band had moved on a lot since then. And it showed that we had learnt something during our brief professional career, that we had a nice, tight brass section. I was particularly partial to the 'B' side, which was more like the Bluesology sound at the time, because that was what we were doing live. We played "Come Back Baby" and "Mr Frantic" live, and the audiences thought they were good songs, and they went down reasonably well, but we were a covers band, so the new songs must have stood out like a sore thumb to the audiences.'

It was during this period of Bluesology, that Reg continued to do the vocals on some of the songs in the band's set list as well as his own compositions but, still feeling unsure about his singing voice, he usually took a back seat and normally only sang about 10% of the time. He never pushed himself in that respect, simply because he didn't believe he had the confidence to take on too many of the vocals. If he didn't think he was a good vocalist, then the rest of the band didn't agree. They considered him to be an excellent singer. It was something that he amazingly wasn't aware of.

Good singer or not, they still managed to end up playing a short residency in Germany at the Top Ten Club in Hamburg. It was a gig that Tendler had set up for them through the Marquee Club in London, because Bluesology used to play there frequently and, at one point, the band's management operated out of the Marquee.

By the time the boys left British shores in March 1966, they knew they were going to be away for a long time but they didn't know for how long, or what the implications might be. 'We had to play for four hours a night and we didn't have enough material to cover the gigs,' remembers Inkpen. 'We had maybe two, forty-five minute sets, so we had a choice to play the set three times or we could do what we eventually did, and that was to play a twenty-five minute blues song with improvisations from Reg using very rude lyrics as the audience was German and didn't know what he was going on about. The manager, who was Scottish, however, did know, and was sitting at the back of the venue having convulsions. It was very funny but rude.'

If you were 18 in 1966, Hamburg was an intriguing place to be, even if you were, like Bluesology, working so much that there was little time for a social life. 'We met one or two of the local ladies, who were charming and delightful,' smiles Inkpen. 'I got to know one girl quite well who took me home to meet her mum and dad for tea. We used to go down to a local Bierkeller and they used to make Reg play the piano, so the Oompah band would get off the stage and the manager got talked into letting Reg play. So, out came the Winifred Atwell songbook again. I can distinctly remember him playing old ragtime favourites which went down quite well. It was a real Bierkeller with wooden trestle tables and big steins of beer and blokes in leather trousers slapping each other about to Reg playing ragtime.' It would have been much like the Bierkeller that you see in *G.I Blues*.

The band played a month's residency at the Top Ten Club in Hamburg, working in tandem with another British band called Linda Laine And The Sinners. The Sinners' keyboard player was Len Crawley and their guitarist was Pete Bellotte. The latter would become a collaborator with Reg, after he had become Elton John, on the 1979 album, *Victim Of Love*.

Long before that, however, on the first night of their month's engagement, Bluesology turned up late, recalls Crawley. 'They had been delayed because they had travelled by train. Unlike most bands, they didn't have a van, so they had to rely on public transport to move their equipment from one gig to another. The band's equipment travelled separately from them, so for the opening night none of the gear had arrived, including Reg's Vox Continental. The other boys borrowed the instruments and sound gear they needed from us, but because we didn't have what Reg needed to play, he just stood on stage trying to look like part of the band without his Vox Continental. They used our drums and bass guitar, and they wouldn't let Reg sing, so yes, he just stood there, in his smart dark blue blazer and clapped his hands to the music. He seemed O.K. about it, but it all seemed a little strange and odd.'

The Top Ten Club was located just off the Reeperbahn and was owned by Peter Eckhorn, who would spend most of his time posing in his Mercedes sports car so most people thought the club must have been raking it in. Even so, there was a curious arrangement for those who worked there. The waiters were employed on a freelance basis and were paid commission on the amount of beer they sold, and each of them had a number of tables to serve. If a good band was playing, they got more money and it seemed that Bluesology and the Sinners fell into that category.

The waiters doubled up as bouncers too. They would be polishing tables and moving glasses around whilst getting closer and closer to the trouble spot and then, without any warning, they would jump on the person who was causing the problem. One would pull the jacket down over his arms and the other two would turn him around face down on the floor and they would pick him up by the elbows and throw him out into the street.

The club was laid out with the stage at the far right as you entered, and there was a seating area and a dance floor. Crawley remembers that 'When it was full, the atmosphere was excellent. Eckhorn treated the bands fairly, but it was hard work. We just turned up and went straight on without any time to rehearse or prepare.'

Bluesology played mainly R&B material, like Muddy Waters' 'I've Got My Mojo Working', but still the band didn't give Reg many vocal breaks. That's not to say he didn't sing at all; he would usually get one or two songs. 'The only one I heard him sing was "My Girl",' recalls Crawley. 'He sounded pretty similar to the way he sang on the "Come Back Baby" single. We all thought he had a good voice, but the rest of the band didn't want him to sing. Stewart Brown was still the lead vocalist and was sounding more and more like a soul singer, in the same vein as Chris Farlowe, and that was why the rest of the band wanted him as the lead singer. At the time, they hadn't yet released the second single, "Mr Frantic", but I do remember Reg telling me that it was due for release when they got back to Britain after the Hamburg gigs.'

Accommodation at the Top Ten Club was pretty minimalist and was situated above the venue. It consisted of half a dozen rooms, some with twin beds, some with single beds and some with bunk beds, so most of the time the boys were sharing rooms and sleeping arrangements. Rooms were all equipped with a communal wash basin and other appliances, such as a kettle to make tea and coffee, most of which was bought and shared by one and all. The only problem, says Crawley, was how they got on each other's nerves because they were living together 24/7. 'There were times when we were even sleeping in the same room, but it was what we had to do because we were not paid enough to stay in a hotel, so we had to stay in this dormitory-style accommodation upstairs over the club. It was clean and tidy, and we each had an iron to prepare our stage clothes.'

Inevitably a lot of practical jokes were played on one another. Crawley remembers: 'Once, someone decided to rewire my bed so that when I jumped into bed one night, I fell completely through it because they had taken all the springs out.' When they weren't fooling around, they would go drinking. 'Reg wasn't a very big drinker, but he decided to join the other band members and have a drink one night. I had never seen him drunk, but we had one or two beers while he had a real skinful. He got so drunk, he ended up passing out on the bathroom floor and was completely incoherent for a short while, before he finally lost consciousness. He wasn't too well the next day!'

Although Crawley and Reg became friends in Hamburg, they only had time for limited socialising because they were playing so late. They usually slept in till at least midday and played until 2a.m. (3a.m at weekends). 'We would eat together at a restaurant next door, but by 7p.m. we had to be on stage.' The respective bands played an hour on and then an hour off, playing a total of four hours each. When they were not playing or sleeping then they would go shopping, and any other spare time they had would be spent rehearsing new numbers because Eckhorn would only let the band rehearse when the club was closed.

'We would also go out to see other bands playing. Reg and I would go out and catch other bands playing elsewhere and always chat about music. He told me he had always wanted to be a songwriter more than a performer and, at other times, we would be dating girls. Reg did meet someone but I don't know whether it was a full-on relationship or not, but he always seemed to be dancing with her. I also remember seeing him with her by the stage all the time we were playing,' Crawley recollects.

After Bluesology completed their Hamburg marathon, they returned to Britain, recorded and released 'Mr Frantic', and continued their frantic club circuit work, often playing two or three times a day. They now had at least three and a half hours worth of material that they could call on, which was certainly enough for a competent set for just about anywhere.

But, the relentless touring was beginning to take its toll on the beleaguered band members. They were still backing the American artists that Tempest was bringing over, with Reg remaining as enthusiastic about them as ever before, especially when they had the chance to work with Edwin Starr. He was thrilled that he had the opportunity to learn so much from them. If anything, he looked up to the American acts, probably because he had always listened to them on record at school, and now, quite marvellously, he had the chance to play with them as a backing musician. As far as he was concerned, it didn't get any better than this, and what was quite remarkable about it all was that the constant grind of touring and learning new material didn't seem to have any effect on him at all. If anything, he seemed to take it all in his stride, unlike some of the other boys in the band.

'We continued to play the small clubs in Britain, when we started working professionally, and these were usually all-nighters,' remembers Mick Inkpen. 'We played at the Ricky Tick, a club in Windsor, which was actually a derelict house that had been a hotel and was now a night club. Everyone played there including the Rolling Stones. It was a rough place and very crude, all very threadbare, but that was the kind of place we played. There was also a similar place in Sheffield called the Mojo Club, and a place in Manchester called the Twisted Wheel that had a good reputation for interesting Blues bands and the kind of stuff that we wanted to play, not the Top 10 type of pop music, but blues-orientated jazz music. I remember we played there with the Move on a couple of occasions; a fantastic band. They all sang in harmony, all spot on, and set a high standard for us.

'We played with Georgie Fame and John Mayall, and I remember one gig they played [John Mayall's Bluesbreakers] with a fresh-faced Eric Clapton when he was in his first few months with the band. He was a stunning guitarist, and he introduced Stewart Brown to the use of light gauge banjo strings for an E string guitar because Stewart wanted to know how he could bend the E string right across the fret board.

'We also played in London clubs like the Marquee. It was very small, just a room with no drinks licence, all you could have was a soft drink, a sandwich and horrible hotdogs. There was a dressing room like a cupboard with all sorts of musicians getting in there, including Chris Barber playing his trombone. I remember him playing with Manfred Mann in the cupboard while the Manfreds were on the stage.'

In addition to the gigs they were playing in and around London, Tendler also managed to come up with another gig in Europe, this time in the South of France. It was at a young teenage night club that had to close at 9p.m., so the kids could get home. It was also where the band would stay in the club owner's house up in the hills in Marseille. They were all very well catered for and looked after by his mother and, this time, unlike in Hamburg, all had the luxury of their own rooms.

Inkpen recalls an idyllic period in the band's history: 'We just loafed around all day then went to the gig, played for 90 minutes and then back home at 9p.m. We really enjoyed ourselves, it was a really nice gig and it had the added bonus of being in the South of France. We did a couple of spots in another night club, to break up the monotonous regime. And we also got dragged out to the middle of Provence in the hills which, because of the picturesque scenery, was like being in the Wild West of America. We went to this farmhouse night club, which had a barbecue, dancing and booze, and we, of course, were the music.'

Although France provided a welcome change of scenery, two weeks later, when returning home to Britain, all it seemed was not well. It was during a gig at the Whisky A Go-Go above the Flamingo Club in London's Wardour Street, that things came to a head, or at least it did for Bishop. Not that it was completely surprising.

He had been unhappy for some time and, unlike the others, wasn't really into the furious gigging, or being a professional musician. He was far more interested in going to university. Even if he had been happy with the band at one time, he never really thought of it as a career. Neither did it help that he was on the butt end of some barracking from Hicks and Murphy. At the Whisky A Go-Go gig, things got a little heated between the three musicians. At the end of one of the sets, Bishop laid his bass to rest against one of the amplifiers, thinking it would be safe from any unforeseen damage, but somehow, someone jostled the amp and sent it crashing into the middle of his instrument, breaking the neck and, consequently, he couldn't finish the set. After a dispute erupted between the three band members, Hicks and Murphy criticised Bishop for leaving his bass where he did, but it was enough to send Bishop storming out of the club, screaming that he'd had enough of the band.

Reg kept a fairly low profile during the row that ensued. He had, by this time, become very single minded as to where his own career was headed, and viewed the Bishop fallout as nothing more than a minor inconvenience. 'I believe he and Stewart already had feelers out for a replacement, so it didn't come as a great surprise to him,' recalls Inkpen. 'When Bishop finally did leave, Reg and Stewart already had someone else they could turn to, a guy called Freddy Gandy. In many ways, Freddy was a Godsend. Not only was he the perfect bassist for the band, but he could drive, so suddenly our transport problems also got resolved.'

As with most bands who are working almost non-stop, it was quite natural that the strain of it all would eventually end in conflict. Neither did it help that there were quite a few age differences and demands on individual members of the band. 'I didn't have the same lifestyle as our brass section, who were older and both had flats in London with independent lives,' continues Inkpen. 'As far as they were concerned, the more they worked, the more money they earned. But, for the rest of us it wasn't like that. We all still lived at home, and didn't need to flog ourselves in the same way, even though we did once Bluesology had got onto the rollercoaster roundabout. It was the only way we could go, so we took whatever was thrown at us. It was either that, or finish the band.

'I was beginning to feel it was a bit of a treadmill and, because I was working all the time, I was losing weight; so by the time I did the gig with Patti Labelle and the Bluebelles, I formed the opinion that my style of drumming was not in tune with what they wanted.' Even though he openly admits that he had been perfectly adequate for the standard Bluesology set, 'It didn't seem to chime with what we were doing with the American artists brought in by Tempest. The rest of them wanted and needed what they would call a funky drummer.'

Inkpen had never heard of a 'funky drummer' at the time, and didn't even know what that meant or how to change his style. 'I was at a loss as to how I should deal with it, I thought I had got it, but apparently I hadn't. So when Patti wanted to hire us again for a second tour, it was on the understanding that I was not in the line up. You would have thought that the other members of the band, including Reg, would have stuck by me and refused the tour, but apparently the tour was more important, so I was asked to leave. But it wasn't the band who gave me the news, that was left to Arnold Tendler to deal with, so he told me and asked me to leave. He had been my employer in the jewellery business, and was very embarrassed about it.'

Inkpen saved his boss the embarrassment by telling him that he was tired of it all anyway, and could do with a break. Inkpen didn't hear from anyone in the band until he met up with Reg about two years later. 'Bluesology had gone back to the South of France, and he came round to tell me how the tour had gone, and to show me what sort of clothes he had bought there, which were a lot more trendy and actually fitted him. Gone were the Hush Puppies, and he had changed his hairstyle. It seemed as if he was beginning to develop his own identity and moving out of his mother's shadow.'

Bassist Freddy Gandy, on the other hand, was the kind of player they wanted in the band. He first met Stewart in Denmark Street. He had seen Bluesology in the clubs backing various acts, so he once told Stewart that, if he ever needed a bass player, he should call him. Stewart replied in a positive manner and, before long, as soon as Bishop had walked out, he was in the band. 'I cannot remember any audition,' laughs Gandy today. 'The band at the time was Paul Gale, who had replaced Mick Inkpen on drums, Stewart Brown, Pat Hicks, Dave Murphy and Reg Dwight.' And although the rollercoaster continued for them all, transport it seemed was still a major problem.

Not that the problem would last for long. Their old Hamburg comrades Linda Laine And The Sinners had a red Comma van that they had bought in 1965. Not long after the German gigs, the band broke up and Len Crawley got stuck with the van, which was still on a hire purchase agreement and he didn't know what to do with it. 'I went to see Bluesology one night and got chatting to Freddy Gandy. I told him that my band had split up and I had been lumbered with this van that I didn't want, because I didn't intend playing in a group any more. I was told that Bluesology needed a van so they paid me the outstanding balance on the HP, and they took the van off my hands.' Gandy's reward for sorting out the transport was to become chauffeur as well as bassist.

Soon after Gandy joined Bluesology, Arnold Tendler set them up with some more gigs in the South of France. This time, they were based in a small town just outside St Tropez where they remained for three weeks. It would be the last time that Tendler would be involved with organising gigs for the band, before he suddenly disappeared. The band remained clueless as to the reason he ended the relationship.

In France, a potentially fatal event occurred when they were shacked up in an old dilapidated villa in the middle of nowhere. Reg electrocuted himself and, according to Gandy, could have easily died. How it happened remains a mystery to this day, but as Gandy explains, it was pretty serious.

'I remember there was a sudden yelp and Reg was spark out. He had touched something live, so we summoned a doctor who gave him an injection in his butt. I remember we turned Reg over and pulled down his trousers so the doctor could give him this injection, while he was still unconscious, but he seemed all right after that. In fact, he recovered from the ordeal so remarkably well, even we were surprised. He was probably somewhat embarrassed about the whole episode, but at least he was unconscious when it all happened. And what was equally remarkable was that the gigs we were booked to do continued with him in good form, like nothing had happened.'

Not long after this 'shocking' episode, continues Gandy:

> We were asked by the gig organisers to move into St Tropez itself to fill in for another band who were not working out as expected. The Nightimers had been playing at the gig's venue and were not going down very well, so we took over from them, which extended our stay in the South of France by a couple of weeks. Our accommodation was a lot better than the villa where Reg almost killed himself. I remember it was a pretty upmarket type of place, a modern low level apartment block about 2km outside of St Tropez.
>
> Unfortunately we didn't have the style of clothes that were really needed for our jaunt to the trendy side of St Tropez. When we left the other club to go to St Tropez, we didn't have any stage clothes to wear, so Reg and I went shopping and decided to steal some. Reg picked up this shirt, and then suddenly lost his bottle so he gave it to me and I shoved it in a bag that I had. It was so stupid. I thought we had got away with it but the minute I got outside onto the pavement, this woman, who I think was the shop proprietor came out screaming after me. I had to pay something ridiculous for these shirts. I couldn't stop cussing and swearing at Reg when I finally caught up with him. He had legged it out of the shop and was at the top of the road waiting for me.

Even so, the boys loved the trip. And on top of that, every night was party night. It was the middle of summer and, as expected for that time of year, the place was full of yachts lined up alongside the quay, carrying passengers who were the jet set crowd of the sixties. 'Yeah, it was pretty amazing,' confirms Gandy. 'These people just wanted to come into the club, dance, drink and get crazy. Then, after the gig we would all go to someone's villa outside St Tropez and the crazy time would carry on. And when we weren't doing that, we would pick up a few bottles of wine and have a party back at our own apartment.'

It was while they were in St Tropez, that Stewart Brown came even more to the fore as the band's vocalist and front man, and would develop his own unique style of delivery. 'Some nights when it got going, we would be running around the stage, and then Stewart would end up running around the whole club. It was fair to say that everyone let loose whilst we were playing,' laughs Gandy. 'One night Pat Hicks even got carried away and threw his trumpet in the air. Normally he and Dave Murphy would stand still like most brass sections, so this was the extent of Pat Hicks going wild.'

One of the things that Bluesology didn't do during this time, noted Gandy, was rehearse. 'We were playing covers of other people's songs, so we just played them like the records. I can't remember any rehearsals. We just played live.'

Like most gigging bands during this period, the boys continued to play the same gigs every night during the week, but it was the weekend gigs they seemed to enjoy most. As one would expect, they were the ones that were more lively. 'We were doing a lot of the Stax type music back then,' continues Gandy. 'And we were also covering the standard disco music of the day, but nothing original. We played a lot of Memphis brass stuff, because we had a good brass section.' But despite all of this, and the vast experience they now had behind them, Reg didn't seem that happy. As usual, he remained fairly subdued on stage and did what he had always done, tucked away with his Vox Continental in the corner, but something, it seemed, had been nagging away at him. He was becoming more and more peeved when he wasn't allowed to sing. It was one of the reasons why he would eventually call it a day, and leave the band.

Even so, Reg still got a lot out of playing live and, although he considered one of the highlights to be supporting Little Richard at the Saville Theatre in London, it wasn't an easy one to play; far from it. It had been organised by Brian Epstein and, if the rowdy behaviour of the audience was anything to go by, it would appear that he wasn't quite experienced enough to take measures to safeguard those performing. Bluesology was the first band on, followed by the Alan Price Set – not that the crowd were particularly interested in either. If anything, they wanted them off the stage so that they could see their hero.

'The place was full of rockers,' remembers Gandy. 'And it appeared that they had brought their motorbikes with them because they were throwing spark plugs, nuts, bolts and all manner of other motorbike spare parts at us. By the time we had finished our set and left the stage, and Alan Price had come on, the rockers had by now grown unbearably impatient in waiting for the headliner of the show to come on, and decided, there and then, to take their frustration out on Alan and used his Hammond organ for target practice. You could have probably made a motorbike with what was left on the stage after we had left it. So, can you imagine what it looked like after Alan had finished? It was dangerous, seriously dangerous.'

Even when Little Richard came on, things didn't really change that much. The audience stormed the stage and were dancing around his piano. The whole thing was out of control even though Little Richard was in no apparent danger. He just carried on playing.

Soon after a prestigious gig at the Marquee, the boys decided to expand the band by bringing in a showman guitarist named Neil Hubbard, but he only stayed for a few months. One of the problems, it seems, was how Pat Hicks and Dave Murphy were not that enthusiastic about Hubbard's antics which, according to Gandy, illustrates the type of people Hicks and Murphy were.

'Being somewhat older than the rest of us, they had been around the music scene for longer than we had, and had come from a more staid music environment, like those in Archer Street in London, where musicians used to hang around looking for session work. These were mainly the old school Tin Pan Alley brass players. And Murphy and Hicks were part of that scene. They had their own little world, unlike the rest of us, who would follow other bands like the Who and the Beatles, they didn't really have any interest, they were far more interested in praising the Big Bands. If anything, they were slightly grumpy old brass players. They didn't really have the same sort of mentality as the rest of us. Reg, funnily enough, came somewhere in between.'

Even though Hubbard was very good at what he did, was an excellent guitarist, and had an enormous stage presence, Hicks and Murphy would always take the piss out of him whenever he threw himself around the stage like the showman he was. 'They would stand there like Archer Street musicians who had been around since the year dot, and taunt him with things like "What's wrong with him, is he having a fit or something." They used to wind him up relentlessly and that is why he probably left – because of Hicks and Murphy. But he bided his time, and eventually walked away from Bluesology soon after he was asked to join another band.'

It was about the same time, that the boys headed out to Stockholm in Sweden for their next European gig. They travelled by boat from Tilbury to Gothenburg, where Reg's competitive nature came to the fore. 'We were on the boat, and he said he wanted a game of table tennis on deck in the middle of the North Sea. It was blowing a gale and raining, we lost thousands of table tennis balls over the side because of the wind, but he was so determined to win a game of table tennis against me because I was a pretty decent player. I remember being out on the deck, in the midst of the wind and rain, but that didn't matter to Reg. I kept saying "Just give up Reg," but he was getting very angry and wanted to carry on. I'm sure he won in the end, simply because I gave up,' Gandy insists.

Known among the rest of the band as the king of the drugs trade, Gandy could usually lay his hands on almost any recreational drug there was, from just about anywhere in the world. In Sweden, it was no different; in fact it was Gandy who introduced the rest of the boys to smoking dope, all except Reg who did not indulge in any kind of smoking.

'I couldn't walk out of the country without some dope, and I remember I scored in Sweden in a railway station. The last thing at night, I would roll a joint and smoke it while Reg was in another room. Quite stupidly, I had left this joint on a table and the woman cleaner came in the following morning and emptied it into a rubbish bin. It was the end of my world. I looked everywhere for this joint, but then, I remembered that she had been into Reg's room and emptied his waste bin and the joint must have fallen out because he found it, and came into me shouting, "There you go, look what I have found," and handed over my joint. I was moaning to everyone about losing it, and amazingly, Reg found it.'

Something else to get lost after the Sweden gig, while on their way back to Britain, was their drummer Paul Gale. 'He just disappeared. We heard that he had taken his drums and boarded a train to Denmark, to be with a girl he met at the gig,' recalls Gandy. Now as they arrived back in England, Bluesology, once again, were without a drummer.

# 7

# LET THE HEARTACHES BEGIN

Soon after the band arrived home from Sweden, the boys were introduced to Long John Baldry, the son of a police officer from Colindale in London who, as his moniker implied, was tall – 6' 7" of him to be precise. He became interested in music simply because he thought he had a great voice, and had also seen it as ideal opportunity not to keep his homosexuality locked away in a closet. Being Long John Baldry allowed him not to make a secret of it anymore.

His regular band, Steampacket, had disbanded in 1966. After losing an amazingly talented line-up that included Rod Stewart, Julie Driscoll and Brian Auger, it seemed as if Bluesology fitted the bill for what Baldry was now looking for – like-minded musicians to work with him as his band. With that in mind, and having seen what Bluesology could do, he approached Stewart Brown during a gig in North London and asked Brown if he was interested. Brown was.

From that point on, Bluesology became Stu Brown and Bluesology for six months of the year, playing their usual type of gigs at pubs and clubs across Britain, and for the remaining six months, they would be on call as Long John Baldry's backing band and remained working with him until just after he scored a number one hit with 'Let The Heartaches Begin' in 1967.

Hicks and Murphy didn't pass muster, so Baldry decided to change the brass section. A new manager was also engaged to replace Arnold Tendler, and who better than George Webb, Baldry's own manager? Formerly a well-known band leader and trad jazz player from the 1950s, he was, as far as everyone was concerned, a perfect choice to take care of the business side of things.

Indeed, when the band agreed to work with Baldry, they were paid a retainer, so the days of relying on the distribution of a 'wad of cash' in the back of a van became a thing of the past; suddenly they had a regular income. Brown informed Hicks and Murphy that they were out, after a gig at the Clook Clique Railway Club in Hampstead,

London. They weren't best pleased about being sacked so, to make things as difficult as they could, they took the van and scarpered off to Germany. Even though the boys were feeling slightly uncomfortable about having to get rid of two of their members, in hindsight, they agreed that they were not really the ideal musicians for Bluesology: Hicks and Murphy just didn't seem to gel anymore.

Stewart Brown introduced the third drummer to join the band. Bristol native, Pete Gavin's real name was Leslie Rowney, but he refused to answer to Leslie as it sounded like a girl's name. He had nicknamed Brown 'Stubber'. 'He was a great drummer and he was one of the first people to have the double bass set up,' recalled later Bluesology guitarist Bernie Holland. 'He had a Ludwig kit with two bass drums like Ginger Baker and Buddy Rich but, for a run of the mill group like Bluesology, it was unusual. He was a very versatile player, who could play swing and blues the way Baldry wanted it played. From the album *Looking At Long John* he could play "Cry Me A River" and "I Love Paris" and a lot of other standards. He was really at home with that style of playing.'

Gavin had already worked with various groups, here and there, but his real passion was to play behind a brass section. It wasn't until he was hanging-out at the Cromwellian Club that he got the chance to sit-in with Bluesology and play the music he loved, from the catalogues of such names as Otis Redding and Wilson Pickett. He remembers that Reg did the vocals on a few songs, as always, and the band had a pretty good horn section. There was something about Bluesology's punchy sound in the Crom's intimate room that really appealed to him.

As soon as he was given the chance to play with Baldry, he decided, then and there, that he wanted to be a permanent part of the line-up. They had by this time also been joined by Marsha Hunt and Alan Walker – two new vocalists to accompany Baldry. The new line up was reprising the Rod Stewart and Julie Driscoll roles from Steampacket. Marsha became involved because of Stu Brown as they were both in some sort of relationship, and Alan Walker was with a local band called the Roadhogs, who used to play in at the Blue Moon club in Cheltenham, where Baldry had met him and offered him the gig.

It was during auditions to find a replacement brass section, that Pete Gavin took a break to get a sandwich and bumped into Elton Dean outside on Oxford Street. Elton and Gavin once had a band called the Soul Pushers. 'I told him to come and try-out with Bluesology,' says Gavin, 'but he said he hadn't played a note in ages. I said, "For God's sake, find yourself a sax and come and audition".' He did, and joined the band as its soprano saxophonist. Elton then brought in Marc Charig – a very well educated ex-public school boy who was a jazz player and had played in a pop group under sufferance and for the money – who was the most serious of the side men about what he was doing. 'Elton and Marc created such a lovely sound and because Elton also played cornet as well as sax, rather than trumpet, the sound was more mellow,' remembers Fred Gandy.

Of course, travelling bands with brass sections were quite a rarity back then. Besides Georgie Fame And The Blue Flames and Zoot Money's Big Roll Band, there weren't that many others. But Bluesology, even without Baldry, were starting to earn themselves a very respectable following. Much of the previous fare had been guitar-based groups in the style of Cliff Richard And The Shadows, so bands with a horn section were a breed apart.

Certainly, when the Bluesology boys were doing their own thing, they would, like so many other London-based bands of the time, still pile into a van on a daily basis, along with *all* their equipment, and trek the length and width of Great Britain to play gigs, just as they had done since they had turned professional. Usually, they would fall out of the van, knackered and half asleep from the extensive travelling, play the gig, and then weave their way back to London afterwards. One day, recalled Gavin, they picked up Reg on route. 'He had a rather nifty suitcase he'd bought at some kind of bargain store, I mentioned it, but that was the end of that particular conversation. A day or two later, when we collected him for another gig, he presented me with an identical suitcase. I'd admired his so much, that he had made a special trip to get me one just like it. That was the sort of person he was: extremely generous and thoughtful.'

According to Gavin, Reg also remained outwardly content about what was going on but, unlike the others, he forged a very close relationship with Baldry, who became a mentor and close friend. Despite his penchant for throwing the occasional tantrum when he didn't get his own way, or becoming frustrated about his role in the band, he was usually fine. Certainly, it was clearer than ever before that he had aspirations beyond Bluesology and, although he didn't discuss them openly with the rest of the band, it was likely that he did with Baldry, just as much as Baldry, renowned for helping young musicians flourish, would have encouraged him. He had, after all, done much the same with a then young and still undiscovered Rod Stewart, whom he had come across busking outside a tube station in the West End. There and then, he offered him a role in Steampacket.

Not that Reg had ever taken to busking. He didn't have to, and although he didn't appear to be any more self-absorbed than any of the other band members, he did keep himself to himself; quite a private person, it seemed. He obviously had in mind what he wanted to do and how he could make it happen. But there were moments of madness, remembers Gavin. 'He would sometimes get a bit nuts in dressing rooms, or at bed and breakfast joints, probably from frustration.'

All the same, Bluesology was a comfortable existence, not just for Reg, but for the entire band and in particular for Gavin. Despite opportunities that came their way, they had regular incomes and a relatively secure future, or so they thought, but with so many difficult decisions made along the way, looking back today they would probably admit that several wrong turnings were made.

'I made decent money, for the time, with Bluesology, and shared a bed-sit with my then girlfriend, later my first ex-wife, and another girl in Westbourne Grove,' explains Gavin. 'One of those wrong decisions, for me, was when a roadie-friend of mine, Richard Cole, stopped by and asked me to come up West and jam for a couple of hours with some guys. He was pretty tight-lipped about the details, and so, not wanting to jeopardise my job with Bluesology, I said if he couldn't tell me what it was all about I wouldn't go. I later discovered, and this was a big "Ooops", that they were putting Led Zeppelin together.'

With a new drummer and a new transit van, the boys continued their arduous lifestyle travelling across Britain from gig to gig. Usually the van, loaded with their equipment, would also take some of the boys who didn't ride with the others in the Ford Cortina they owned. To help matters on the travelling front, they had also taken on Barry Lawrence as road manager. He had equipped the van with a stereo system complete with a hand-built ten watt amplifier and speakers situated under the rear seats, which blasted out blues songs while they were on the road. And when they weren't listening to music, they would be drawing up a set list for what they were going to play that evening.

The band normally played two forty-five minute sets with a break. In between the Bluesology slots, especially if there was another band playing, Reg and the guys would just sit back and be entertained. Otherwise, it was a case of sitting it out in a make-shift dressing room in a dusty village hall whilst the kids in the audience listened to the local DJ playing records. Usually gigs would end at about 11.45p.m., when Lawrence dismantled the equipment and dragged it to the stage door to start, quite meticulously, loading each piece into the van. His idea was to maximise the space so that it would be as roomy as possible for all those who travelled with the equipment. Much of this happened while the boys discarded their sweat-sodden stage clothes and had a wash down. That was, if they were lucky enough to have access to water. If not, the journey home was certainly a rather aromatic ride.

As Bluesology started to do more tours with Baldry, it was quite clear that a 'them and us' situation had been established. Whilst John Baldry, Alan Walker and Reg went in a separate vehicle, Stewart Brown and Marsha and the rest of the band travelled in the band bus. Marsha was a woman with ambition, and as soon as a decent opportunity for bigger and better things came along, she was off. One of those things, remembers Gavin, was a run in the London production of *Hair*, during 1968.

It was at the gigs with John Baldry that Stewart Brown, Alan Walker and Marsha Hunt, as well as Baldry, all took it in turns to do the lead vocals, on at least one number each. One would wander on, do a song, and then wander off. It was all orchestrated by Baldry, of course, who in effect was also the musical director. Certainly, with Baldry, Bluesology were being treated to a better class of gig than ever before, simply because Baldry was highly regarded and respected on the circuit. Suddenly, they were playing a lot of university and college gigs and getting well paid for it. But Reg didn't seem to be that happy about the arrangements. He was getting more and more disillusioned with it all, because he never got to sing much and also, more importantly, their gigs with Baldry were turning into the sort of shows you would see at a cabaret lounge.

And with all the other singers that Baldry was bringing in, it was unlikely that he would ever have the chance to use his vocal chords in the way he wanted, to front a song of his own. 'Although, he still did the backing vocals, and the occasional lead vocal, he was still not happy,' says Gandy. 'I remember he and I sang the backing together on "Morning Dew", but his voice was so loud, it was deafening. He had a hell of a voice and, because we used the same microphone, it was pretty hard-going for me to be standing next to him.'

To many, Baldry was a larger than life character. On stage, he was always waving his arms about and often would get a kick out of winding Reg up. Not in the serious sense, more a fun thing, but luckily Reg always took it in his stride. If anything, he was influenced by Baldry, especially by his flamboyance. Nor did it bother Reg that Baldry was outwardly gay and, even though it was pretty much forbidden in those days (The Sexual Offences Act decriminalised homosexuality in 1967), Baldry didn't care who knew it and would share his exploits with the other members of the band, who were highly amused at his antics. Certainly, it had a significant impact on the still impressionable Reg.

'When I first met Reg, he was a fairly subdued and quiet character,' remembers Gandy. 'In those days, everyone was image conscious, but not Reg. He was quietly dressed down, until the Baldry period, when he suddenly became as flamboyant and loud as Baldry was. I am sure it influenced him.' To an onlooker, it was not difficult to spot how well they bonded, and how close they became even though Baldry was always taking the piss out of Reg, not that it seemed to matter to him. Why would it, when he treated almost everyone the same?

There was one gig, however, when he almost pushed Reg's patience a little too far. They were playing a college, where one of the classrooms was being used as the dressing room. Baldry was a good sketch artist and he used to love drawing Reg's face so he drew it on the college blackboard, but when Reg came in and spotted it he was none too pleased. 'The rest of the band however thought it was hilarious. It didn't help that we were all falling about laughing at it, not because it was bad, but because it was so good. Reg was O.K. about it in the end and took it in good stead,' laughs Gandy. 'Although, in later interviews, Baldry would describe Reg as a very shy person, almost introverted on stage, and certainly that was true.'

At the time, Len Crawley and Pete Bellotte of the Sinners were still keeping in touch with Reg and so it was no surprise when they turned up to see Bluesology with Baldry at the Marquee. 'Reg had changed his image quite a bit by then. He introduced me and Pete to his mum and she was thrilled to bits that they had started making a name for themselves,' recalls Crawley. 'It was one of the few times she had seen him perform. It was also the first time we had seen him wearing fancy clothes. He had ditched the blazer look, which in turn, appeared to give him a completely different personality. It was very interesting to see.'

Another of those 'interesting things to see' was how he started to socialise with Baldry a great deal more. There was a club in Wardour Street called Le Chasse and it was run by the owner of the Marquee club. Baldry called it the 'Pooverama' as it was renowned for being the big gay hangout. 'It was usually Baldry, John Gee, Billy Gaff, Reg and Jack Barry who would all go there together. In many ways, it was their club,' recalled Gandy. 'All the same, we were not aware that Reg was gay and so we didn't think much about it. Besides, we knew he was with his girlfriend, so why would we think any different? It was not until he became Elton John that we became aware of his sexuality.'

It was around this time that Stewart, now Stu Brown, went back for another recording session, to record a song Kenny Lynch co-wrote titled 'Since I Found You Baby', though nobody seems to remember much about the song or the session that produced it. The only thing that can be said about it is that it is clearly Stewart Brown on vocals. Gandy revealed that there were a lot of drugs around at this stage and there was a lot going on musically, so they were in and out of studios recording all kinds of different material all the time. Whether Reg was on the record remains a mystery, but the sequence of events that are known would suggest he was.

After the single sank without trace, Stewart Brown decided to leave the band. Now disillusioned with his role in Bluesology and playing second fiddle to Baldry, he came upon the idea of pursuing a solo career. Perhaps, as far as the other band members were concerned, it was no surprise. 'He was a kind of mellow type who didn't care much for the trappings of commercial success. He didn't even like the 'London Scene' anymore. Bluesology had meant a great deal to him, but he had gradually become disappointed with the whole thing, with the direction the band had taken,' Pete Gavin recollects.

And even though he did eventually re-emerge, a couple of years later as a solo singer, it was short lived. He later hoped to re-launch himself with 'I Can't Go On Living Without You', penned by two new songwriters on the block: Elton John and Bernie Taupin, and produced by Gary Osborne. The track was never released due to contractual issues with Dick James, who had submitted the song for the *Eurovision Song Contest* at the time.

Osborne was 19, and had a job as a staff A&R man for RCA. 'I used to see Bluesology down the clubs, where Elton and I were on nodding terms,' recounts Osborne today. 'When I joined RCA, Brown came into see me and told me that Bluesology had split, and Reg had gone off to write songs. Brown gave me one of those songs, and asked me whether he could record it for RCA. I loved the song, and Brown had a good voice and was good looking, so yes, we went off and did the song. We actually made a rather good record.' The arrangement was done by another friend of Brown, Jimmy Horowitz, who had replaced Reg in the Bluesology line-up before the split. 'He had a manager called

Billy Gaff and I introduced Billy to Kenny Jones and that's how Billy became manager of the Faces. And then, when the Faces split, he stayed on as manager for Rod Stewart for many years.'

Osborne remembers the record 'was pressed up and it was just about to be released when the song got entered into *Eurovision* and made the final six that Lulu was due to sing. And once a song has been released then anyone can cover it, but to get the first release the publisher needs to sign a release form and, of course, quite rightly Dick James refused, because *Eurovision* was a much bigger deal at that time. Everyone submitted songs for *Eurovision* in those days and even if you didn't win you still sold a lot of records, so James said to RCA "I can't let you release it, because it may be the *Eurovision* entry." RCA were very understanding, but it was unfortunate from Brown's point of view because there were 5,000 copies of this single pressed and ready to go.'

Someone had to carry the can. That was the end of Stu Brown at RCA, and Osborne was lucky not to be kicked out as well. 'We should have released it after it failed in *Eurovision*,' says Osborne, 'but RCA had gone cold on Stewart, and while my boss, Terry Oates, understood what had happened, the accountants upstairs didn't like the fact that we had made an expensive record with a big band, horns, strings and backing singers, and we were now stuck with 5,000 unsellable singles.'

It was quite a different story in 1967, however, when Baldry had a hit with 'Let The Heartaches Begin', and even though they were perfectly capable of playing it, Bluesology were replaced with a recorded backing track at live gigs. Baldry believed that the song, which featured an orchestral-based arrangement, couldn't be reproduced faithfully live. To make matters worse, Bluesology hadn't been involved in the studio session when Baldry had recorded it.

'We waited on stage or in the wings with egg on our faces as John lip-synched to the track,' recalls Gandy. 'We did not play on the record of it, which we were a bit pissed off about anyway. After all, we were his band and yet he gave us no indication that he was going into the studios to record it. I remember he was singing to this tape one evening and it went wrong, and Baldry was left embarrassed. So, we were all given a copy of the record and told that we had to learn it and, after that, we would join him on stage. When the record first became a hit, I remember going round to his house with the band to pick him up for a gig, and he was saying, "I have a hit record, but I feel no different to how I was yesterday."'

As a result of the Baldry hit, the band were now more financially sound than ever before but, because of Baldry's hit single, they found a completely new niche, and that was playing the cabaret circuit for the blue rinse and chicken-in-the-basket brigade. In order to fit in with that scene, Baldry took the boys to Carnaby Street and fitted them out with a suit each, which consisted of a dark olive green jacket and trousers with a shirt that had frilly cuffs. 'The new suit lasted a week. We all hated it,' laughs Gandy. 'You have to remember, this was 1967, and the whole hippie thing was now in full swing, and perhaps what was surprising is how well the band took to that scene. In no time at all, they were into Afghan coats, Hendrix and the Blues. And Baldry was riding high in the pop charts with a schmaltzy ballad.'

'Even though we had to wear those bottle green suits from Lord John in Carnaby Street on stage, off stage we were hippies,' raves Caleb Quaye, who was soon to become the lead guitarist. As one observer noted, it was a schizophrenic series of gigs where the boys would show up wearing hippie gear and then they would change into these cabaret outfits and become different people entirely. 'We would be trying to turn the sound up a bit,' continues Quaye, 'and Baldry would be flapping his arms about and shouting, "This is not psychedelia, for God's sake, turn it down."'

Their set would usually include a fair amount of jazz, and then Baldry would throw in his single at the end just to please the punters. After a while, the band got fed up with it and decided to do their own original music. The collapse of Bluesology came pretty quickly after that.

Caleb Quaye had joined Bluesology before the collapse and, for a short time, was the lead guitarist, while Reg busied himself with sorting out his own future. It was quite clear to the others, and indeed Baldry, that he now had plans of his own, which didn't include playing in a band, but did include Quaye. By 1967, he was firmly in a position to play more than just a supporting role in Reg's then immediate future.

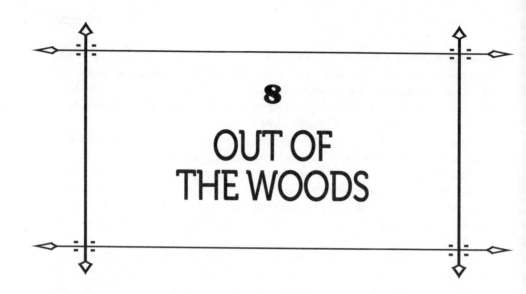

# 8

# OUT OF
# THE WOODS

Bernie Taupin had no idea how his letter to Liberty Records would change his life, or the history of popular music. It was the kind of showbiz fairytale that one could only dream of. Was it really possible that one day he could be a farmer's son, jobless, bored and frustrated, and the next, he was on the road to becoming one of the most prolific lyricists in popular music? It seemed a far cry from the life he had so far known.

At the turn of the twentieth century, the original Taupin family, French by origin, moved from their homeland to set up a wine importing business in London. Despite some success in their ventures in London, the family gravitated back to France leaving one of the brothers, Henry Taupin, in London to look after the business. Another brother, Robert, who was the father of Tony and Bernie Taupin, also stayed in Britain. 'My father, without any reason or history in the family, decided he wanted to stay in England and become a farmer,' explains Tony. 'He went up to Scotland to do his basic training, pre-war, and got a job in a small village called Kirton, near Boston in Lincolnshire. Then, when the Second World War broke out he signed up and went off to fight.'

Tony and Bernie's mother, Daphne, came from a traditional middle class background. Her father was a teacher, but had previously been rector at a church in Sale, Cheshire (now part of Greater Manchester). She had spent most of the war living in Switzerland, and then, when she returned to Britain, found work as a governess for the Taupin family in London looking after the six children who would eventually become Bernie and Tony's cousins. Indeed, she was working there when their father came back from the Far East after the war, and that's when they met. They did their courting in post-war London, marrying in 1947. Taupin senior resumed his work in Lincolnshire at Hubbard's Bridge near Boston, where Tony was born.

In many ways, the Taupins could never be described as a conventional family. They always seemed to be transient, always on the move due to Taupin's work as a farm manager, working for the Dennis Estates. It was literally a case of having to move from place to place, to wherever the work was. Their second home was located in the rural and secluded setting of Flatters, near Market Rasen in Lincolnshire, they moved there in 1949. This is where their second son, Bernard, or Bernie for short, was born on 22 May 1950. Flatters was a semi-detached house with a gamekeeper living on one side and Taupins on the other. 'There was a farm on its own, and no village nearby,' explains Tony, 'so the big influences in our lives were our parents and our grandfather or, as we called him, Poppy.'

It was a most idyllic setting for children to grow up in. It was safe for them to roam around neighbouring fields and do what boys did in those days, enjoying simple pleasures. Open fields, fresh air and a fertile imagination ensured that the Taupin boys were occupied most of the time. 'There was very little scope to do anything else,' recalls Tony. 'Bernie, I remember, was always into the American West with his toy gun and his cowboy hats and with an almost permanent scowl, especially when my parents were taking photographs of him; whereas I was into football and most things that were sporty. As brothers, we fought tooth and nail; Bernie was the naughty one while I was always the goody-goody. Although our father would often tell us off for fighting, he very rarely grounded Bernie for his other escapades though. The only inside entertainment we had was when our father bought the family a television set in 1956; it was amazing. We both came home from school one day, and there was this television set. I remember one of the first things we watched was *Muffin The Mule*.'

By the time the Taupin brothers were old enough, they would catch the bus into Sleaford, the nearest town, where the local Roman Catholic primary school was situated. It was here, after a carol service, that the boys gave their parents the fright of their lives, when they decided to walk back home on their own. 'It was a freezing cold winter night,' laughs Tony. 'Luckily, someone we knew picked us up and took us home.'

Bernie's romantic dreamy side seemed to be derived from Poppy who had a literary background. He was a fine old gentleman who was very knowledgeable about all sorts of things. He would take the young boys to the ornate bridge by the side of Flatters and during the short walk along the narrow lane they would fly kites and talk to Poppy until they reached the bridge. It was there that Poppy taught them to play Pooh sticks, taken from the books by AA Milne about a bear called Winnie The Pooh, which became one of Bernie's favourite things, because, says Tony, he was quite whimsical.

The Taupins moved again to Rowston Manor, which was a big Queen Anne house that they had rent free because Robert Taupin was now the farm manager. Having a tied house rent free was one of the perks of his senior position. Entrance to the house from the road was accessed via a large five bar gate, which Tony remembers spending many hours sitting on and watching the world go by.

'It was a grand house with central heating and lovely grounds but, like Flatters, was right in the heart of the country with very few other children around. This was great, because we could have games where we played together; there were spinnies to play in, a vegetable plot, stables and plenty of places for us to explore.' With Tony always wanting to play football and cricket with his friends, and Bernie being into Cowboys and Indians, there was a lot of squabbling and eventually the two boys didn't hang around together much because they were so different. 'Bernie was a bit solitary at this stage, and didn't have that many friends. But generally, it was a great way to grow up. We had this very simple life in the middle of nowhere, and we had very caring and loving parents so, for us, it was perfect.'

By 1959, Robert decided it was time to try and have a stab at running his own farm. Once again the Taupin family upped sticks and, with Jill their sheepdog in tow, moved to the small Lincolnshire village of Owmby by Spital to a ten-acre farm whose main income came from battery farming chickens for their eggs.

'The original house was an old farmhouse and was very primitive,' remembers Tony. 'During the first year in Owmby, we were living in the farmhouse which was a real culture shock for us after the splendour of Rowston Manor. It didn't have any heating or flushing toilet and we were resentful of our father at first, because he had taken us to these awful surroundings while he built a new prefab house on the land next door which, when it was finished, the old farmhouse would be knocked down.'

The move also bought a change of primary school for the boys, who once again, were forced to leave behind their fellow pupils and teachers at Sleaford, and now journey to their new school in Normanby by Spital, the adjoining and neighbouring village. Tony spent a term year at his new school, while Bernie, had another two to endure. Although Tony thrived at the school because the headmaster liked him, Bernie hated every minute of it, especially the headmaster, simply because he was a strict disciplinarian and Bernie wasn't one to toe the line. All he could do was grin and bear it.

He was always going against the grain and kicking against authority, whereas Tony was the complete opposite. He walked away passing his 11-plus and ended up at the Aston Grammar School in Market Rasen: for Bernie, it was a different story. He failed his 11-plus and, as a consequence, was enrolled into the local secondary modern school. He didn't enjoy school and rarely did his homework – unlike Tony who never failed to finish his on time. In the end, Bernie left school without any qualifications. Tony, on the other hand, did a great deal better than his brother and ended up going to university.

Although it was clear to his parents that Bernie was no academic, he certainly showed a flair for creative writing, which he appeared to enjoy more than anything else that he studied at school. His lack of attention in the classroom, however, resulted in his spelling, punctuation and general grammar being pretty atrocious, but he had a creative streak from his mother's side of the family, as Tony explains: 'He loved, from an early age, writing creative poetry, and at school creative writing was all he was interested in because he had a very fertile imagination. He would write the occasional pseudo epic piece of work and our mother would correct his grammar, spelling and punctuation, and especially before he sent lyrics to Reg in the early days of their partnership. Most of his early work was based on the American Wild West and make believe, Tolkien type verse as well as essays.' One of Bernie's teachers recalls that his writing had character and he was always able to use words vividly.

For the first ten years of his life, Tony Taupin had only one brother to contend with but all that was about to change. 'We were 10 years old when Kit was born, in the front room of the house in Owmby of all places, which doubled up as a living room, and when Bernie wrote "The Greatest Discovery", it was about our awareness of a younger brother. I was starting at grammar school at the time and I took umbrage with my parents that we were going to have this noisy child disturbing my studies, not that it would have bothered Bernie though.'

Tony believes that a lot of Bernie's early lyrics are autobiographical, about places he knew locally and events that took place in his life and 'The Greatest Discovery' was just another example of that. 'He was influenced by his environment and what he witnessed in his younger life.'

'He became a bit of a tearaway in his teenage years,' says Tony. 'It always amazed me how patient and tolerant our parents were with him, because he did push their patience to the limit. I remember he formed a gang of sorts with three other mates, the West Brothers and Pete Hayes, from Spridlington and Bernie was the leader; it was his gang. They were pretty much inseparable and did get themselves into all sorts of unbelievable scrapes.'

There is little point in having a gang in isolation and there was, indeed, a rival gang from Caister that was the nemesis of Bernie's gang. 'Whether there were any major fights between the two gangs I don't know, but both gangs used to go to local youth clubs and pubs, such as the Aston Arms in Market Rasen, and get into all sorts of trouble, simply because he was always rebelling against authority. Certainly this period of Bernie's life was the inspiration for the song, "Saturday Night's Alright (For Fighting)",' Tony asserts.

Life at Owmby though proved to be a better period for Bernie. He found his own circle of friends, and spent much of his time engrossed in Western games in the fields behind the farmhouse and then, in his adolescence, his time was more or less taken up with his gang. Living in a village, as they did, there appeared to be much more scope for both boys to make friends with others their own age and develop their own interests. Bernie played his American West games and Tony indulged in his sporting activities.

'And then,' says Tony, 'Bernie started drinking and that was when my parents showed a great deal of patience and tolerance with him. My father was a very introverted type who didn't really socialise at all, and although Bernie had some of those traits, he was in other ways the complete opposite. He wanted to do things his way and on his own terms. Father used to be called out on various occasions to collect him from under a hedge because he was so drunk and, on other occasions, would regularly fetch him after a drunken night out, but I think that was more out of duty than anything else. Dad wasn't too pleased about any of it, but he did it all the same. But despite all of that, Bernie had a charisma, and everyone would follow him. It was the same with the girls too. He attracted them quite effortlessly.'

After leaving school, Bernie seemed to show no desire to want to work as Tony explains:

> He was employed in the print works at the *Lincolnshire Echo*, which was his one and only real job. He thought he was going into some journalistic career at the time, but he was soon disillusioned by that notion and left after about three weeks. After a period of unemployment, he then worked temporarily on a chicken farm. He worked really hard for a time, raising chickens in a broiler house. He was feeding them and when they were fattened they were taken away for slaughter. He would also clean out the shit and other stuff while he was there and so, yes, he did show an aptitude for being capable of doing some really intense labour work. But overall he didn't really have any fixed work when he left school and showed little interest in our father's smallholding. He didn't do any work on our farm, but then again, neither of us did, we weren't natural farmers and when our father realised that, that we were not going to take over the farm, he decided to sell up and went to work for the Ministry of Agriculture. It's funny, because Bernie always talked about farming in lyrical terms, but he didn't really want to be a farmer or the hard graft that went with it.

One area that his parents encouraged him in, was the idea of his going to London to stay with his extended family in Putney to see if he could find something in the capital. It just so happened that one of his cousins was working in the television industry as a film editor and it was agreed that he would stay with him and try his luck in London.

Bernie made his move to the 'Smoke' in 1967, a year when anything and everything seemed possible. And, after all, the streets were paved with gold ... weren't they?

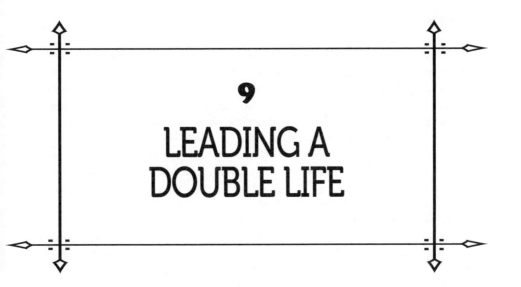

# 9
# LEADING A
# DOUBLE LIFE

As anyone in the music business could tell you, Tin Pan Alley, was the Mecca of the British music scene, and anyone who wanted to get into it, usually started off there. But it wasn't only music publishers that took up residence in the now famous street. Not long after the first music publishers had moved in, other music-related businesses such as *Melody Maker* and *New Musical Express* followed suit. It was an ideal place to be as they could be in the centre of what was happening as it happened. Location, location, location, as they say.

*Melody Maker*, of course, was one of the premier music papers of the period, which started life at 9 Denmark Street in 1926, and the *New Musical Express*, or *NME* as it became known, launched its first issue from the building at No.5. Another music publishing house, Peter Maurice Music, was at No. 21 where Lionel Bart wrote songs to be sold by the publisher to artists like Marty Wilde and Adam Faith. In the basement of No.22, bands like the Small Faces and Manfred Mann made their first recordings, while upstairs at Rhodes Music, Jeff Beck, Eric Clapton and Pete Townshend bought the tools of their trade. At No. 25 was Denmark Productions who had bands like the Kinks and the Troggs frequenting their studios on a regular basis. There were two recording studios; one was Regent Sound where the Stones and the Kinks made their first records, and the other was Central Sound.

'It was quite a remarkable area,' remembers Caleb Quaye, who visited Denmark Street on a daily basis to see how many music stars of the day he could spot frequenting the Giaconda café. 'Anyone who was anyone in music was in and out of the Giaconda, because it was just a few doors down from Regent Sound. Whenever a band was recording in there, they would at some point, go down to the Giaconda to take a break. You would see the Kinks, the Small Faces, the Stones, and Donovan in there and, especially in the summer when the kids were off school, they would be outside the Giaconda signing autographs. It was a happening place.'

Nature abhors a vacuum, and by the end of the 1960s music publishers had started to expand their businesses to fill the ever increasing spaces between finding new songwriters and publishing music. By now, Tin Pan Alley publishers had also started to dip their collective toes in the waters of record production through their own labels or via independent record companies which, to all intents and purposes, led to the massive restructuring of the British music business at that time. For instance, David Platz, the managing director of Essex Music, formed Straight Ahead Productions and regularly used Denny Cordell, then an already well established record producer in his own right, to produce Procol Harum, the Move and Joe Cocker, while Gus Dudgeon produced John Kongos and David Bowie for Platz.

In many ways, it is surprising that Platz ended up in the music business at all. With no formal music training, and not really having a love of music, his first job out of school was in publishing: not books, as he had hoped, but music. Aged 14, he found himself working as an office boy for Southern Music. All the same, his early business awareness soon took him through the copyright department, then to the Latin-American music division, as manager. A few years later, when a new managing director of Southern Music was required, Platz, at 28, was considered too young for the post and was turned down.

When one door closes another opens, and an opportunity arose for him to front the British division of Essex Music for leading American publisher Harry Richmond. He started it from a pokey little office in Denmark Place, which he shared with band leader John Dankworth. But, in a very short space of time, he turned Essex Music into a huge success story, almost from the start, due solely to his personality. If you asked anyone at the time what their general impression of a music publisher was, most would answer, a brash, cigar-smoking individual with a dismissive and largely pessimistic view of most new music that came his way. But that was not the case with Platz. Regarded by many as a softly spoken individual, he exuded confidence and honesty, and those attributes brought budding songwriters to his door and turned him into the pioneer publisher to see at No.4 Denmark Street.

The Rolling Stones were among his early conquests and, where they led, others followed. Platz encouraged talent regardless of musical genre. The Moody Blues, Procol Harum, the Who, Johnny Dankworth, Ralph McTell, Dudley Moore, Lonnie Donegan, David Bowie, Marc Bolan and even Paddy Roberts all joined him.

The Stones had been signed to Essex in 1965, after Alan Klein got involved. He had reportedly told the band that he would get them a £1million for their publishing rights which he did by going to Platz, who, in 1966, bought Immediate Music, the Stones' publisher. This is why Essex still own the rights to the early Stones' records to this day. Over the years though, Platz became slowly frustrated by the lack of interest shown by the major labels, so he formed his own label.

His son Simon Platz takes up the story: 'Bolan and Bowie were creating music that was so different for the time, and the larger labels just didn't seem to get it, and so my father formed his own label and was largely responsible for setting the scene for the introduction of producers to become the next big thing in the music scene. He was the first person to actually sign producers and hire them out to other record labels for significant financial benefit to Essex Music.' Visconti started working with the likes of Bowie and Bolan in the early years and when, in 1970, Platz's new label, Fly Records, was established, Essex Music Limited became Essex Music International.

The first producer who was signed by Platz, and employed exclusively by Essex Music, was a young man called Gus Dudgeon who was introduced by Visconti and became his junior. 'He later became a partner in a subsidiary company called Tuesday Productions, but we also signed Denny Cordell as well,' explains Simon. Dudgeon produced the first four albums for Elton John and *Space Oddity* for Bowie which, as combined projects, achieved great success for the company. As an employee of Essex Music at the time, Dudgeon's work on Elton's first albums meant that Essex Music earned and continues to do so from those albums. 'My father had a knack of looking outside of the box and seeing ways to improve on things and do things that had never been done before.'

What is interesting to note, though, is that when Essex Music signed a deal with EMI Records and had formed its own Fly label to launch Marc Bolan and Tyrannosaurus Rex, Dick James had already started record production, through one of his subsidiaries, Page One Records, that was headed by Larry Page with artists like the Troggs, whose first record, 'Wild Thing' had become a massive number one hit.

'That was funny,' laughs Page today. 'Even though they had a few of their records banned, like "I Can't Control Myself", we still made them into the nice kids of rock rather than bad boys, like the Kinks were. They would be very courteous, open doors and stand up when ladies entered the room, and pull chairs out for them when they went to sit down. It was the sort of disciplined behaviour that was taught at private and public schools in the 1960s. Good manners and courtesy to our elders was all part of the education back then. And of course, no one would believe that a pop group could behave like that, so it really worked a treat. We even changed the names of some of the band members to Reg Presley and Ronnie Bond, just to create an impact. Again, it was funny, because some people actually thought Reg was related to Elvis.'

That was when Page's working relationship with Dick James really started. 'He wanted me to form a company with him,' remembers Page. 'So I asked around, and everyone told me that Dick was the most honest guy in the world and was a fantastic man to work with, who had a lot of financial backing from the City behind him, so it seemed to me like it would be a good move. And then, when Ronnie Bron recommended me to him, I decided to take the plunge, and that is when we formed Page One Records. It was a sort of handshake deal, no contract or anything like that. We signed some artists up and had some big hits. One day I read in the *Record Retailer* that Dick James had formed his own record label. For me, that was the beginning of the end.' Page went on to form Penny Farthing Records that

September in 1969, and continued to manage the Troggs who remained with Page One Records.

At the same time, Dick James had moved his headquarters to New Oxford Street in London and renamed the building 'James House.' The idea was that the new building had additional space for his expanding publishing empire. His son, Stephen, turned some of the spare space into a recording studio and with a small budget managed to bring in a stereo tape machine, some microphones and started to offer a demo recording service. Later, when he added 8-track recording, the studio started to operate 24 hours a day to cater for the then growing demand by musicians and songwriters for recording facilities.

As expected, Dennis Berger, who had previously worked with Dick James at Sydney Bron, took over the running of the production at Page One on behalf of Dick James Music. Stephen James was in charge of the administration. James junior, who had been carefully forging a career for himself within his father's company, had established his own label called 'This Record Company', (an anagram of hits or shit) in 1967. One of the first artists to work for This Record Company was Elton John, who had recorded the song, 'Lady Samantha', which was released on the Philips label in early 1969. It enjoyed significant radio airplay but sold fewer than 7000 copies, but it was still enough for James to be impressed. He had also negotiated a deal with Pye Records that led to the formation of the DJM label which was soon to be distributed in Britain through a new Dick James Organisation company called DJM (Distributions) Ltd.

One of the first artists to sign for James' new label was Zack Laurence, an arranger and songwriter. Although he didn't have a major hit himself, he was instrumental in the label's first smash following James' visit to the States to purchase a song that the label could cover called 'Groovin With Mr Bloe'. The song was originally demoed by Hookfoot and Reg Dwight. Produced by Steve Brown, it didn't quite work, so Laurence was commissioned to re-score the song, and with the help of some Tin Pan Alley session musicians, the track was released in February 1970 and became an instant hit. More of that later,

It also helped that it was a hit during the same period that Dick James' publishing empire was expanding with the acquisition of several other publishing interests, which included Maribus Music, owned by AIR, a publishing concern that had been set up by George Martin, Don Richards, Peter Sullivan and John Burgess. They also held the publishing rights for Alto Music, the company that looked after the songs of Hollies front men, Allan Clarke and Tony Hicks, and had previously traded under the name of Gralto Music, when they owned the Clarke and Hicks songs they had written with another Hollies band mate, Graham Nash. There was also Cookaway Music which had the songs of Roger Greenaway and Roger Cook. All in all, it was a pretty impressive collection.

*Top:* A young Reg Dwight in Bluesology. © Geoff Dyson

*Above:* Honky Tonk Piano - Northwood Hills Hotel. © George Hill

*Top:* Tony was the sporty brother, Bernie was a fan of the American West from an early age. © Tony Taupin

*Middle:* Flatters, the Taupin family home: before renovation in 1949 and after in 1954. © Tony Taupin

*Left:* Bernie and Tony Taupin, going back to their plough. © Tony Taupin

*Top:* The class of ... probably 1962 with schoolboy Reg. © Pinner Grammar Old Students Association

*Above right:* Reg's first job was at Mills Music, Denmark Street. The very heart of Tin Pan Alley. © Unknown

*Above:* Dick James. © Stephen James

*Right:* Publisher David Platz (sitting down wearing glasses) at the legendary Julie's Café. © Stephen Platz

*Above:* Relaxing after rehearsals -
Stu Brown singer and guitarist with
Bluesology. © Geoff Dyson

*Right:* Through the keyhole shot
of Bluesology rehearsing at a
church hall ... © Geoff Dyson

*Below:* ... here they are in full swing.
© Geoff Dyson

*Opposite top left:* Loading the van for another gig. Reg and Long John Baldry in the
background. © Unknown

*Opposite top right:* The Bag O'Nails where Elton got talked out of marriage. © Unknown

*Opposite below:* Life after Reg. Bluesology in 1968. © Bernie Holland

SPRING 1968 - LONG JOHN BALDRY & "BLUESOLOGY"

Back Row from Left to Right : Marc Charig -
Bernie Holland - Fred Gandy - Pete Gavin - Elton Dean -
Jimmy Horovitz - Foreground : Long John Baldry.

*Top:* Without this ad in 1967, Elton and Bernie might never have met. © Keith Hayward

*Below:* Elton and former manager Ray Williams, who placed the ad. © Ray Williams

*Above:* Loot, the forerunner of Hookfoot L-R: Roger Pope, Caleb Quaye, Dave Glover. David Wright seated. © Roger Pope

*Right:* Hookfoot press conference prior to the last US tour. © Roger Pope

*Top:* Elton in classic pose in the studio, taken by his cover designer
David Larkham. © David Larkham

*Above:* Krumlin 1970 - the festival that Elton took by storm. © John Wharton

Also in the picture at this time was Ray Williams, a 17-year-old follower and friend of Cliff Bennett And The Rebel Rousers. He could always be found at the band's gigs wherever they played, which then was most frequently at Botwell in Hayes and Burtons in Uxbridge. It was while he was at one of the Southall gigs, hooking up with the band backstage, that Cathy McGowan suddenly appeared to ask them if they would like to appear on *Ready, Steady, Go!*, and would Williams like to go as well, (simply because McGowan liked him)? He obviously jumped at the chance, and went to the recording of the programme at the Associated-Rediffusion Kingsway studios. After the show, he was asked whether he would like to go back the following week. He agreed, and after that, he went back every week.

Things went so well for Williams that he became an integral part of the show's production team, and found himself travelling to places like Brighton to find dancers for the show. With his good looks, he suddenly found he was getting as much attention as the bands that were appearing on the show and, before long, was being sought for photo shoots by such magazines as *Titbits* and *Festival*.

Things for Williams got even better, when Michael Aldred left the programme. That was when Cathy McGowan introduced Williams to Brian Sommerville who was the publicity manager for the Beatles, and had started his own company near Denmark Street. He was also managing the Kinks and, eventually, took over management of Sonny and Cher. Sommerville needed an assistant, and Williams seemed perfect, so he got the job. The first assignment he was given, he remembers, was working with the Kinks. 'That was when we heard that "You Really Got Me" had hit number one. It was their first, so everyone was very excited. But it still makes me laugh to think there I was with the number one group in Britain, hurtling down Streatham High Street in an old beaten-up Austin Princess going to a gig at the Locarno.'

After the Kinks, Williams next worked with Tommy Roe, an American singer-songwriter from Atlanta in Georgia who had been a constant name in the charts since 1962 with such hits as 'Sheila', 'Everybody' and 'The Folk Singer' and, at the time Williams was working with him, was still some years away from his biggest hit, 'Dizzy'. 'Tommy had been supported by a lot of bands in his time, but I guess the most famous was the Beatles, even though they were still unknown at the time. The gigs during my time though, included working with Cilla Black, Sounds Incorporated and P.J. Proby,' explains Williams. 'I can still remember very clearly how Proby got kicked off the tour part way through, because he kept splitting his velvet pants. The guy from the ABC Cinema chain booted PJ off before a gig at Wigan and, of course, when that happened, we had to change the artist line-up. We bought in a new young singer called Tom Jones who stayed with us for the rest of the tour. It was quite amazing because when we played in Cardiff, Tom's hometown, the crowd went wild.'

It was after the tour had finished that Tommy Roe asked Williams if he wanted to go and work for him and Bill Lowery in Atlanta. 'When I told him I was interested, he told me to hang on for about six weeks at which time he would contact me so, in the meantime, I continued working for Brian Sommerville, who by this time had asked me to assist Sonny and Cher. I remember one occasion when I was out with Sonny, how he was asked to leave the Mayfair Hotel in London for wearing an unsuitable jacket. Something you wouldn't come across today! I bet Katy Perry has never been asked to do that, because her dress was too short, or because she was showing off too much cleavage!'

Williams got the call to go to America. 'I was invited to stay with Sonny and Cher who, by this time, had returned to the States and had asked me to record a song with them, but I turned it down as singing was not my strong point.' Not that he was worried. At the same time as the Sonny and Cher offer, another project was on the table, which was to help manage Buffalo Springfield for Bill Lowery. Williams accepted.

'I remember one night, going to a club in Los Angeles with one of the band members, and as soon as we got there he told me that he had just seen someone he knew and whom I should really come over and meet. So we walked over to this roped off area where this person was. Can you imagine my surprise when this guy turned round and it was Elvis Presley? We spent some of the evening inside Elvis's private area in the club talking with him.' Although Williams can't remember exactly what was discussed, he suspects it would have been largely based around music, Hollywood and the Beatles.

As much as Williams was impressed with meeting Elvis, Lowery was impressed with Williams. Soon after spending an evening in the company of Presley and friends, Lowery asked him to establish and run Lowery Publishing in Britain and to work through Chappell and Co, an established British music publisher not best known for pop music. Suddenly, Williams found himself working in Hanover Square in London trying to establish a music publishing business for 1960s music and musicians in an environment where his colleagues were dealing with classical music and scores for orchestras.

'It was difficult, to say the least,' laughs Williams today. 'While I was with Lowery, I created a public relations company in Mayfair with Simon Hayes and Ben Stagg and, over a period of time, we earned ourselves a good reputation among most people in the music business.' Even so, Williams wasn't quite as happy as he hoped he would be, so he decided to look around for a new challenge. He came across it sooner than he thought. Bob Reisdorf had his own Dolton Records label in America, which later merged with Liberty Records. He had three artists signed to the label, the Ventures, the Fleetwoods and Vic Dana, but as Reisdorf was planning his retirement, he asked Liberty Records boss, Al (Alvin) Bennett, to front a Liberty Records operation in Britain.

Williams was called in to an interview as Head of A&R, a job he viewed with some trepidation. 'At the time, most A&R people were artists in their own right and could play an instrument and pass well as a musician. I was neither of those, I couldn't play anything. I had also been economical about my age. I said I was 19 when I was really 18 because I was worried that I would look too young for the job. But to my surprise,

I got it and was made the first and possibly the youngest Head of A&R in Britain. I was given an office in Albemarle Street in London, and all I had were a few Picasso prints on the wall and a desk. I was also asked to look after a grey parrot that belonged to Billy Fury.

Williams was in something of a fix. His job was to find new acts to sign, but he didn't know of any. So if the mountain wasn't going to come to Williams, he would have to go to the mountain. He placed an ad in the *New Musical Express*. 'I had thousands of responses: post bags of mail and telephone calls. I can honestly say I went through every single response to ensure that I didn't miss any talent. As this was a publishing company I was looking for artists, writers, composers, anything.'

Having cast his bread upon the waters, it came back buttered. From the results of the ad, Williams signed Idle Race with Jeff Lynne, the Bonzo Dog Doo-Dah Band and Family. Interestingly enough, the drummer on the Do-Dah Band's Gorilla album, was 'Legs' Larry Smith who later went on to be a tap dancer for Elton. 'I also remember auditioning Paco Peña. He was an exceptional Flamenco guitar player and he played for me for about ninety minutes. Unfortunately there was just nothing I could do for him at Liberty.'

One letter, in particular, aroused Williams' curiosity. 'It was from someone called Reg Dwight. In his letter, he told me that he was with a band called Bluesology playing keyboards and that he would like to meet me. By this time, I had an upright piano in the office, so I invited him over and asked him to play for me. I remember he had a wonderful voice, but he didn't look anything like a pop star. He sang "He'll Have To Go", a Jim Reeves song, and a couple of others. He then talked about his career and told me that he was frustrated, because Bluesology wouldn't let him sing and he felt lost in the environment that he was in.'

Liking what he heard, Williams booked a date a few days later with a local recording studio for Reg to make some demos for him, but little did Reg realise what an impact the demo session would make on his own future, or indeed how an old colleague and friend from his past would also play a part in what was to happen next.

Caleb Quaye remembers the occasion well. It had probably been about a year since he and Reg had spoken after their less than amicable parting in Denmark Street. And it just so happened that Quaye was on a recording schedule at DJM for the many bands, artists and singer/songwriters that were coming in to the DJM studio to audition to get signed up to a recording deal. At the time, DJM published all the Beatles songs via Northern Songs, which instantly made them the company to get in with if you were a singer or songwriter. One day, recalls Quaye:

I had a client booked in by Ray Williams, who worked for Liberty Records at the time. He came into the studio with this new singer-songwriter as he wanted to record some demos with him, so I met this guy who looked somewhat familiar, but I couldn't quite place him. If he was who I thought he was, then he had certainly lost some weight and grown his hair a lot longer than when I knew him. I was setting up the mics as he was going to play the piano and sing, so I obviously had to set up two mics, one at the piano and one for his vocal, and all the time I am looking at this guy, and he is looking at me and then looking away. I think we both recognised each other but didn't want to say anything. I could tell that he was thinking, 'I know this guy, he was the one that laughed at me when I joined Bluesology.' I recorded his demo and that was when our music relationship really first started. When he had finished, I remember, we laughed a lot and agreed that the piano playing was nice and the songs were O.K., but his voice sounded like Sandie Shaw. It was so high, but it was a good start. We made quite a few demo records, one of which was 'He'll Have to Go' which Williams had cut onto an acetate and took back with him to Liberty.

After Reg had left his office, Williams convened an A&R meeting with Bob Reisdorf and the Head of Publishing for Liberty to discuss his new discovery. He played them the demos and Reisdorf didn't like them and the Head of Publishing just couldn't see it. 'I could see some potential in what I had heard, but no one else did. I discussed the outcome of the meeting with Reg, and that's when he told me he could write music but that he couldn't write lyrics. I told him that I'd try and find someone for him. I initially introduced him to two young guys called Nicky James and Kirk Duncan, who were writing songs at the time and I thought it would be good for Reg to write with them to see if anything happened.'

Soon after the introductions had been made,' continues Williams, 'I opened another letter, which was amongst the thousands that I was still receiving from the advertisement, and it was from a guy called Bernard Taupin. His letter said something like, "Dear Mr Williams, I am basically a poet, but I think my words can be set to music." I found out later that he had written the letter but didn't want to send it, so he put it on the mantelpiece above the fireplace at his home, where his mother spotted it, and posted it for him.

'Attached to the letter were some lyric sheets which I read, but I couldn't make head or tail of them, but I then thought of Reg Dwight, and it seemed natural to put them both together; one can write music but not lyrics and the other can write lyrics but not music, so I wrote to him and invited him to London to meet Reg. I wanted to sign Reg as a recording artist for Liberty and Reg and Bernie to a publishing contract for their songs with Metrics Music, which was a sister company to Liberty run by Alan Keen, and so I went back to Bob but my suggestions fell on stony ground'

Williams put Bernie in touch with Reg and that is when, says Williams, they started sending each other stuff. But that is not quite how Stephen James remembers it. He claims that by the time Williams had introduced Reg and Bernie, he was an employee of DJM. 'One of the guys in the office had the awful idea of putting an advert in the paper for writers and this guy from Lincolnshire applied and we invited him down and put him and Reg together. They went out to have a coffee and came back friends. They were getting on very well so we paid for Bernie to come down and stay with Reg and he was with him for about three weeks during which time he was writing lyrics. Suddenly Reg's songs were improving dramatically.'

What is certain, is that Liberty Records turned the songwriting team down but Williams was impressed by what he had heard and kept in touch, so did James, who would later sign the songwriters to DJM. It is likely that Bernie joined Reg on the Gralto payroll with Graham Nash until he joined DJM after what became known as 'The Great Purge'.

It wasn't long after Bernie had landed his £10-a-week job at Dick James Music that he moved in with Reg, his mother and stepfather at Frome Court. He packed his bags and left the relatives he had been staying with and headed over to Pinner. The idea to move in with Reg, was simply so that they could spend more time writing songs. As brother Tony Taupin correctly observes, 'It was a huge twist of fate that Reg and Bernie had written at the same time, in reply to the same advert, and that Ray Williams had the foresight to see them successfully working together.'

Soon after meeting and working and living together, and indeed becoming good friends, Reg and Bernie started making regular trips to visit Bernie's family in Owmby. The visits usually coincided with Tony coming home from university to play his beloved football on the local football pitch at the back of the family home. When Reg came to visit the Taupins, says Tony, 'If I was home, then we would usually all go to the Bottle And Glass pub in Normanby by Spital, as there wasn't a pub in Owmby. I remember Reg would always play the piano there.' In many ways, it was a throwback to the time when Reg played piano at the Northwood Hills Hotel as a youngster.

On one visit to Owmby in 1968, when Tony was about to leave home to go and live in Spain as part of his university course, where he was studying Spanish and French, things didn't quite go according to plan. 'Yes, I was going out to Seville that September to do my placement abroad in the third year, so we went to the pub for a farewell drink. We were then going to go to a dance at an RAF camp via Gainsborough to pick up my girlfriend. While we were in the pub, someone spiked my drinks and, because I had these drinks I couldn't drive, so Reg drove and picked up my girlfriend. I was so ill. I couldn't make the dance, so Reg drove back to Gainsborough to take my girlfriend home and then back to Owmby. He really did make himself useful that night as a chauffeur.'

Every time Tony was at home from university, he would follow the career of his younger brother and Reg. 'I always remember in 1968 when Elton was in Bluesology and playing in Sheffield with John Baldry, I drove over with a girlfriend and it was at the time when Baldry had the hit, "Let The Heartaches Begin". I watched the show and then afterwards, we sat with the band having a few drinks, and that's when Bernie told me that Baldry fancied me something chronic. We just chuckled about it. I also remember the gig at York University in 1970 before they went off to LA. That was the first time I had seen them play as the Elton John Band, so it was an exciting time for me and, obviously, a very exciting time for Reg and Bernie as they kind of knew that their careers were about to take off.'

'When I first met Bernie, he was this "hick" from Lincolnshire,' recalls Quaye. 'He was a poet and very talented, but he was a country boy who didn't know anything about the music business or living in a big city.' He spent a lot of time with Reg in the studio working alongside Quaye and helping put together some demos of his songs. At DJM, the studio was in one room, and the control room was across the way in another room. The only communication between the two rooms was through a television screen with cameras in the studio.

'I remember when we started doing the DJM demos early on in Elton's career, we were laying down the vocal and the track for a song, and I could see the vocal mic with Reg on one side and Bernie on the other trying to play the tambourine. Bernie had never played a tambourine in his life and I am sat at the control panel looking at the screen thinking, "What is he doing?" It was all out of time, so through the communication intercom I told Bernie to stop what he was doing as it looked like he was swatting flies with a tambourine. He stopped at that point, but Reg fell about laughing.

'What some people forget, or don't realise, is that Bernie was a poet not a songwriter, or even a lyricist. He wrote poetry.' According to Quaye, 'He was smart and intelligent and read a lot but in many ways, he was a closed book. I was not really that close to Bernie even though we spent a lot of time together, but then no-one really was close to him. He was in his own world most of the time, but he was happy there.' Even so, Taupin was an important member of the band, because of his lyrical contribution, but he was not someone whom the rest of the band would immediately hang around with. He was a poet who wrote the words first, and Reg quite often had to edit and rearrange the words to fit the song.

Gary Osborne, who would later become a lyricist for Elton by the end of the 1970s, explains the dynamics of how Bernie and Reg created their songs:

It was common knowledge how Bernie and Elton wrote together and I did watch it happen. Bernie would send him a sheaf of what were at that stage poems really, because it's not a lyric until it has a tune. Elton would stick it on the piano and start doodling around and singing a bit here and there. He didn't necessarily understand or care what the poem was saying or what it was about. He saw it as a bunch of words, and he would cut out a word here and there, because he is getting a tune now, and the line is a bit long and would take out an entire line or cut out an entire verse, and then suddenly, he would have a song.

He ended up with songs which had often been edited in this haphazard way, but were perfect for the 1970s because this bizarre editing of Elton's made the songs feel rather mysterious. Maybe, when Bernie wrote it, it had a beginning, middle and an end, but now, although it still had the skeleton of Bernie's theme, he had turned it into something else. The system worked brilliantly, because the tune Elton came out with was always dynamite. If I had been involved in that process, I would have insisted on going back and saying 'Now you have written this tune based on my lyric I am now going to rewrite the lyric based on your tune' so that the words would make perfect sense. But I would have been wrong, because of the way they wrote, those early Taupin/John songs have a magic.

Certainly that was true. And part of that was down to the fact that Reg wrote the songs so fast and so spontaneously, continues Osborne. 'He told me that he wrote every tune on the *Yellow Brick Road* album in one weekend, which is incredible genius.' Danny Hutton of Three Dog Night agrees. He can still remember the time when Reg described how his songwriting process worked. 'Bernie would give him the lyrics and then all the music would come flooding out. If it didn't, then it didn't work, and the lyrics were scrapped.'

Before Bernie arrived in London, Nicky James and Kirk Duncan continued to write with Reg, with the support of Williams and, although nothing came out of the relationship, some of the songs were put onto demos. It was an ideal situation for Reg, as it gave him the opportunity to experiment with his own music and set it to lyrics by other composers.

Duncan takes up the story: 'We ended up writing two or three songs together and as a result Graham [Nash] signed us to Gralto Music with an agreement that if we could introduce writers to Gralto and make £10,000 from combined copyright for our songs, and any songs introduced by us from new artists, then a new company would be formed called Niraki. The whole arrangement was underwritten by Dick James, who would administer the publishing through DJM, and so he drew up the contracts and signed them and off we went in search of new songwriters to work with.' Gralto was another of Dick James' many companies.

Williams named the would-be company Niraki, which was more or less an idea he had borrowed from Gralto by using the initials of the names of those involved. Formed in 1965, Gralto derived its name from Graham Nash, Allan Clarke and Tony Hicks of the Hollies.

Reg, at the same time, was also working with Caleb Quaye, and got to lay down the songs during all-night sessions at DJM's recording studio. As Gralto had premises in the DJM building, and Reg was working with Nash, he had access to the DJM studio even though he didn't have a direct deal with Dick James. It was during the same period, that the studios were having a trail of musicians, singers and songwriters popping in and out of the studios, after dark, to make demos and recordings without the knowledge of either Dick or Stephen James. The arrangement, however, was soon to be cut short.

It was something that would disappoint Kirk Duncan. He began his musical career at the tender age of 4, when he started playing the piano by ear. Realising his talent, his parents, and in particular his father, who was also a musician, arranged for him to have piano lessons. He then progressed to playing in bands at school, where he would practice in the school hall, after the teaching had ended for the day, with the assistance of a forward thinking teacher who introduced them to rock'n'roll and the art of personal expression. Within a short time, and the help of the teacher, the boys went from being a skiffle group to a rock'n'roll band.

After a spell in the army, where Duncan sustained a back injury during a training session on an assault course, he went back to music and hopped from band to band until he met up with Nicky James who had enjoyed considerable success as a solo artist, and was one of the founding members of the Moody Blues. Their meeting gives an interesting insight into how Tin Pan Alley worked in those days.

'I was sitting in the Giaconda making my coffee last as long as I could, when Nicky came in and asked if there were any musicians available to do some session work with Graham Nash. I volunteered, not really believing that anything would come of it, but during the journey to the studio, Nicky told me he was writing songs with Graham. I was invited to the studio to meet him and sure enough, he was there.'

The idea that Niraki would eventually be supported by Gralto and administered by DJM seemed an excellent wheeze. But, to make ends meet whilst the search for talent ensued, Duncan and James were signed to DJM on a retainer and 'it was agreed that Nicky and I would get 25% of any publishing rights for songs that we found or wrote and so we started to get people in,' continues Duncan.

'Dick, at the time, was running Gralto as well as other companies that were part of the DJM Group, so we were confident that he would back us.' Following the formation of the agreement, Ray Williams did all the studio work with the writers, and when Reg joined in 1967, 'I was in on the demos with him from the start, with Caleb Quaye as the engineer. "Scarecrow" was the first thing we did with Reg, and when Bernie joined Reg, we booked them in for sessions at DJM and recorded their songs,' Duncan remembers.

Indeed, Duncan would spend a considerable amount of time in the studio with Quaye and Reg, writing songs and recording demos of the songs they had written together, and, later, with Taupin when he came along with his compositions. 'Most of Elton's work was piano and vocals,' Duncan says of the early sessions. 'To get other sounds we would improvise. For instance, to get a good bass sound I would get a plastic chair and thump it to the tune of the piano, so if you hear a thumping sound on the demo it's me with the chair. My memory of that time, was that Elton took himself very seriously whenever he was in the studio, as we all did, but the amazing thing was, he never took more than a maximum of three takes per song having worked on it himself for a while, before coming into the studio.

'We could tell from the moment we started working with him, that he was something special, but he didn't have the image, he really didn't. We thought that he would never be a big star because of how he looked, but we did feel he was a good prospect to sign up to Gralto and then to Niraki. He would have moments of complete madness in the studio, though. One afternoon, I recall, was when he had recorded a really good song called "One Time, Some Time, Never", and when we were listening to the playback, he got very excited about it and started running around the rooms of DJM saying he was going to be a star. He got that sort of madness from Caleb. He would do that sort of thing as well, even when he was walking down the High Street going for a coffee.'

During the same period, Duncan was actively looking for a management deal for Reg as he was clearly impressed by what he was hearing in the studio. He had discussions with Graham Nash and Spencer Davis and there were movements for Reg to sign for the Spencer Davis Management Company and introduce him to America as early as the end of 1968. However, everything was about to change.

Duncan's social and studio life was beginning to take its toll. During the day he would be in the studio working with Quaye and Reg until at least six o'clock at night. Then, after work, he would go out with James and Nash to the clubs, such as the Bag O' Nails, where Nash would buy them spirits by the bottle, and they would all stagger home in the early hours of the next morning to start all over again.

'Yeah, Nicky and I were running on empty and it took its toll on me and I collapsed. I went to Southend to recuperate for a while, and when I returned, things had changed. When I got back to DJM on 7 November 1968, I was told that Elton and Bernie had signed to Dick James Music. On the previous day, November 6, Dick had decided to use the excuse that he didn't know that Reg and Bernie were using the studio to sign them.

'There may have been some truth in the claim that he didn't know that they were using the studio at night as, during the day, Reg and Bernie were booked into the studio by Gralto. I told Dick that he couldn't sign Reg and Bernie as they had a contract with Gralto, and they were writing for part of our catalogue to form Niraki, which Dick was already aware of, having signed the original agreement, and was administering the arrangement. We asked for a meeting with Dick, during which, I told him that we had a contract to introduce writers but Dick wouldn't budge. I said some choice things to him and as a consequence of speaking out, I lost my contract and retainer, and was told that I was excluded from the studios from then onwards.'

However, he was soon back at DJM, despite the ban from James, to work with the Mirage on keyboards with Dee Murray and the Hynes Brothers. The new venture led to Reg joining forces with Murray on bass, Hynes on drums and Quaye on guitar for his first live gig at the Marquee club in late 1968.

Quaye's take on how they all got rumbled for using the studio nocturnally is enlightening . 'I was managing the studio, and had all sorts of musicians coming in and out, saying that they had a band and wanted to do a demo, but didn't have any money to pay for studio time. I was letting people come in after hours and Reg and Bernie were part of that arrangement. A lot of the stuff, what are now called the *Dick James Demos*, was recorded after hours. I gave bands a lot of studio time for nothing, and let them make demos and acetates. Being a musician, guitarist and engineer, I understood what was needed and what sound was required to suit each individual band, so I was able to provide what was wanted in the studio.'

But it was not quite as simple as that. The studio was situated directly above the Midland Bank, so if anyone worked at night it was down to Stephen James to inform the security people that the studio was being used after normal office hours. There was, however, one night that no one told him that they were going to be working late and, as a result, nobody warned the security people, who would later call DJM's office manager, Ronald Bron, halfway through the night to ask him. As far as he was concerned, the answer was no; the studio was not being used. If it was, James would have told him, and he in turn would have told the security team. All the same, Bron decided to check it out for himself and hurtled over to the studio. And that's when he discovered that the studio took on a life of its own after hours.

Remembering the incident today, Stephen James recalls arriving at the office the next morning to be greeted by a rather annoyed Bron. 'He raged at me as if I was a naughty schoolboy about to get a detention. He told me that I had slipped up by not informing the security at Midland Bank, and that I had no right to let others, musician or other publishing concern, use the studio.' And of course, he was right.

'It was quite bizarre,' explains Quaye. 'I think Stephen was told to control his staff, as Bron was running the studio and the office. He was like most office managers at the time, like a Sergeant Major who we all feared. He was basically in charge of the day to day running of the place, and literally controlled everything and everyone to the point that we had to ask him even for a toilet roll. He had every cupboard and door locked, and he held the keys, so no one could get anything unless they asked him. And, of course, it didn't help that James knew nothing about the clandestine arrangements, so I got called into Dick's office. I thought I was going to lose my job. He got very angry, telling me that he was losing money and told me to throw them all out unless they were signed to the company. The result was that we had to have a clear out of those that had nothing to do with DJM. And that's why it became known as The Great Purge.'

Quaye agreed to put a stop to the late night sessions, but also alerted James to an artist that he considered he should listen to. 'I told him his name was Reg Dwight who was recording under the name of Elton John. With Stephen also in the room, they both asked me to get the tapes. When I returned and played them, I was standing there, sweating like a waterfall, while they listened. All I could think about was, if they don't like them, I am done for. Luckily, they did like them. Dick said he thought the tapes were very good, and he wanted to sign them, so in a way I got Reg and Bernie their first contract with DJM on a retainer for about £10 a week. And the funny thing was that, if it hadn't been for Bron complaining, the office manager that most of us avoided at all costs, then Reg and Bernie may never have been signed at that time.'

'After listening to the tapes,' says Stephen James, 'I thought the lyrics were pretty awful, but the melodies had something quite different, original and interesting. I told

Caleb to arrange for Reg to meet me as I wanted to talk to him about the demos, so he came round at about six that evening and that's when I told him he couldn't use the studio unless he signed to DJM, or he paid for the time. I knew he couldn't afford to pay, so instead he signed. It was quite simple really; he couldn't sign to the company and carry on working for a competitor around the corner, so I also gave him the ultimatum that he would have to give up working at Gralto. They were paying him eight pounds a week, so I told him I would get him ten pounds and he would have to pack in his job at Gralto.'

The deal was really just an advance against royalties earned by the two songwriters, which meant that James would recover his investment from whatever royalties were earned from Reg and Bernie's songs, but there was also a risk as far as James was concerned. 'We may not have recouped our investment, but it was something we were prepared to take a gamble on.'

Reg, of course, agreed to the deal and while James prepared the contracts with Geoffrey Ellis, he went home to collect his mother who was required to sign and witness the agreements. At 20, Reg was still under age in Britain to sign a legal document without the signature of a parent or guardian.'

When Reg and Bernie were initially signed to DJM, it was with a view to eventually recording as Elton John but, before any of that happened, they first had to earn their crusts by being staff writers, writing songs to be sold to anyone prepared to buy them from James; no different really to what many other songwriters in Tin Pan Alley were doing. At this stage, and quite ironically, it seemed that Reg had come full circle, and had returned to Tin Pan Alley, only this time he was on the songwriting treadmill.

Rather than hawking sheet music around, he was now hustling songs for publishing for his new employer Dick James Music. 'I used to take the songs written and performed by Reg and try and sell them,' recalls Stephen James. 'I went to Johnny Franz at Philips and played him the songs. He said they were really tough songs for artists to sing and suggested I record Reg instead.'

Before that, however, in the summer of 1967, Reg was still playing with Bluesology, and was about to tour with Baldry again, who was milking the success of 'Let The Heartaches Begin'. It was at this point that Reg seized his opportunity to bring in Caleb Quaye when guitarist Neil Hubbard left. Now, Reg and Caleb could be working on songs together whilst they were touring. After the gigs, they would usually work with Bernie's lyrics at DJM late into the night. And then, in between gigs, they would go back to the DJM studio and put the songs onto tape and disc. It soon came to a point where the Baldry thing became old hat, and Reg, who no longer wanted to be part of it, developed other plans for his future.

When Baldry took them under his wing, Reg now found that he had the time to become involved in other things. Instead of the frenetic touring and doing everything themselves, they had acquired people to help and so it all became a lot more organised. It was an ideal situation for Reg who was looking to further his career elsewhere. 'We had roadies by this time, so we didn't need to carry and set up our gear,' recalls Fred Gandy. 'Reg was going up to the studio at DJM with Caleb, who was, by now, a tape operator and that is where Caleb met Roger Pope and from where Hookfoot started.'

In fact, when Reg was recording with Caleb and needed musicians they first thought of Bluesology. Pete Gavin remembers that he got a call from Reg to go to DJM and audition for his band, but Gavin was drinking heavily at the time, so nothing came of it. 'If I'd been a bit more professional I might well have stayed with Reg. But it was not to be,' says Gavin.

As Reg's new career was starting to emerge and he and Caleb were beginning to look to a future without Bluesology, Reg came across the idea that he should perhaps find a stage name for himself. 'He needed a working name,' remembers Quaye. 'Reg Dwight was not the right name for a singer/songwriter. I used to laugh about it and say to him "You can't call yourself Reg Dwight in this business". There was a cycling champion at the time called Reg Harris and Caleb kept telling Reg that the kids were just going to think of Reg Harris and expect him to come on stage riding a bike. So we decided to find a name for him.

'I remember we had flown down from Scotland to London, after Bluesology had done a gig in Glasgow, and we were on the airport bus. Reg was writing some names down and included Elton John amongst them. He showed me the name and told me he got the idea from Elton Dean and John Baldry. He asked me if I thought they would mind and I said I didn't think so, and so we went with that name.'

When Elton Dean was told, he just laughed at it, and said he thought Reg was crazy. At the time no-one took it very seriously and certainly didn't expect what was to come. One day, Gandy remembers, 'Reg said "I am leaving the band", he wanted to take just Elton Dean's name at first, and Dean told him to "fuck off." I still remember how Reg just said "O.K., I'll use your name and John Baldry's then." When he told us that he was going to call himself Elton John, we all fell about laughing, and said, "You must be mad!" Not that it put Reg off. He was pleased with the name and he was determined that he would stick with it.'

Mick Inkpen was another to know that he was thinking about changing his name. 'He was getting ready to form a band and he was planning to change his stage persona and his new name would be at the centre of that change.' But he hadn't really done much stage work on his own, except for doing session work and filling in for other band members. He didn't have a band of his own.

Len Crawley, the guitarist with Linda Laine And The Sinners, was still in regular contact with Reg. 'He invited me to DJM to make demos, he told me he was thinking about forming his own band and he was going to leave Bluesology. He actually said in the letter that he was thinking of changing his name from Reg Dwight to Elton John because he had offers of gigs for £68 a night as Elton John.'

Mick Inkpen also remembers the transformation. 'He was going to get a makeover, get some stage clothes and have his hair done, and he was adamant that he was going to change his name to Elton John. I told him not to be so silly.'

It was not long before the Elton John persona began to take hold of Reg. To those around him, it was quite remarkable to watch the metamorphosis from shy caterpillar to confident butterfly. Out went the blazer and slacks and in came a strange Noddy shirt. By this time, his wit and humour was common to all in DJM and his outgoing personality made him a hit with his work colleagues. As the Elton John project continued, so Reg's personality began to change with the style of music he was now making.

Crawley went up to see him at DJM. 'We couldn't believe what we were seeing. He had completely changed his image from the one he had in Hamburg. Now he had fancy shirts that were flowery and flamboyant, and we said to him, "What's all this then, where's your slacks and blazer?" And he said, "I have been told that I have got to change my image." He had grown his hair, and his glasses had changed to look like ones that John Lennon had at the time and he had traded in his Hillman Husky for a more prestigious Austin Somerset. He was writing his own songs by then, but he hadn't met Bernie at that time. It all seemed to change after he left Bluesology.

When he was working with Quaye in the DJM studio, Freddy Gandy and Stewart Brown had a chance meeting with him. 'He came around the corner, he had a shirt with Mickey Mouse all over it and silly coloured trousers, he had suddenly hit the colour barrier and we thought "If the fashion police were around they would have arrested him" and so we said to him, "What the hell are you wearing?". He was slightly put out about it but as far as he was concerned he was on his way by then, so he didn't care what others thought; but it was a big change. It was like his Elton John persona was already taking him over.' But soon, someone else was to take him over too.

# 10

# FIRST LOVE

Linda Woodrow was living on the Meadowbrook council estate in Sheffield with her mother and stepfather when she met Reg. 'Nothing specific was happening in my life. I worked almost every night and went out with my friend Jackie two or three times a week. I remember on Monday nights we would go to a club called the Penny Farthing, and that is where we met Joe Cocker as he usually appeared there most Monday evenings.' Woodrow was also working as a DJ six nights a week at the Silver Blades Ice Rink, which was located in the basement of the building that housed the Heartbeat night club on the floor above the skating rink. For her, it was a good place to work, but it wasn't the only place she spent her time trying to make a living. 'I also worked with my friend Jackie, who owned a hairdressing salon, and who, in the evenings, was working in the Heartbeat. If nothing else, life for us seemed pretty normal.' But all that was about to change.

Born in Lauder, Berwickshire, Linda had attended private boarding school in Reigate, Surrey, from when she was 8 years old until she went to a finishing school in Eastbourne, Sussex, aged 16. That was before she moved back to Sheffield to be with her family. Her father's step-brother, Robin Wood, had something to do with Epicure Foods, which is why she was dubbed a 'pickled onion heiress', not that she would receive a penny from her uncle when he died. The only sum of money that Linda received would be some time later, in the form of a small trust fund from her aunt.

Woodrow had been making a name for herself on the Sheffield music scene, simply by being associated with local celebrities. One of these was Chris Crossley, the resident 'Jock' at the Locarno, who went under the name of the Mighty Atom due to the fact that he was just 4' 8" high. 'He called me one night and told me that Long John Baldry was appearing at the Fiesta night club and would I like to go and see him? Crossley was quite well in with the people in the club scene and knew all the right people, so yes, I agreed to go with him and this is where I met Reg Dwight,' she explains.

Reg was at the Fiesta with Bluesology for one of their club circuit tours with Baldry. He had, by this time, teamed up with Bernie Taupin. It was during the time that he was working closely with Caleb Quaye, firstly at DJM and now as part of the Bluesology line-up, so it would have been difficult for Quaye not to have noticed how Reg and Linda were becoming smitten with each other: 'She was his first real girlfriend, although for some reason, I kind of remember it being at the Cavendish Club, not the Fiesta, when Linda came onto the scene. We were definitely on the Bailey Club circuit at the time, and they were just crazy gigs to do. I thought she had a boyfriend at the time, who was the midget DJ guy, the Mighty Atom, but not so. It's so easy to get the wrong idea with things like that.'

At the same time that Reg was growing fond of Linda, Caleb was starting to fall for a waitress at the club: 'It was all part and parcel of the business at that time, whether you were a disc jockey or with a band, it was easy to pick up a girl because they were kind of all over you, because of what you did or who you were, and being with Baldry certainly made us a good pull. Everyone had turned up to see Baldry and afterwards at the bar we would be having drinks with quite a few girls, but Reg, I remember, was talking with Linda most of the time. We were playing in the club for about a week, so on those sort of gigs we got the chance to do a lot of drinking and a lot of socialising, and hanging out with whoever took our fancy. Reg had certainly taken a fancy to Linda, so I guess it wasn't any surprise that they seemed to be hanging out together most of the week that we were playing up there.'

But according to Woodrow, meeting Reg was really down to the fact that he was sitting with Long John Baldry when she and Crossley were introduced to Baldry. 'Reg was a very shy person. I remember during our initial conversation, how he told me that he had never been to the Yorkshire Moors, so I offered to show him around. And that was our first date, showing him the sights of Sheffield rather than the Yorkshire Moors. I think I drove him around, just showing him some of the sights that Sheffield had to offer.

'At that time, we were just friends and were enjoying each other's company. I also watched him rehearsing with Bluesology during the day. After that first date, he invited me to the next gig and the relationship began to build from there. He was just a nice person, and the more I saw him, the more I liked him. Never in my wildest dreams did I ever imagine that he would become so famous. I was young, actually I am three years older than Reg, and I suppose I was flattered because of who he was, and that he took an interest in me.'

It was why every night after Woodrow had finished her disc-jockeying stint at the ice rink, she would head straight over to the Fiesta to meet Reg. During the day, it was a different story though. The pair would just hang out together, because neither of them had much money to do anything. In the evening, Woodrow would go back to her family whilst Reg went back to the small hotel he had booked for the week long residency with Baldry.

While it could never be described as love at first sight, Linda, young and impressionable, really liked Reg a great deal and that is how their friendship started during those first few days in Sheffield. After Sheffield, when Bluesology carried on with more gigs across the North of England, Woodrow would either travel with Reg to a gig, and when she couldn't do that, she would be calling him on the telephone. Usually after the shows, Reg and Linda would go out together, either just the two of them or, on other occasions, with the rest of the band. Everyone that is, except Baldry. Indeed, Woodrow quickly became a popular member of the Bluesology entourage, and got on so well with the rest of the band that she was a welcome addition.

When the tour of the North was over, and Reg was due to go back to his home in Pinner, he told Woodrow that they should keep in contact, and that she would have to come and stay with him at his parents' house at Frome Court. Even though they kept in touch with each other as they said they would, it wasn't long before Woodrow had left her family in Sheffield and moved down to London to be with Reg. Having already stayed at Reg's family home on several occasions, they didn't want to be apart for too long.

'I used to come down from Sheffield and stay with Reg and his parents before I made the decision to actually move to London,' reflects Woodrow today. 'His parents were very nice to me, when I used to visit at weekends. It was like when we were in Sheffield, we really didn't do very much, because we didn't have that much money. I remember how he used to play the piano nearly all day. He had a very small bedroom, but it was still big enough for him and Bernie to write songs in. It probably helped that we weren't sleeping together at that time, simply out of respect for his family.'

Woodrow didn't make the decision to move to London on her own without first discussing it with Reg. 'He seemed genuinely excited about the idea of moving in together. It was a decision that was made by both of us. As I say, he was quite excited about it all and was ready to leave home. At the beginning, my parents weren't too happy about our relationship but once they learned we were living together, they just accepted him. They even invited him to Newcastle to spend the evening with us at my brother's twenty-first birthday party so, like any other couple's first months together, it was a very exciting time for both of us.'

From scouring the local North London newspapers, Woodrow eventually found an ideal flat to rent in Furlong Road, Holloway. 'It was the basement of a house where you went in through a gate to a little courtyard, and then when you went in the front door, to the right was the kitchen. There was also a large living area with a back door that led to a very small yard, a large bedroom, and at the end of the hallway, a bathroom.'

It seemed the perfect home for a young couple, and Woodrow, understandably excited by the whole thing, was ecstatic. She had found the man she wanted to live with and had located an ideal home for them to nest in, so what more could she ask for? 'The flat was already furnished when we moved in. The only things we took to the apartment were our personal belongings. We were both very excited about living together.'

Soon after she had reserved the flat and moved in with her two dogs, Reg followed and, soon after that, they were joined by Bernie Taupin, who decided to occupy the large bedroom leaving the couple to share the living room as their sleeping accommodation.

'Unfortunately, I can't remember my first meeting with Bernie. I think it was Reg who suggested that Bernie should move in. He paid a very small amount towards the rent, but every penny was helpful.'

It was helpful, because Woodrow paid the rent and the household bills. 'He didn't really have a job while we were at Furlong Road and that's why I had to pay most of the bills. Neither of them had a job other than composing songs and spending a lot of time at DJM writing music and recording, so it was down to me to pay for most things.'

In many ways, it was very fortunate for Reg and Bernie that Linda was working at the time, at the Evening Newspaper Advertising Bureau, in Holborn. 'Yes, I worked for a guy who was retired from either the army or the marines. Major Grogan was his name and I was his personal secretary.' Not that she had much left out of her salary since she had paid everything out each week, to keep the boys fed and off the streets. 'Most times were good; sometimes they were not. Sometimes I felt Bernie got in the way but, as they were busy writing and composing songs, they really needed to be together. And it obviously helped that we were all quite good friends but, sometimes, I got a little frustrated with Bernie, probably because he was always there, so Reg and I never really got to spend too much time on our own.'

An animal lover by nature, when the boys were out working on their songs Woodrow would be kept company by her dogs. 'Reg would play with them as well, when he was home, but Bernie didn't very much. He always used to say that the dogs used to mess everywhere, but I totally disagree with him. They didn't at all. I am to this day, still very house proud.'

Not that Caleb Quaye was completely convinced about it all and recalls that Linda wasn't as put-upon as she makes out. 'I remember when Linda moved down from Sheffield to be with Reg and that's when it got serious. To me, their relationship was comical. She appeared to me to be very dominant, and a controller, and had a very strong personality. I recall how she would make him walk her two little dogs. And on one occasion, when we had gone out to lunch and were on our way back to the studio, I was walking behind them. He has these two little dogs on a lead pulling him along, and I was just laughing. It was hilarious. Reg knew that I was laughing at him and that I thought it was funny. We knew it was never going to work. They were just a total mismatch.' Not that Woodrow would completely agree. 'Looking back, maybe I was just a little controlling at the time, but I was the one that used to suggest many of the things we did, but I don't believe that could be called controlling. If I was, then Reg certainly didn't say so, it was never ever mentioned.'

While Reg and Bernie spent most of their days and nights at Dick James' studio, Woodrow would either be at work in Holborn or at home in the flat. She recollects, 'I have always been very domesticated. After boarding school, I was sent to the Eastbourne School of Domestic Science and this taught you how to be a lady, how to clean properly and cook. Just as well, as I don't remember getting too much help from either Reg or Bernie.'

In the evenings, Linda would often go down to DJM to watch Reg and Bernie composing and recording. 'It was quite an exciting time. I sometimes went inside the studio with them, mainly because I wanted to be with Reg, and also because he and Bernie would stay quite late at the studio, and as I had to be up early for work the next day, I needed to be in bed at a certain time. It was simply thrilling to see and hear Reg working on the songs with Bernie. I was very proud of him. And it was great fun to watch how they put a lyric and tune together. All Reg ever wanted was to be a success, but I am not sure he ever expected to be as successful as he became. It is amazing to think about where he is today, because all he ever really wanted to do was to be a composer.'

The one thing that Reg and Linda didn't do much of was socialising and if they did, Bernie was in tow. 'I remember we would sometimes go to a club in Bond Street to see some of his friends, and I think that is where I met Rod Stewart for the first time. But Reg really wasn't into the club scene at that time, though.'

At home in Furlong Road, it was a different story. Reg would spend most of his time in Bernie's quarters writing songs and listening to a lot of different types of music, both for interest and inspiration. Reg and Linda never took vacations together, either, apart from the occasional journey, like the time when they went to the twenty-first bash for Woodrow's brother in Newcastle. On another occasion, she and Reg were invited to Bernie's parents, but even the journey to the little village of Owmby by Spital in Lincolnshire was fraught with problems. 'We were travelling along the A1 motorway when another car ran into us,' remembers Woodrow. 'I hurt my arm and an ambulance was called, but I was treated on the spot; I didn't have to go to hospital.' Bernie was travelling ahead with his then girlfriend.

Overall though, life at Furlong Road was pretty good for Linda. She was playing the domestic goddess around the flat, usually tidying up after the boys, and providing them with meals, and generally being a housewife and supporter for her beloved Reg. 'He never intimated that he was unhappy with me, in fact, we were planning on getting married, and he seemed very happy with the idea.' Quite understandably, Linda was more than happy to support her boyfriend in his quest for success. After all, they had discussed getting married and she was over the moon as most young girls would have been in finding the man she wanted to spend the rest of her life with. 'He never actually proposed to me, we just discussed the idea of getting married. I had to go out and buy my own engagement ring as Reg had no money.'

The wedding date was set for 22 June 1968 at Uxbridge Registry office. And Reg, remembers Woodrow, wrote and told a friend, on 7 June, that he was about to tie the knot. 'He considered it was the thing to do as we had been living together for some time. We had, by that time, found a flat together in Mill Hill, and had been out and bought furniture for the new place, but I had to be pretty strict about Bernie's accommodation. Bernie certainly wasn't going to come and live with us. He had several girlfriends at that time and I thought he could move in with one of them.

'My parents, of course, were a little concerned; they knew that I had been paying for everything, so their reaction was very hesitant, but they accepted it as they knew that I loved Reg.'

It didn't help matters that at the time of the wedding plans, Reg was having problems over his contract with DJM. He was writing songs that he didn't want to write, and his career, once again, seemed like it was going in no specific direction. He wanted Ray Williams to become his manager and buy out the contract with DJM, but the idea was proving more difficult than he thought. He was becoming very down with the way things were panning out, and with life in general.

'One of the reasons he was getting so depressed,' explains Woodrow, 'was down to the fact that his music wasn't catching on as he wanted it to, and the day I walked into the flat and found him lying on the kitchen floor with the gas oven on, I was in total shock. But it had all been thought out very carefully. He had placed a cushion in the oven to make himself as comfortable as he could, and had also left a window open. So I suppose he was never really serious about trying to end his life.

'I am not sure whether his parents knew how badly depressed he was. Quite naturally, his mother was devastated and somewhat surprised when she heard. He never sought any professional help for his depression, and he "just got over it." But it was hard work, because Bernie and I had to keep reassuring him that one day he would make it.'

The night of his breakup with Woodrow was another occasion that she remembers quite vividly:

> It was three weeks before the wedding, at four in the morning. Reg, Bernie and Baldry had been to the Bag O'Nails club. It was where both Baldry and Bernie had told Reg that he was making a big mistake getting married. Both Bernie and Reg came home very drunk and Reg was quite tearful. Bernie, I remember, scurried off to his bedroom to avoid the impending conflict that he knew was about to happen.
>
> Reg came straight to the point. He told me that he didn't want to get married and that he was moving out, it was that straight and to the point. We were both in tears. My reaction was hurt, devastation and pure amazement. I didn't expect anything like that to happen. I probably blurted out that I was pregnant just to try and keep him. It was clear from whatever happened that night at the Bag O'Nails, that Reg's mind was made up. He just went into the living room and began to pack his stuff and I was hoping all the time that he would change his mind.

The next morning, Woodrow continues, he called his stepfather to come and collect him. 'I pleaded and pleaded, but whatever Baldry had told him the night before had completely changed his mind. He and Bernie packed up all their things and headed off with Fred in his van. I kept trying to talk to him but his mind was made up. We may have spoken only once or twice after he moved out.'

It may well have been for the best though. Even Tony Taupin remembers that Reg had doubts about the marriage: 'I recall Reg bringing his girlfriend with him to

Owmby but they didn't stay with my parents, they booked into a hotel in Market Rasen called the Gordon Arms. We knew that Reg was planning to get married to her, but even at that late stage, he was agonising over whether he would go ahead with it.'

After the boys had moved out and gone back to Frome Court, Woodrow remembers, 'I only rented the apartment, and I don't remember staying on there for very long after the breakup. My mother moved down to London to be with me and we lived together for a short while, I then met someone after a few months and unfortunately now realise that I married on the rebound; it only lasted a couple of years.' Linda has been married three times and has three children and three grandchildren and is now living happily on her own in America.

Mick Inkpen also remembers how Reg disappeared from the Pinner map completely during this period. 'I didn't see him at all for a few years. He later moved back into his mother's house in Northwood and we started seeing each other again. Bernie had moved back as well.'

'According to Reg, after he had become Elton,' says Gary Osborne, 'he said he was getting engaged to this girl, in spite of the fact that he had a crush on a male friend of his. It happened when Long John Baldry suddenly says to him, "My dear boy, why are you getting married when everyone knows you're a poove?" and I believe those were his exact words. Poove was a piss-elegant way of saying poof and at that stage the word "poof" was not considered to be offensive like it is now. And at the time, he kind of knew that he was gay and Baldry crystallised it for him in that sentence.' Someone else who agrees with that summation is Stuart Epps. 'The story goes that on his stag night, Baldry convinced Elton that he was actually gay.'

Even if Baldry did manage to persuade Reg to self-examine his own sexuality, and it seems he did, he was still attracted to women. Even after his relationship with Woodrow was done and dusted, he would still meet up with women here and there. One was the new secretary at DJM, Sue Ayton. 'They went out a few times together, but we were never sure whether it amounted to anything,' confirms Chrissie Cremore, then DJM's Press Officer. As far as Ayton was concerned, the friendship began soon after she started at DJM as one of Dick's personal assistants.

'As Dick was a very powerful man in the music business during the sixties and early seventies, he would get copies of recordings from all over Tin Pan Alley and from all of the artists across Britain and America,' explains Cremore. 'Elton would regularly rifle through the racks of records that were kept neatly by Ayton and, with Dick's permission, take the ones he wanted. That is when the friendship with Ayton blossomed into a relationship.'

Reg was charismatic, amusing and fun to be with. It seems the attraction was mutual. He was definitely attracted to her, but all it seemed to be was a brief relationship that he probably thought would be fun to pursue. Long after the relationship with Ayton fizzled out, and long before the defining gigs at the Troubadour in Los Angeles, Ayton could often be seen at some of the smaller gigs that Reg was playing on his own or, on other occasions, with Hookfoot, or when Dee and Nigel were his backing band, just before the historic trip to Los Angeles.

# 11

# THE DEATH OF
# BLUESOLOGY

Long John Baldry wasn't surprised when Reg decided to leave Bluesology. If anything, he had probably been waiting for it to happen. He was well aware of the clandestine recordings at DJM, and Reg's budding partnership with Bernie Taupin, so in many ways, as far as Baldry was concerned, Reg's departure was inevitable. 'He was a competent player, yes, but really all we were losing was just a keyboard player,' remarks Freddy Gandy. 'We weren't losing Elton John. Besides, nothing could really faze Baldry. He was above it all.' Before Reg and Caleb Quaye departed, however, they auditioned two young hopefuls as their replacements.

One was Bernie Holland who, at the time, was working as a semi-professional guitarist in Cheltenham and had played with bands, mainly as a bass player and, on occasions, as a drummer – though the guitar was his preferred instrument. 'I just wanted to get into a band so I would play anything,' recalls Holland.

Holland was best-known for being a regular at the Blue Moon in Cheltenham during the era of the Mods, from whom he gleaned an appreciation for their sophisticated tastes in music. They were huge fans of all the imported albums and singles from America, by such artists as Chuck Berry, Aretha Franklin, the Temptations and Lee Dorsey, which in turn influenced British musicians such as Georgie Fame, John Baldry and a lot of the other R&B groups like the Artwoods. Like Holland, all these solo artists and bands were into R&B, but what Holland really enjoyed was the organ-based stuff like Brian Auger, because like Auger, he was also into Jimmy Smith.

'I remember seeing Bluesology as a kind of expansion to that music with brass, trumpet and sax in addition to the standard organ, bass and drums. At the time when I met Baldry and Bluesology, it was Baldry on vocals and harmonica, Fred Gandy on bass, on drums there was Peter Gavin, and on organ was Reginald Dwight.' says Holland. 'He didn't have a Hammond like most bands did, he had this horrible Vox

Continental that had a rather nasty nasal sound. It was almost cheap and nasty but it had a stop on it that sounded a bit like a Hammond. He just played organ, he was a side man and you wouldn't give him a second glance. Everyone got a solo, including him. And he had this characteristic, when he was playing his solo, which demanded concentration for a particular skill, where his nostrils would flare up and hence he was given the nickname, "Piggy", which, of course, he hated.'

The guitarist, remembers Holland, was Caleb Quaye: 'I got to know him pretty well during the Bluesology gigs at the Blue Moon, and would often buy him a drink. We enjoyed swapping notes about all the different guitarists of the day. And it was during one of these conversations, during the interval at a Bluesology and Baldry gig, that I was approached as a possible replacement for Quaye.'

Quaye had joined Bluesology after Neil Hubbard had left and, although he became a popular member of the band and a well respected guitarist, it was clear to the rest of the band that it was just a stop gap for him whilst Reg was getting ready to go solo. 'He never heard me play,' continues Holland, 'but because of the people I was talking to about the things that I liked, he got the impression that I might be a candidate for an audition. He gave me an inkling about this, and I think that he was thinking of leaving the band, but he didn't want to leave them in the shit, so he wanted to find someone who would make a smooth transition. He said to me, "I am getting my own band together and I am working with Reg and he's going solo."

'Reg had decided at this point that he wanted to be a solo artist and he no longer wanted to be part of the Bluesology-Baldry treadmill anymore. It must have been in early 1968, as I was still in Art College at the time and going out to these clubs, and I told Caleb I was interested. He said that I needed to go to London for an audition and of course I jumped at the chance, who wouldn't?'

From that conversation, Holland was invited to an audition that was held at the Ken Collier Jazz Club, which was in Studio 51, a basement club with a bar, in Great Newport Street in London. Holland can remember how the place was decorated with nicotine-stained photographs of all who had played there on the walls, and 'I remember there were two old ladies who cleaned and made sandwiches watching the auditions.' Holland gives a fascinating account of the audition process:

> Reg was in charge of the general audition but specifically looking after the organ auditions, and Caleb was there to give approval on guitar. There were at least six guitarists there, all of who I thought were streets ahead of me, but I remained hopeful and confident. I was 17 years old, but some of the other guys who auditioned were in their 20's. We had a list of things we were going to do, we were asked to give a straight swing type of twelve bar blues thing. If we didn't know a twelve bar blues chord sequence, then we may as well have gone home! We had to play a piece of our choice that we had heard the band do and that the band knew. I chose a blues song, then we had a piece which we were given a chart to sight read. It was sight reading chord changes. Had it been notes, then I would have needed more time but with chord sequences we just had chord symbols and that is a lot easier to deal with.

So, Reg handed out this chord sequence for this Horace Silver number called 'Song For My Father' and he counted me in. I started playing and about twenty bars into this, he stopped me and asked if I was sure I was playing it right. I said it's what I have got here, pointing to the chord sheets, and he said 'Well something doesn't sound right', and I said 'Well I'm playing what you have written', and he said 'Sorry', and he changed the chord from a minor seventh to a major seventh, and he asked me to do it again, and it was fine.

After the audition, Caleb gave Holland a wink as if to say he had done well, and he would be in touch. By the time he got home to Cheltenham, the phone rang. It was Caleb and he asked Holland if he wanted the gig. 'I couldn't believe my luck, especially because I had auditioned with other guitarists who were, I thought, miles better than I was. Caleb told me that the band did not want to carry people who had any drug habits, and he knew that I would be O.K. and was a good player. Any shortcomings that I had with my playing would be backed up by the rest of the band, including Baldry. They gave me a month to sort myself out, so I gave my notice at the Art College and that was it, I was on my way.'

Holland soon discovered that there were two types of Bluesology gigs. One was when they played a residency in a night club, normally in the North of England with a typical noisy and blunt Northern club audience, and the other was with Baldry. 'We would be on the bill with a magician or a hypnotist type of act, and we would play things like, "Cry Me A River", "How Sweet It Is To Be Loved By You" and "Let The Heartaches Begin", as backing to Baldry. Although Baldry was an excellent singer, he was also a brilliant entertainer, who could hold the audience in the palm of his hand. He was very witty, and it was amazing to watch how quickly the audiences would warm to him.'

Baldry was amusing off-stage too. On one occasion, Holland recalls, when they were playing Mr Smith's club in the centre of Manchester, 'The doorway was less than six foot high and there was a gas lamp converted to oil above the door. We were doing a one week cabaret at this place and Baldry, one night, had picked up a couple of young lads, and had been drinking a fair amount of vodka. He walked into the club and hit his head on this oil lamp which was lit. It set fire to his hair and had burnt most of it, so he had to go out and buy a Stetson that he then had to wear on stage for the rest of the week. He turned it into his image. Baldry used to drink a lot of vodka, and he was terrific when he was drunk. He was louder and more outrageous,'

Another incident, recalls Holland was 'when we were playing somewhere and after a drinking session, Baldry was found wandering out to sea in a white tablecloth. We had to go and rescue him, we had no idea what he was trying to do.'

When the Olympic Games were held in Mexico in 1968, Baldry decided to jump on the bandwagon and recorded a song called 'Mexico'. It became the official song for the British team and consequently gave Baldry another hit. 'I will never, never forget that song, it will torment me for the rest of my life,' laughs Holland. 'It was a gimmick, but we still had to play it wherever we went.'

But more than anything, Baldry always went out of his way to make sure his gigs suited the audiences he was playing to. If he was doing a mod club with young people, he would change the set to suit them. If he was doing a cabaret club, then he would do all the jazzy stuff. 'He could sing anything as he was a brilliant artist,' continues Holland. 'He was as good as Sinatra, he knew all about working with a big band, and working with a small group, and he knew how to work with a quartet with organ, bass and drums. He was a complete professional, and on top of that he had a huge heart. He really did care about his musicians, the people he worked with day in and day out.'

The only time that Baldry read his audience completely wrong, was when he and the boys went to Southern Ireland. He was on stage and made a comment about the Republicans. It was meant to be a witty comment, but the audience took it the wrong way and started throwing coins and beer glasses, and the band had to flee the stage to avoid getting seriously hurt. Never mix music and politics!

The success of 'Let The Heartaches Begin' though, helped the band to secure gigs at better places for better money than they had so far done. 'When "Heartaches" was a hit, we were given a brand new six-wheel transit which, in those days, was the best vehicle to have for touring bands,' says Gandy. 'We had various roadies as well, so we didn't have to load and unload and set up equipment, it was a dream. Baldry, by now, had stopped travelling with the rest of us, got himself a driver, and a Bentley. But he was generous to a fault. When he had his number one hit, he got himself a roadie, who was a bit of a sharp character. When he realised that we had all got a bit of money, he told us that his uncle owned a second-hand car showroom, so we went down there and I bought a MK10 Jaguar, and Pete Gavin bought a Rover. I remember driving around London in my Jag, on many occasions when I shouldn't have, but I never scratched it once.'

After about a month of their new lifestyle, Baldry called a meeting with the band. Fred Gandy, who by now was the organiser and unofficial band spokesperson, remembers it very well. 'I rang everyone and told them that John wanted a word with us all. He sounded very upset. We were all worried, and wondered what could have happened. So we all headed into London to meet John. He was in tears and very distressed. He said, "I'm sorry guys, this is terrible, but you're all fired. I'm sorry, I've got no money, and I can't pay you." We all looked at each other in shock and wondered where had all the money gone? Later, there were the usual claims and rumours of bad management and corruption, but the fact was that Baldry was a ruined man financially, and Bluesology were now in the firing line to follow next.'

Indeed, when the Baldry relationship came to an end, Bluesology were left to make their own way, and ended up working with groups like the Fantastics and the Paper Dolls. They had lost their retainer and were now back to getting paid gig by gig. Not that it would last long.

'Not long after Baldry had made his announcement, we were doing a week's cabaret spot in Manchester and were staying in some apartments with a young girl group called the Paper Dolls. We did one rehearsal in the afternoon of the gig in each club, and then we would check into the digs where we would be staying, and then head back out to the club later for the gig. We played at places like the Fiesta, and the Batley Variety Clubs, and while the cleaners were cleaning up and the tables were being laid out, we would be rehearsing,' says Gandy. 'They had their manager who would hand out the music charts, a couple of songs were their original hits and the rest were covers. The place was packed out with people as it was a social club, but it tended to consist of old men out for the evening to ogle at the sight of the nubile and scantily dressed young Dolls.'

But for Bluesology, it was the beginning of the end, remembers Holland. 'They were awful one hit wonders, and there were three of them: Tyger, Copper and Spyder, and it really was a case of they were touring because they'd had one hit. And behind the scenes, it was no better. Their road manager was the partner of one of the girls, but he was also allegedly having an affair with someone else and she found out. I remember one evening, seeing one of the Dolls running down the road in her night gown, sobbing; it was very sad. And to make matters worse, the cabaret gigs weren't going much better.'

Neither did it help that Bluesology were, by this time, into drugs. Gandy would supply the rest of the band with whatever they needed and the others just took every opportunity to take advantage of his generosity. But when Gandy could not supply what they wanted any more, they found alternate suppliers, and that is when it really got out of hand. Bernie Holland once dug up a car park when he was on Demerol. 'Yeah, it was cough medicine, and it was amazing stuff if you drank a whole bottle. I got up in the middle of the night and dug a great hole in this car park. The next morning we found a car in the hole where a businessman had come back and backed into it. We would take anything at the time, just for a laugh.'

On another occasion, after one of the Paper Dolls gigs, 'We were taking drugs and smoking pot in the front room of a hotel when police cars started patrolling up and down the road,' recalls Gandy. 'We had drugs in the apartment so, of course, we were looking for ways to hide it. We turned off all the lights and pretended that no-one was in. Certainly, the gigs with the Paper Dolls didn't help – they were pretty awful and not our scene at all. Although they were attracting a good following, and were very talented in their own way, it was not the kind of gig that we were accustomed to. It was all working men's clubs.'

The Paper Dolls gigs were certainly not what Elton Dean and Marc Charig wanted either. They too called it a day, and left the band after they had finished the round of gigs they were booked to do with the Dolls. They both went back to the world of jazz which was their spiritual home. The organist Jimmy Horowitz, real name David Horrocks, who replaced Reg also disappeared. He was living at a place in Belgravia with Rod Stewart's manager Billy Gaff and they used to hang around with John Gee, then the owner of the Marquee Club. Fred Gandy, Pete Gavin and Bernie Holland stayed on and persevered for a while until, eventually, the whole thing fizzled out due to the lack of money and bookings.

What had started off as a promising hard working band had finally come to an end through personnel changes, bad management, drugs, lack of money and not enough gigs. It's a common enough story, of course.

# 12

# THE GAFF

In 1938, when Dick James was 18 years old, he was a professional singer and had just auditioned for the Henry Hall Band under his stage name of Johnny Sheridan. One year later, just before the Second World War broke out, Hall signed him up. For James, like so many, the war was nothing more than an inconvenient interruption to a career, but at least he could continue to do what he loved, and that was to sing. He had a dodgy eye that prevented him from aiming or shooting a gun accurately, so he was enrolled into the medical corps and also flown out to the Middle East to help entertain the troops.

By the time the war had come to an end, in May 1945, James had decided to move on from Henry Hall and, one year later, he was offered the role of lead singer with bandleader Geraldo who, at the time, was one of the most popular British dance band leaders. But Geraldo didn't like the name Johnny Sheridan, simply because it was too long and wouldn't fit on billboards, so he offered James the choice of being called Dick James or Dick Jones. 'My father, whose real name was Reginald Vapnick, phoned my mother and asked her whether she wanted to be known as Mrs Jones or Mrs James. She said she didn't like either, but if she was going to have to pick one it would have to be James. So overnight, my father became Dick James,' explains Stephen James.

'He sang with Geraldo from about 1946 until 1950, and then he formed a group with Cliff Adams called the Stargazers. He was with them for a short period before going solo and into variety. It was when he was offered the theme tune to *Robin Hood* in 1955 that he was introduced to George Martin, who would later become the recording manager for Parlophone Records. At the same time my father was developing a career along the lines of becoming a Tin Pan Alley star, which he successfully did, singing sing-along songs. *Robin Hood* went to No.1 and through that, he became a worldwide star,' says Stephen.

By 1956, when rock'n'roll seemed to take over the world with the likes of Bill Haley and Elvis Presley, James didn't feel he could compete with that kind of music. So, deciding that he'd had enough of travelling up and down the country doing summer seasons, he took a job working for Sydney Bron Music, a music publishing company in the heart of London's West End, where he was employed as the Exploitation Manager from 1958 to 1961. His main duties included finding songs and then having them recorded by the artists of the day. It was because he enjoyed a considerable amount of success while he was at Bron that he decided to form his own music publishing company, which he named Dick James Music, or DJM for short, and secured premises at 123-125 Charing Cross Road, right on the corner of Denmark Street.

Although DJM's start in music publishing during the first eighteen months of business left a lot to be desired, and only enjoyed minor success with unknown Tin Pan Alley writers, James was about to strike it lucky. 'When Brian Epstein brought the Beatles down to London from Liverpool, he hawked them around all the major record companies but didn't get a deal, until he eventually got them signed to Parlophone and George Martin,' recalls Stephen. 'Their first single, "Love Me Do", was released in 1962, and was given to EMI's music publishing arm to sell. But Epstein was disappointed with the result. Although many bands and artists at the time would have been thrilled to have a record reach the Top 20 at No. 17, Epstein wasn't. He thought that EMI didn't do enough promotional work for it, so when it came to release the follow-up single, "Please, Please Me", he said he didn't want EMI to publish the song and asked Martin if he could recommend anyone. He said he could.'

In Martin's eyes, DJM was perfect for Epstein's needs. 'They are a hungry company looking for something to make their name with,' Martin told Epstein. And it just so happened that Martin knew Dick James. Indeed, he was very confident that he would be able to give Epstein everything he wanted. But of course, DJM wasn't the only music publisher being recommended. Another publisher was also in the running, so Epstein visited both firms. 'He was booked to see the first publisher at ten, and Dick at eleven. When he turned up for his first appointment, he was kept waiting for twenty-five minutes, so he walked out and went to meet my father. He arrived at DJM at about 10.35 and although early, he would sit and wait, but my father came out of his office immediately to meet him,' Stephen relates.

The two hit it off immediately. James was given a finished master of 'Please, Please Me' and Epstein told him it was being released the following week, and if he could get the song to No. 1, he could have the Beatles' publishing contract. So whilst Epstein was still sitting in the office, James demonstrated that it's not what you know, it's who you know. He called Philip Jones, who had worked with James previously during his years as a singer with Parlophone and just happened to be the producer of *Thank Your Lucky Stars* – only the most popular pop music show on British television. He told Jones that he had the manager of the Beatles with him and that although their first single had stalled at No.17, their next single was due to be released in a few weeks and was a potential No.1.

Would Jones like them on the programme? Jones asked to hear the record to make sure he liked it, so James played it down the phone to him. And Jones loved it. The single was released on 19 January 1963, and the show was due to be broadcast on the

20th. There and then, he confirmed that, yes, the Beatles were on the show on the requested date.

Dick put the telephone down and told Epstein that the band were on *Thank Your Lucky Stars* on 20 January, whilst probably mentally thanking his own lucky stars. Epstein couldn't believe what he was hearing. In the space of a twenty minute meeting, James had secured the Beatles a prime spot on the most watched early Saturday evening television show. 'Please, Please Me' reached No.1, and a grateful Epstein gave DJM all the publishing rights for the Beatles songs. This in turn helped DJM to become an overnight success and Dick James the shining new star of Denmark Street. The moral of this story is that it pays not to keep people waiting!

After it became clear that the Fab Four were destined to become the biggest thing since sliced bread, James decided that it would be of benefit to Lennon and McCartney if he was to set up a separate publishing company for their songs. Epstein agreed and, before his very eyes, James created Northern Songs. He gave a share of the company to Lennon and McCartney and a small share to Epstein. The split was 50% to DJM, 20% to Lennon, 20% to McCartney and 10% to Epstein, which in comparison to what Colonel Tom Parker was said to be raking in from Elvis's music publishing interests, made Epstein's cut look quite modest.

Indeed, DJM looked after the composers very well, and thus ensured that every song that Lennon and McCartney wrote up to 1973 was published by Northern Songs. But, by 1965 James was becoming concerned that the rate of income tax, a huge 83% of earnings, being charged by the British Government would leave a sting in the Beatles' tail. To overcome what Lennon and McCartney would pay out in taxes, James consulted his tax advisor Charles Silver who suggested that James should make Northern Songs a public company and float it on the stock exchange. This would give Lennon and McCartney a capital gain rather than taxable earnings income. It was a brave move, because the City at that time didn't really understand how music publishing worked, but it was floated at 7/9d a share, which was a bargain.

On 27 August 1967, Epstein unexpectedly died from an accidental drug overdose at his home in London. The news not only shocked the Beatles and Dick James, but the whole world. Even worse, was the fact that without him the Beatles seemed rudderless. In the end, it was inevitable that the most famous of all pop groups would go their separate ways. And when that happened, James decided he would sell the music publishing arm of the Beatles to the highest bidder.

Not that it was going to be an easy sell, far from it. James was concerned that the financial heads in the City would not understand that even without the Beatles Northern Songs could still turn out to be a most profitable going concern. But, as expected, there was a dramatic fall in the share price when it came to selling time. Lew Grade at ATV had been asking James to sell Northern Songs to him for some time, and so, perhaps it was no surprise when James let him have it at a bargain price of 33/6d a share, which despite the fall was still five times the value of its original share price and therefore a nice little earner.

'It is a well known fact that Lennon and McCartney were not happy with my father for selling off Northern Songs without giving them the chance to buy it,' explains Stephen James. 'However, at the time, there was no way that they could have bought it because they weren't talking to each other. There was an offer on the table at the time from Lew Grade, so my father felt that if he didn't take the offer, and the opportunity at the time, he might have lost out. It benefitted Lennon and McCartney, because of the shares they had in Northern, and it goes without saying that they made a pretty sizeable profit.'

Even though James sold Northern Songs in 1968, the same year the Beatles began the long and winding road towards break-up, DJM entered into a management agreement with Lennon and McCartney which lasted to 1973, when it was taken over and run by ATV Music.

With all the success from publishing the Beatles songs, perhaps it was a surprise that Dick James didn't expand into other areas of the music business until 1969. He opened a recording studio, which he gave to his son Stephen James as a project for him to get his teeth into. Stephen, however, was not a musician, he was more an administrator who was being groomed to eventually take over the company from his father. Caleb Quaye was to be Stephen's saviour.

Stephen James started working with his father in the summer of 1963, having dropped out of school at the age of 16. 'I was very privileged to sit in on a lot of the Beatles recordings sessions at Abbey Road Studios with George Martin,' smiles Stephen today. 'I remember sitting in on the sessions for *Sergeant Pepper's Lonely Hearts Club Band* and most of the other albums they did before then. There was a lot going on with the technology moving from 4-track to 8-track and things like that. At the time, there was friction between all the Beatles as individuals but as a team they were fine. A lot of the songs were written separately by this time, or partially written separately, but everything was always credited to Lennon and McCartney and the royalties split down the middle. We never differentiated between the two, regardless of who was the main influence in the song.'

Dick James, who by now had firmly installed himself as managing director of Northern Songs with Charles Silver as the chairman, was under pressure. The flotation of Northern Songs as a public company was what bought the new pressure, not that James had any qualms about it. Extra demands for any expansion to the DJM empire could be handled by Stephen.

## ▐▐ ▐▐▐

In 1965, Caleb Quaye sought his fortune in Tin Pan Alley. 'One day I was delivering some music to Francis, Day & Hunter, when I met with a friend who worked there in the music department. He asked me if I had heard about a vacancy at Dick James Music in Oxford Street. I was in the middle of my rounds at the time, and was supposed to report back to Paxtons with my deliveries and orders, but instead I took a risk and shot round to DJM.' It probably helped that Dick James knew of Quaye's pedigree as he was offered the job as office boy on the spot.

'It was good that Dick James interviewed me, because he asked me what my name was, and when I told him, he asked if I was related to Cab Quaye [a leading jazz musician of the time]. I told him I was, so in a way that was what sort of got me into Dick James Music. The Beatles were at their peak and all their singles of that year, "Ticket To Ride", "Help" and "Day Tripper" had all gone to number one. They were the biggest thing in music at the time, and although no one would have ever imagined it happening, they were even bigger than Elvis. They all used to go in and out of DJM all the time, and were considered by the staff, and me in particular, as the "Four Gods".'

The introduction of the recording studio at DJM also introduced a change to Quaye's career. 'Dick James called me to his office and told me he would like me to run the studio, because he could see that I was keen and had an aptitude for it. I was promoted when Stephen could no longer run the studio as he was being trained to do the more administrative aspects of the business. I was Stephen's understudy, so I gradually progressed from being the tea boy to now helping out in the studio learning all the different aspects, such as cutting acetates on a disc cutting machine, and then, when the studio was up and running, I learned about sound very quickly.' Eventually, by the time Quaye was 17, he was appointed studio and official A&R manager for DJM.

'There was a lot going on between 1965 and 1970,' continues Quaye. 'I was given an amazing chance and I am still thankful to this day for that opportunity at DJM's studios, or "The Gaff" as we called it. During the five years that I was studio manager, things were really changing in the recording and publishing business in Tin Pan Alley, and my aim was to learn every aspect of it that I could. I always wanted to be a musician, especially as I grew up in a musical family, but when the Beatles came along, I noticed how everything changed. One of the things that I observed, was that jazz musicians who could only play jazz had problems when rock came in, because they couldn't make the switch.'

Quaye intuitively knew that to be successful in the music business, you needed to do more than just play an instrument. 'I knew that Dick James Music would be a great opportunity for me to learn every aspect of the business from song writing to recording and playing. There was a term that we used to use back then, about learning what was going on, we used to call it "on both sides of the window." The "window" was the glass window in the recording studio that separated the studio from the control room. And I was determined to learn about playing, arranging, putting the music together, different instrument functions, miking instruments up, sound engineering, production ideas, and to plan how the sound should come out of the studio as a recorded work. It was a survival mentality, but I liked music so much that I wanted to stay in it, and thought that if I had more than one string to my bow I would survive any changes.'

The new offices in New Oxford Street were an ideal fit as they provided a central location to house both the music publishing and recording arms of DJM. 'It was still an old fashioned type of Tin Pan Alley building, but it was slightly better than any place you would find in Denmark Street, because it had its own 8-track recording studio, and that was where most of the activity was,' remembers Freddy Gandy.

'It was a very small place really, there was a large office where Dick was, and he had these gold plated taps in his en-suite bathroom. I remember we were always taking the piss out of him. We used to go in there some nights as someone had a key, probably the engineer, so we could get in there whenever we wanted a session or a smoke. But the place was more of a publishing office than anything else. On the first floor were offices with a reception area and that's where Dick's office was situated. It was more like a management suite really, with a general office and typing pool. Anyone using the studio, had to go through this area to get to the control room. Dick really didn't know much about music, but he was very knowledgeable about the workings of publishing and sheet music. If anything, DJM was traditional Tin Pan Alley for the new free musicians, and most of us we did our own stuff. Dick couldn't understand that really to save his life, and why should he?

'It was progressive rock or blues, or whatever you want to label it. But we used to play there all the time, whenever we could and get totally wiped out as well. You could smell the dope before you got to the door and the corridor. The studio itself was a converted office and, when you went through the studio door, there were mobiles hanging everywhere and pictures of nude models. It was just a rock'n'roll den of dope, drugs and sex and God knows what else.'

'The drum booth,' continues Gandy, 'was away from the recording studio but you had to walk down the corridor to get to it. It was formerly an office complex that had been broken up to make a recording studio. It was fine going in there, but it was coming out again, and going through the office that was the interesting bit, if you had been in there all day. We used to go in there after working hours and we had the run of the studio. Caleb was in charge and he told me when we first met to come up and meet the guys, so I did, and we started playing and working at about 8p.m. We would set up in the studio and start jamming with anyone else who was there. We would be smoking dope and end up under the control desk completely stoned.'

Next door to DJM, and sharing the same building, was Page One Records, the label that had been launched by Larry Page. He had a publishing arrangement with Dick James, which was one of the reasons why there was always a flow of musicians in and out of the studio. Most were signed to Page and, of course, for Reg and Bernie it was ideal. Whenever they needed musicians for their demos, they would have plenty to choose from. People like Roger Pope, David Glover and Caleb Quaye, who, alongside Reg, formed Hookfoot. Tony Murray was another, before he joined the second incarnation of the Troggs, as was Nigel Olsson, who did the same with Plastic Penny, the Spencer Davis Group, Uriah Heep and, eventually, the Elton John Band.

Equally significant were the Mirage. They were a psychedelic band consisting of the Hynes brothers and bassist Dee Murray, who, like Olsson, hooked up with Plastic Penny and the Spencer Davis Group for a year in 1968, and recorded an album together.

All figured in Reg's career when he later became Elton. Tony Murray ended up playing bass on *Empty Sky* simply because he was the only bassist in the studio; Dave Hynes played drums on most of Reg's demos; Caleb Quaye was the guitarist for all the early compositions, and Pope, Glover, Olsson and Murray played their parts too. In those early days, Reg didn't need a band as he was always spoilt for choice with the wealth of musicians he surrounded himself with; musicians who worked with him because they all loved music and loved creating it with each other.

As has already been discussed in previous chapters, one of the significant bonuses of working in Tin Pan Alley if you were a songwriter, was the benefit that you could wind up as a staff writer for music publisher and would have the potential to write songs for artists like Tom Jones, Lulu or Engelbert Humperdinck and have your name on their records as the composer. The downside, of course, was that if it wasn't a hit, you wouldn't receive much in the way of royalties or earn much more than your retainer. Nine times out of ten that was the case. Being a staff songwriter in Tin Pan Alley was hard work. And for Reg and Bernie, it was no different.

Not that their songwriting would impress Paul Griggs, then the vocalist for Octopus, and later, for Brotherhood Of Man. Although he was interested to hear what they had written, when he heard one of their demos it didn't make Griggs jump up and down with excitement. 'It was in January 1969, when we visited DJM in New Oxford Street to see Tony Murray, who was going to play us some songs that he thought may be suitable for recording. While we were there, Dick James asked one of his writers if he had any songs that we could record. The writer was a guy with glasses whose face was familiar to us from the times we had been to Musicland in Berwick Street, a record shop where we had seen him working behind the counter. He told us we may be interested in a song he had just written, and handed me an acetate of a song called "When I Was Tealby Abbey".'

It wasn't suitable for Octopus to record, and consequently they turned the song down, but kept the acetate [which still exists to this day in the author's private collection]. Certainly, it would be true to say that Reg was not very happy with what he was doing, and with James noting that he was having little success in selling any songs, frustration soon set in. All the same, Ray Williams and Quaye could still see a future in Reg and Bernie's work. It probably helped that Reg had seen Williams as someone who could help him with his career. Although nothing had come out of the Liberty arrangement, it had encouraged Reg and Bernie to become more involved in the DJM set up. 'I continued working at Liberty Records,' recalls Williams. 'But I kept in touch with Reg and Bernie and often went to see Reg at his mother's home in Frome Court.'

Another to encourage Reg and Bernie was undoubtedly Caleb Quaye. He was probably one of the few people at that time who did more than most in recognising Reg and Bernie's potential. It also helped that he was able to work alongside them in the recording studio and bring out a completely different side to their sound. It was something that would not have been expected in those days when the Tin Pan Alley sound was very predictable, which to Quaye, Reg and Bernie, was something they were against.

One of the reasons Quaye was able to come up with the sound he did, was very simple. He became more creatively involved in working with them, and therefore was able to create something quite special on most of the recordings he made with them, and preserved onto acetates and tapes. It is how so many DJM demos got to be made. 'There was something like thirty songs that I actually produced,' remembers Quaye. 'In many ways, I became Reg's first record producer for Dick James.'

But what was strange, was how Reg and Bernie wrote their material for recording. Even when Bernie returned to his family home in Lincolnshire, he still continued to send poems to Reg in the post, who would then put the words to music at his home in Frome Court. 'Yes, it was weird,' confesses Quaye. 'They didn't sit down together and it was the most unusual working arrangement, but it worked. Every time Reg had new songs to record, we would go into the studio and grab Dee Murray and Dave Hynes.'

As Paul Griggs had noted, Reg was also working in Musicland on Berwick Street at the same time that his career at DJM was starting to evolve. It was a part-time job, explained Willy Morgan, then the general manager of the flagship store of 1967. The main plan for Beat and Commercial Records, who started and owned the Musicland chain, was to be best known for its American imports, selling records on labels such as Stax and Atlantic. Soon after the store was opened, the style of music changed and psychedelia started to become popular. Musicland pulled out of the Atlantic and Stax based music and started to stock rock records by the likes of the Doors and Jefferson Airplane.

Indeed, much of Reg's life outside the recording studio revolved around the music store, simply because it was renowned as one of the few places to stock American imports before they were released in Britain. Following Reg's example, designer David Larkham also became heavily influenced by the same type of music. 'We would be the first in the country to get the first Leonard Cohen album, *Songs Of Leonard Cohen,* which we would take down to Steve Brown's house at the weekend and we'd drink our Merrydown Mead and then later in the evening, when we were all very drunk, we'd listen to it.

'On another occasion, I remember a call from Musicland for Reg at DJM one day to let him know about a great new album by Crosby Stills and Nash, so we would all run down to the store to listen to it.' If nothing else, Reg got a big kick out of listening to music no matter what genre it was. The American artists, though, were his big inspiration.

With Reg firmly placed in his jobs at DJM and Musicland, and now earning a regular salary, he no longer had to worry about going out and playing live gigs, either on his own or with a band. He could now do what he and Bernie had always dreamed of, and that was to write songs. After Bluesology, they were able to continue working with Caleb in putting together an album, which to this day remains unreleased. Most of the songs on the album were the songs that Caleb and Reg had put together during the latter years of Bluesology, and before Bernie came into the picture.

Another to come into the picture a little later was DJM's new office boy, Stuart Epps. The first time he met Reg was during the making of his first album. 'One day the door opened to the studio and there was this guy called Reg Dwight, who was one of a number of singer-songwriters around,' explains Epps. 'He was a strange guy with a Noddy shirt and a long Afghan coat. When I first met him, he was making demos in the studio with Caleb Quaye, who was one of the finest guitarists I had ever heard. They were making an album together, and what I was hearing at the time was just amazing, because it was the kind of stuff I had never heard before. From that point on, I very quickly got into what they were doing and, as I say, the music was just stunning. I suppose it was hippy music, which was heavily influenced by what the Beatles were doing at the time, but it was also very representative of the psychedelic music being produced, which I guess, to all intents and purposes, is what the Beatles were then experimenting with.

'Reg was writing his own words, which I remember thinking were pretty terrible, and Caleb was also writing words, which weren't much better than Reg's. At some point during the recording of the album, Bernie came in.' It was when Epps found himself promoted to be DJM's disc cutter, that he was allowed in the studio to witness for himself, what he today describes as very beautiful songs being recorded. 'When Bernie started writing words for Reg, the songs took on a totally different meaning.'

But of course, it wasn't only Reg's music that was creating a buzz. 'I remember a lot of musicians used to hang out with Reg and co. in the copying room next door to the studio,' Epps recalls. The Mirage, a DJM band who would later lose their bassist Dee Murray to Elton John, was one such group who were completely mesmerised by the sounds they were hearing. They were also totally intrigued by the advanced production techniques which Caleb used to create Reg's album.

Another to be seduced by it all was Clive Franks, then a young soon-to-be sound engineer who, like Epps, had started life at DJM as an office boy. One of his first tasks was to take the latest album cover art for the Beatles' *Sergeant Pepper* to the home of Neil Aspinall, who was then the band's road manager and PA. He couldn't help taking the cover out of its brown paper wrapping while he was in the cab on his way to Aspinall, and being totally amazed by what he found, as you would be.

'Certainly,' continues Epps, 'if *Sergeant Pepper* made us think that it was the most important rock'n'roll album ever made, then listening to the *White Album* in the small cutting room at DJM one year after *Sergeant Pepper* would be a completely different story. This was the album that made the Mirage seriously consider whether they wanted to continue making music. In their eyes, the Beatles had done it all and what was there left to be done? Not that it would deter Reg. Hearing great records like that only made him more determined to make great records himself.'

It is one of the reasons that he continued writing with Quaye and producing songs for his first album. 'I remember one song we wrote together was called "I'm Just Sitting Doing Nothing",' recalls Quaye.'

At the same time that Elton and Bernie were starting to craft songs together, Quaye was making his own music, and ended up releasing his own single on the Philips label in 1967. It was called 'Baby Your Phrasing Is Bad' on the A side, and 'Witch With The Half Strength Powers' on the flipside. Quaye realistically admits that it was never the kind of song that was going to take the charts by storm. Not that Quaye can remember if Reg played any part in the song. If anything, it still remains a mystery.

Equally mysterious is why the album Quaye had produced for Reg and Bernie never saw the light of the day. 'It was ready for final production when I decided to leave DJM, and Steve Brown, from the promotions department, came along to manage the studio and replace me as Reg's musical mentor.' However, the good news is that most of these songs have survived and surfaced on bootleg albums and as a collection of CDs called *Elton John: The DJM Demos*.

For Epps though, it was entirely different. Being at the centre of the British music business with one of the most prominent publishers of the period was all he ever wanted. Following in the footsteps of his old schoolmate Clive Franks, who would regularly tell him some amazing stories of what it was like to be working in the music business, Epps joined DJM during the height of Beatlemania, when the emergence of the singer-songwriter was probably at its height. It was an industry bursting with creativity and talent.

'I was very in awe of Franks' job, not necessarily because it was a glamorous job, but because it was in glamorous surroundings.' When Franks was promoted, Epps was called in to see Ronald Bron, the office manager, for two interviews, as Franks' replacement. Needless to say, he got the job, for £6 a week, but as he soon found out, it was not all glamour and red carpets.

'It was nice to leave school and it was exciting travelling to work for the first time, but the job itself consisted of emptying coffee machines and dustbins, in fact emptying the dustbins was one of the first jobs I was given,' laughs Epps. 'I had gone to work in a three-piece suit on my first day. I was shown the bins and told how horrible they were, and that it was my job to take them back to the kitchen. So I had to carry two bins up the steep stairs to the DJM offices, trying to look cool, walking through the reception and past the beautiful reception girls, who were all looking at me.'

Epps would regularly make his way round the corner from DJM to Denmark Street and places like Campbell Connelly, running errands and delivering sheet music – very much following in the footsteps of Reg, in fact. It wasn't rocket science, but he had got his foot in the door of one of the leading music publishers, and witnessing the whole process of taking a song and producing the sheet music for sale in the local music stores. If anything, he considered himself very lucky.

The Holy Grail for Dick James was to have his in-house songwriters come up with a song that he could get into the *Eurovision Song Contest*. The publishing deals that could come out of scoring a successful or winning song in the competition were worth their weight in gold, so there was a lot of pressure on Reg and Bernie to deliver something commercial that would be a *Eurovision* contender. Something, they were told, that the likes of Tom Jones or Engelbert Humperdinck would want to record. And, as far as James was concerned, that wasn't the type of music that Caleb, Reg and Bernie were experimenting with behind closed doors.

'There was a real artistic dichotomy going on, because we were not interested in that commercial sort of stuff,' explains Quaye. 'We were listening to the Beatles, the Stones and Hendrix and all the rock stuff, and Reg had no interest in writing more of the "stupid stuff" as we called it. It was really difficult because most of us at DJM were listening to the American singer-songwriters, such as Joni Mitchell and Laura Nyro, who were both a big influence at the time. And of course, the Beach Boys had become very influential when they released their *Pet Sounds* album. It was an amazing step forward in popular music, because of all the elaborate layers of vocal harmonies, sound effects and unconventional instruments they used. We had never heard stuff like that before so, yes, it was pretty amazing and, as a result, we got switched on to all that kind of musical creativity.

'We also loved Lennon and McCartney's "Strawberry Fields Forever", and we were very heavily influenced by that sort of sound, which is where songs such as "Regimental Sergeant Zippo" came from. So we had our artistic vision but the company was saying it wanted more songs for people like Cliff Richard. It was out of that sort of pressure that "I Can't Go On Living Without You" came from.'

That ditty, penned by Messers Dwight and Taupin, was one of six songs previewed on the *Happening For Lulu* TV show over a six week period. The winning tune would go forward as plucky Blighty's 1969 *Eurovision Song Contest* entry. In a special show, hosted by Michael Aspel, in which she performed all six, one after another, Elton and Bernie's tune came last in the viewers' postcard vote; not that it mattered. It was later recorded by Cilla Black, Sandie Shaw, Polly Brown and Elton himself as well as, ironically, Marie McDonald McLaughlin Lawrie, a.k.a Lulu.

The first time Tony Taupin became aware of Bernie's impending success, was when he got an excited call from his parents telling him that Reg and Bernie had written a song that was in the last six as the possible UK entry for the *Eurovision Song Contest*. 'I was abroad in Paris and my parents told me that they had a song that was to be considered by Lulu for the *Eurovision*. Bernie and Reg had come last, but at least they were in the six that were being considered, so obviously it was a thrill for my parents to hear and see their names in print.'

According to Lulu, her bravely answering Britain's call to enter *Eurovision* all came about because she had a series on television at the time. 'Bill Cotton was the Head of Light Entertainment at the BBC, and he said to my manager, "I'd like Lulu to do the *Eurovision Song Contest* on the series." And she came to me and I went "Why? What do I want to do that for?" And she said that he said that "you'll get good ratings, and he is the boss." Maybe I could have said no, but I felt I didn't really have a choice in the matter. And I thought, ratings aren't what it's all about. But, you know, Elton and Bernie wrote a great song that didn't go through.'

The song that beat Reg's attempt was 'Boom-Bang-A-Bang', written by Alan Moorhouse and Peter Warne. 'It was a typical Tin Pan Alley song, although I actually thought it ruined *Eurovision*,' admits Martin. Not that he was any more complimentary about 'I Can't Go On Living Without You'. 'I gave Reg a scathing report in the *NME* for his *Eurovision* song,' confesses Bill Martin. 'I said it would come last, as it only consisted of the title and little more. Lyrically, they were trying to write formula Tin Pan Alley, songs like Phil Coulter, Barry Mason, Roger Greenaway, Roger Cook and myself did, but they couldn't do that. They were not trained in that way.' Martin knew what he was talking about as, along with Phil Coulter, he had penned Sandie Shaw's winning entry, 'Puppet On A String' in 1967.

'All the same,' muses Mick Inkpen, 'like any songwriter would be, despite his aversion to the *Eurovision* type of commercialism, Reg was very pleased that he had a song submitted for the contest. We had run into Lulu when we were with Bluesology, so I think she knew Elton. There was much excitement about it, when she sang the song on her show, especially in the Dwight household and, of course, we were all hugely disappointed when it didn't win.'

It seems, however, that Reg and Bernie took Martin's criticism to heart. They now realised they were not cut out to write songs to order, like most Tin Pan Alley songwriters could. Their remote way of writing songs was totally removed from the way most other songwriters worked.

According to Martin, the difference was that he had the gift for writing *Eurovision* type of songs. 'When I won the Eurovision in Vienna with "Puppet On A String", I wrote the song in tribute to my idol Sammy Cahn, he always wrote songs with internal rhymes all the time. He put more words in Frank Sinatra's mouth than anyone else and, when I met him, I asked him, about all the internal rhymes and he explained it to me and that is the basis for "Puppet". He taught me that you don't have to put the rhyme at the end and that's what made it so different, but the melody was so strong as well.'

When Martin was at the dress rehearsal for the *Eurovision*, in the year his song won, he heard another song that was actually much better than 'Puppet On A String'. Recognising a good song when he heard one, he told his publisher to buy the song, which they did for £100.

'The song was called "Love Is Blue", and it went to No.1 in America,' continues Martin. 'That is what publishers did though, they would search out and buy melodies and then get someone to write the lyrics. Johnny Mercer, for instance, wrote the melody for "Autumn Leaves", and the melody for "La Mere" would become "Beyond The Sea", which became a big hit for Bobby Darin, and that's how it worked. A publisher would find good melodies and then the song would then be written on top. A Tin Pan Alley publisher would now go to the States, rather than run from building to building in Denmark Street, and try and find another publisher. They would meet some obscure publisher and say they had a song and the publisher would buy it for about $100. This happened with hits like "I Left My Heart In San Francisco".'

This soon became the norm. Producer Mickie Most used to fly out to the States on a Saturday and by Monday he would be in the office of American publisher and producer Don Kirshner listening to all of his songs. He would cherry pick the best, buy them and fly back to Britain and demo them in Regent Sound and sell them on for a profit. 'That's how he found "I'm Into Something Good" for Herman's Hermits, and gave them their first No.1 in 1964. Mickie had great ears and the trick was to try and get to Mickie to hear your own songs,' says Martin. 'Publishers were very important in the Sixties for finding songs, and they would scour the world as well as Tin Pan Alley.'

After the *Eurovision* heats failure, and following the advice of Stephen James, DJM decided that if they couldn't sell Reg and Bernie's songs then they would record them themselves. 'I've Been Loving You' was the first single Caleb produced with Reg right after the Great Purge when he had signed to DJM. It was released on the Philips label because DJM didn't have their own label at the time. 'I played guitar and produced the single,' confirms Quaye. It was credited as a John/Taupin composition though on Bernie's website he claims not to have written the lyrics. The lyrics may have been written by Reg and credited to Bernie in a generous gesture. Either way, this type of song, according to Quaye, 'Came from the pressure to be commercial from DJM and was not the type of work he was doing in the late night sessions.'

Not that it mattered. The single with 'Here's To The Next Time' on the flip side was withdrawn shortly after its release and, in most quarters, was regarded as a flop despite some investment in promotion with print advertising in some of the popular music press such as the *New Musical Express* with a marketing ploy that claimed Elton was '1968's Great New Talent.'

# 13

# THE GAFF
# PART II

With the failure of the first single behind them, Reg, Bernie and DJM carried on with business as usual. As part of their roles as staff writers for DJM, Reg and Bernie were also expected to perform certain public relations duties. As James was hardly making a fortune out of their songwriting, he would give them other tasks, and one of those was some PR work. They were sent to meet a prominent American music business executive from Heathrow airport. 'They were early so they came round to my house to pass the time,' recounts Mick Inkpen. 'Bernie had a particular liking for my home made beer so we decided to have a drink before they left for the airport, so we drank and chatted until they left, a little worse for wear, but not too bad.

'The next day I got a call from Reg who was cursing me about my beer. He said that it had a delayed reaction and by the time they got to Heathrow they were completely out of it, especially Bernie. Neither of them could remember which flight this person was on, what his name was or which terminal he was landing at. They, of course, missed him, and DJM were furious that they couldn't do a simple job of meeting an executive at the airport. As far as they were concerned, it almost beggared belief.'

Not that Reg was too worried. He had other things to be concerned about. Having to write Tin Pan Alley songs, suffer the lack of response from music publishers and artists, and the disappointment that he was not getting the chance to record his own material, were all contributing to making Reg miserable. It started to show in both his personal and professional life. 'I knew that he was unhappy about being a staff writer,' says Inkpen, 'and although he respected Dick James, and appeared grateful that he had looked after him at the start of his career, Reg still decided to have a showdown with him about his management.'

With the Wisdom of Solomon, James agreed to release him from the management agreement, but only if he could come up with the money to buy himself out of it: which wasn't likely. Although James gave Reg a way out, it was not going to be easy and might even be impossible. His career was going nowhere and he was more or less enslaved to the life of a staff writer, writing songs to order rather than from the heart.

The turning point and, in some respects, his saviour from being a Tin Pan Alley writer came from a most unexpected source, and one that would lead to his introduction in the American music market. 'I went into DJM studios and Reg and Bernie were very down and depressed,' recalls songwriter Roger Greenaway. 'He [Reg] said that nothing was ever going to happen so I asked him to play me some of his songs. He played me "Tealby Abbey" and "Skyline Pigeon".' Both Greenaway and his writing partner Roger Cook were impressed with the songs and Greenaway recorded 'When I Was Tealby Abbey' and Cook recorded 'Skyline Pigeon'. It was released in August 1968 as a single on the Pye label by Guy Darrell and simultaneously by Roger on Columbia Records, and was the biggest breakthrough yet as it took a John-Taupin song across the water for the first time.

Because Cook and Greenaway were such well-known songwriters in Tin Pan Alley, and Dick James could see how much of an encouragement they were to Reg and Bernie, he agreed to give them the publishing rights to both of the songs. 'Dick said if we were going to record them, we could have the songs because we were taking such an interest in Reg and Bernie,' remembers Greenaway. As a result, it not only relieved the pressure on Reg and Bernie, it also gave them the lift they so desperately needed. But they still needed a manager to help them get where they wanted to be and Dick James, they believed, wasn't that man. However, another person at DJM who was taking a keen interest in Reg and his music could be.

Lionel Conway left school in 1954, when he was just 15 years old, and landed a job with Dick James at Sydney Bron Music. He moved over to work with James when he formed Dick James Music. 'There were a great deal of very talented people back then, both artists and entrepreneurs, rather than the music corporations that dominate today's music business,' he explains. 'Talent is hard to find these days, but there are something like 50,000 bands and artists surfacing on the internet every week, whereas during the sixties the business was smaller and being talented was a prerequisite of being in a band. The artists needed to know how to play their instruments or sing and how to get that talent over to an audience. To do this, the bands needed to be constantly gigging up and down Britain's motorways. At any one time you could stop at the famous Watford Gap service station on the M1 and find several bands in there, taking a break from the arduous journey from gig to gig. It's not like that in the current music business, not at all.'

In 1968, Conway worked for James as the creative guru for about a year, during which period he took more notice of what Reg was up to more than anyone else at DJM:

He was always in the studio recording, with Zack Laurence doing the arrangements, and Caleb Quaye playing with him and operating the studio equipment. What I'd heard I thought was good, so I decided to take an interest and get to know the guy. His songs were so different to the music that was around at the time. You could tell that he was influenced by American music and bands like the Band and Robbie Robertson, which were not all that commercial, especially songs like 'The Tide Will Turn For Rebecca', which was something I eventually recorded. It was then I went round to the BBC and got some interest in him and organised some live dates. I remember I got him some work with a BBC radio producer, heralded as the pioneer of music radio, called Aidan Day, who helped launch Radio 1 and went on to produce shows for DJs like Emperor Rosko and Stuart Henry, and then the Radio 1 Club. And it was from these programmes I was able to get the interest of John Schroeder, who was working as an assistant with Norrie Paramor at Columbia with artists like Helen Shapiro and Cliff Richard And The Shadows, and who wanted to sign him to his label.

Up to that stage, continues Conway, James didn't really think Reg was a commercial writer and didn't really put any pressure on him to write commercial songs, but as soon as Schroeder showed an interest, so did James. 'Although he was recording for hours in the studio with Zack, Caleb and others, Dick wasn't really interested in what he was doing, probably because it wasn't costing him anything because he was doing everything in-house.

'There wasn't a vast amount of money going into Reg's pockets, and he was on about £20 a week, earning it as a gofer. I used to have daily contact with him, and played tennis with him in Rickmansworth. I knew him really well and he and Bernie used to come to my house for dinner. He thought no-one was going to take him seriously, especially Dick, and that's when, because of my efforts, he agreed to finance the first single.'

At the same time that all this was going on, of course, Reg was also recording his own material as well as doing some session work and writing songs for other artists. 'He just wanted to do anything,' confirms Stuart Epps. 'He wanted to get somewhere. Caleb, on the other hand, was very choosey about what he did.'

As well as keeping an eye on Reg, Conway was also busy with all the promotional work that needed to be done for DJM, and with the publishing side of it doing so well at that time, Conway needed someone to help him and recruited Steve Brown. 'Steve came recommended by some DJs and producers that I knew, so I brought him in as my right hand. I introduced him to Reg and told him that Dick wasn't that interested in him but we needed to change his mind. I remember taking Steve in to meet Reg in the studio and he played him some of his songs. Steve thought they were unbelievable, and I agreed, and that started the relationship with Steve and Reg.'

It was during his time at DJM that Conway found another singer called Brian Keith, who had just released a cover version of a song called 'Everything I Am', under the name of Plastic Penny, which was already climbing the charts. There was no such band, and as Keith needed to tour the single around Britain, he needed to create a band, so Conway stepped into the breach. 'Brian wanted to bring some guys in from Sunderland and I agreed. The only problem was that the drummer, a guy named Nigel Olsson, was only 16 and we would have to find a safe place for him to stay.' Nigel had been drumming with some local bands in the area, but nothing was going on with his career until he met Keith, when it looked like his Box Tops cover was about to be a hit.

'I met him with his mum and he came to stay with me and my wife,' adds Conway. 'He was a nice lad, very well brought up. Nigel continued living at my house at the time and a lot of bands wanted him for sessions and gigs. He did some gigs with Elton and Spencer Davis, as well as Uriah Heep who were a heavy metal band on Bronze Records.' In fact, Uriah Heep wanted him to join the band. 'Nigel was managed by me at the time so he came to me to discuss which of the three options he should take. Elton was a singer-songwriter at the time but not going anywhere, but despite that, I told Nigel to stick with him as he was the best of the three. He has always credited me for that.'

Brian Keith, born Brian O'Shea, remembers, 'I was with a show band called the Universals, and we played mainly in clubs. We made a record for Larry Page's Page One label. Me and Paul Raymond, now with UFO, were from the Universals and we were writers. We had written a song which we had demoed and we were playing it to Dick James to get it published. Lionel Conway and Larry Page were there with Dick James, and Larry liked my voice, so he took me to his office and played me this song by the Box Tops which was the flip side of their second single, which didn't do anything, called "Neon Rainbow". The flip side was called "Everything I Am".

'Plastic Penny were formed with members from the Universals as its core .We had a drummer who was very good but he didn't look the part, and in those days looking good was almost as good as playing the instrument well, so we had to find a drummer. We were in Newcastle and I picked up a guitarist called Mick Grabham, even though "Everything I Am" didn't have guitar on, but we were going to be touring, so we needed a guitarist. I asked him if he knew any good drummers and he said there was a local boy called Nigel Olsson. We had *Top Of The Pops* coming up so I told them to come to London on the Monday having not heard Nigel play.

'They all turned up at DJM and we went on from there. Paul and me were the original members of the Universals and we added Mick Grabham, then billed as Mick Graham, and Nigel to form Plastic Penny. Nigel was only a 16-year-old kid, and he couldn't believe, that overnight, he was in a band with a hit record. We then went on tour, which culminated in an appearance on stage at the first Isle of Wight Festival in August 1968, and made an album called *Two Sides Of A Penny*.'

In the end, Plastic Penny didn't have another hit single and although they released three albums, they soon disappeared into pop oblivion. Keith went into session work, including backing vocals on several of Elton's early albums with Tony Burrows. Keith would also feature as the lead vocalist with Congregation on 'Softly Whispering I Love You', a hit in 1972.

'George Martin's company produced that for Roger Cook,' says Keith. 'I said to George "What the fuck do you expect me to do on this?", and he replied that he just wanted me to rough it up, so it was a combination of sweet and sour; the sweetness of the choir and the roughness of my vocal'

In 1968, Quaye left DJM, which dropped Stephen James right in it as he now needed to find a new studio manager if he was to continue with the expansion plans for DJM to produce the acts that were now signed to their label. He turned to Conway's protégé to help. Steve Brown, hippy in looks and nature, had previously been with EMI Records as a record plugger and then in charge of Artists & Repertoire.

His claim to fame was being responsible for turning busker Don Partridge into the most unlikely pop star ever, and taking his self-penned single, 'Rosie', to number four in the singles chart in February 1968. When the song became a hit, Brown's stock rose. It was just what he needed to turn him into a name to be reckoned with inside the hallowed walls of EMI's Manchester Square building.

'Steve Brown was a massive turning point,' recalls Epps. 'When I first met him he was going round DJM meeting everyone. I was in the disc cutting room and was introduced to him as the cutting room boy. Steve asked to hear what Reg and Bernie were doing, and I remember him coming into the studio with Reg, Bernie and Caleb. We played him what we considered to be the best songs, and when they had finished listening, the three of them went out without making a comment. Later I heard that Steve didn't think that the songs were that great and we, of course, all thought he was mad. I think the problem was that he considered them too commercial and poppy and not written from the heart.'

Brown was very into counter-culture at the time, and listened to music by the likes of Bob Dylan and Leonard Cohen, so he suggested to Reg and Bernie that they should write from the heart, rather than pen what was expected of them. On Brown's advice, Reg and Bernie started to write songs for a totally different album to the one planned with Caleb Quaye.

They came up with new songs which were different; the words were deeper because they were Bernie's words. When Quaye departed DJM in January 1968, soon after work had begun on the new album, Frank Owen, who had previously worked at Island Records' studio, became the DJM engineer just when the studio was ramped up. Brown stepped up to become Reg's producer using Caleb's new band Hookfoot as the main musicians. But then there were more changes as Frank Owen left and Clive Franks became the new engineer. Epps was promoted to be his assistant, and the newly recruited Jeff Titmus took over as DJM's disc cutter.

Not only was Steve Brown now firmly in place as Reg's producer, but also as his manager. He quickly started involving himself with all aspects of his career, from promotion to recording and planning gigs. Certainly by this point, Elton, or Reg as he was still known, was being treated by DJM as a proper recording artist. 'I was very involved in the business by now and, in particular, with Reg's music and career,' confirmed Epps. 'I got on well with Steve Brown and in no time at all I was being asked to start plugging songs for DJM, an activity I didn't do too well at, but I was meeting people like Ray Williams, Lionel Conway and Stephen Ames, and got to know them all very well. I then went to work for Steve Brown as his assistant and during that time I was involved in the inauguration of DJM Records. We held a reception at the Revolution Club in London, which I put together with Hookfoot performing with Elton, whom he was already gigging with at the time, but Steve was also getting him gigs on his own as well.'

▐▌ ▐▐▌

When the album *Empty Sky* was finally released in June 1969, it quickly became popular among the college crowd and with Radio 1 disc jockeys like John Peel. At the time the music Reg was making wasn't regarded as pop. It was in a different genre to that, not that Elton appeared to be concerned, but Steve Brown's influence took him underground; he wanted him to work the singer-songwriter furrow ploughed by the likes of Cat Stevens.

Long before the idea of a new album came up, Stephen James was still hawking Reg's songs around music publishers in true Tin Pan Alley tradition, and was repeatedly being told that Reg would be better off recording his own songs rather than trying to sell them for other artists to cover. 'I went back to the office and said to Steve Brown that Reg has got a good enough voice to record in his own right, and do you fancy taking him into the studio and doing a few tracks? Steve was very interested in producing at the time, so it seemed a perfect arrangement,' recalls James. 'He agreed and recruited Caleb and some of the other musicians that were around at the time, mostly the members of Hookfoot. They started recording some tracks in January 1969, most of which were to become the basis for *Empty Sky*.

Also in January 1969, Elton's second single was released. 'Lady Samantha' featured Quaye on guitar, Roger Pope on drums and Dave Glover on bass, so in many ways, it was a very Hookfoot-influenced sound. 'It was the first successful single I played on with Reg,' recalls Quaye. 'He asked me if I would record this song with him, and could I get a bassist and a drummer, so my job was to put a band together for the single and arrange the music, with Steve Brown producing it.' The week before, Quaye had been in the studio with the Loot, and had been rather smitten with what he had seen during the sessions. As a result he recruited their rhythm section of Pope and Glover to play on Reg's single.

When he called Roger up to ask him if he was interested, he jumped at the chance, and joked that he would probably pick up three endorsements on his driving licence in his hurry to get there, so desperate was he to play with Quaye. Although it could never be called a commercial hit, it was certainly more successful than the previous single, and the airplay for it from the usual DJs was certainly more encouraging. More importantly, it introduced what many considered to be the real Elton John sound. It was what Reg and Bernie had wanted to create for ages, rather than turning out mediocre Tin Pan Alley songs that weren't going to take their careers in an upwards direction.

Steve Brown co-produced the single, even though he had no previous experience, and, it was said in some quarters, this inexperience showed. However, the single did pick up some fair reviews and a lot more radio play than the previous single. It probably helped that Brown had some good contacts here and there, and most notably at the BBC with people like John Peel, who instantly loved the record and added it to his playlist. If there was any disappointment, it would have been that sales didn't quite match the general enthusiasm of the media.

Reg's first two singles had been released on the Philips label and many considered that the lack of promotion which accompanied each single was largely to blame for them not being as successful as they could have been. Dick James was also aware of it and, to counteract any further missed opportunities, decided the answer was to launch his own record label so every aspect of record promotion could be kept completely within their control.

Steve Brown was picked to run the label, assisted by his then already deputy, Stuart Epps. The official launch of the label took place at the Revolution Club in London and both Epps and Brown were given strict orders to make it work, no matter what. 'I can actually remember putting on a Neil Young album while people were coming into the club,' recalls Epps. 'This was very much the kind of artist we were trying to turn Elton into, to be regarded as Britain's Neil Young or a James Taylor or a Crosby Stills and Nash.' And that's how the DJM record label was basically formed, with the promise that all future Elton John releases would be released on their own label.

‖ ‖‖

In the same month that 'Lady Samantha' hit the shops, Brown was back in the studio making the album. It was recorded on a 4-track machine at DJM by Jeff Titmus and Clive Franks, who was the assistant engineer but who, quite amazingly, created a new role for himself during the sessions, and became the chief whistler on one of the tracks! On another occasion, while they were recording 'Skyline Pigeon', Brown came up with the idea of putting a weird reverb on Elton's voice, so it was recorded on the fire escape leading to the roof of the DJM building, because it had a metallic echo that everyone loved.

'Certainly,' says Tony King, 'that was a very special moment, when he wrote "Skyline Pigeon". I plugged the Roger Cook single version because I thought it was a great song but I could also see that Reg was becoming a really good songwriter.' It also helped that

Brown was now taking control of Reg's musical career. They became good friends and Reg trusted him no end, which was largely due to Brown realising that he had what he called a brilliant songwriting team to nurture and, from that moment, things started happening at an amazing rate.

Brown became hugely responsible for generating and styling the publicity that would be needed to showcase the launch of the album, so he decided to recruit other specialists to help him achieve his goal. One of those was David Larkham, a photographer and graphic designer who had worked at the *Evening Standard* after he had finished art school.

Larkham remembers that 'Steve phoned me up and said he had got these songwriters and he needed some publicity material for them, so I went over and met with them and took some photos around the DJM building of them: on the roof, fire escape, all the clichéd places to take photographs.' During the shoot, Larkham could sense Reg had a sense of humour and his knowledge of comedy was almost as good as his knowledge of music. Afterwards, Reg, Bernie, Larkham and Brown all became good friends, and at weekends, they would descend *en masse* to Whyteleafe, Surrey where Brown lived with his wife Jill.

'We would meet up at the DJM offices on a Friday afternoon and catch the train,' continues Larkham. 'We would go to the nearby Purley Odeon to watch films like *2001: A Space Odyssey* and *A Clockwork Orange*, and then have fish and chips on the way back to Steve's house.' Larkham very quickly became an integral part of the Elton John phenomena both as the art director at DJM as well as friend and confidant.

'The sessions for *Empty Sky* were good fun,' remembers Quaye. 'We were never sure what we were doing was going to be a hit in the commercial sense, but we knew that what we were doing was musically very interesting and relatively new for the time. We were pulling on all of our musical influences, and we just had this feeling that, yes, we were doing something very fresh and very interesting. We couldn't wait to get into the studios, because we all believed in Reg and Bernie as songwriters and what they were now doing, but we had no idea where it was going to go or end up. But it was also a great opportunity for Reg, me, Gloves and Roger to play together and of course we bought in Tony Murray from Plastic Penny to play bass.'

It helped of course, that they were all signed to DJM with Reg, as they could all hang around the studio and basically make demos and work with each other. Murray explains how it worked for him:

Paul Raymond and I wrote some songs and I remember that Reg sang some of the stuff for demos. It was just the sort of thing we did at the time. Bernie and Reg were around all the time and we just worked and socialised together, I really enjoyed their company. When Reg got to recording *Empty Sky*, he needed a bass player, and as I was around and he knew me he asked me to help out. Recording with him and Bernie was simple and a pleasure. Both were really normal down to earth people and I loved them very much. Basically Reg would turn up with some lyrics that Bernie had written. He had some idea of what the melody should sound like and he just started playing it on the piano. I simply watched his left hand and started playing bass to his piano. It was as simple as that. Much of the playing was impromptu stuff. It really was like watching a song being written right in front of you.

After hours, of course, the DJM studio would turn into a different place, once Dick and Stephen James had left the office and gone home. That's when the reefers would come out. 'When I became a full time employee,' recalls Larkham, 'I was given a tiny little office near the studio, so during the day, for privacy, there would be quite a few people coming in and out to use my room to roll a spliff and smoke it with the door locked from the inside so Stephen or Dick wouldn't find them.'

Another small room of interest was located in between the studio and the reception where the engineers would run off acetates of countless demos. That's where there was an Aladdin's Cave of early Beatles out-takes with conversations between the Fab Four that had been put onto acetates. 'It was a very loose atmosphere at DJM and in the studio,' continues Larkham. 'Caleb organised a lot of demos for his friends, and it was through Caleb, who was organising the demos for the Elton stuff, that much of the *Empty Sky* album came from.'

Again, it was down to Steve Brown who persuaded Dick to loosen the purse strings to make the album and, once he agreed, that's when the recording sessions would go on long into the night. 'I would hang out with the guys watching them recording into the early hours, then we would go to the Wimpy Bar and occasionally to the pub for a pint.' And when the sessions finished late, long after public transport had finished running, the entourage would descend on the home of Brown's father, which was a flat near Oxford Circus in Hanover Square, where Larkham spent his weekends with Brown's sister, who he was then dating. They would usually all spend the night there as Brown's father was the officer-in-charge of the Salvation Army Hall, and the flat, which was large and stretched across three floors, came with the job.

When the album was completed, Larkham was given a meagre budget to try and publicise the new work. 'As I had worked for the *Evening Standard*, I knew music columnist Ray Connolly, so I set up a lunch with Elton and Ray, and although Ray didn't rate *Empty Sky* that much, he did compare Elton to the Beatles, saying that the Beatles songs were about everyday things, while Bernie's lyrics weren't. All the same, and despite his lack of enthusiasm for the album, he still called Elton a talent to watch out for, when his piece appeared in the *Standard*.'

If Connolly's article and review of the album wasn't exactly what Steve Brown had hoped for, he wasn't too concerned. He already had allies from the 'Lady Samantha' single. One of those was Radio One DJ, Tony Brandon. He and his producer Keith Stewart were very impressed with the single. 'Not only did Reg have a very distinctive vocal style but we were very intrigued by the lyrics. A very large percentage of records at the time were made by groups, so it made a welcome change to hear a solo artist.' Brandon played the record regularly, so it wasn't long before DJM's representative for Reg, Dennis Berger, arranged for Brandon and Reg to meet for lunch to discuss the forthcoming album. The meeting took place at a small restaurant in Soho.

'I recall Reg being a very modest and intense young man, he spent most of the lunch talking about his childhood, which I understand wasn't altogether a very happy one,' remembers Brandon. 'He told me that his father was a strict disciplinarian.' Following the lunch Brandon was invited to write the sleeve notes for the *Empty Sky* album as a result of his positive reaction to 'Lady Samantha'.

The album was released on 3 June 1969, and was described by many music critics as a folk rock album, which didn't really seem to make much of an impact despite Larkham's valiant attempts to produce a unique album cover. He had taken one of the early promotional photographs of Reg playing the piano and turned it into a striking illustration. 'The whole *Empty Sky* project was approached a bit naively,' remembers Larkham. 'Steve recognised how to put things together, but he didn't have much experience of how to produce it.'

Mick Inkpen remembers hearing the album at Frome Court with Reg and Bernie, when it was first released: 'It came as quite a revelation to me as I had not heard the new Elton John band sound, or anything about the songs. I also remember how very excited Reg and Bernie were about the release.'

Despite regular airplay, the album disappeared into the bargain racks pretty quickly. As it was so different it did cause a buzz in the industry, but that wasn't sufficient to propel it chartwards, even though Elton still regards 'Skyline Pigeon' as one of the best songs he and Bernie have ever written. The song had such an impact on Paul Buckmaster, who would soon contribute to the success of the Elton John phenomena, that he persuaded Elton to re-record it with new Buckmaster arrangements. Although the new version was never released, it did make the B side of the 'Daniel' single four years later in January 1973. 'Whenever I listen to that song it still makes me cry,' confesses Buckmaster.

Tony Taupin remembers, quite vividly, when he and his father first heard 'Skyline Pigeon' on the car radio. 'My dad stopped the car to listen to the song, as it was one of the first times my father had heard their names on the radio. From then on, every mention of Bernie's name was seized upon with pride. They were immensely proud of him.'

Despite the lack of commercial success for *Empty Sky*, most of the negative opinions about Brown's production abilities seemed to dry up, and not only did he become Reg's record producer, but also his mentor. It wasn't all plain sailing though.

'There were times when Reg's temper would get the better of him to the surprise of the studio team,' says Epps. 'I remember when we were recording one night at DJM with Steve, and Reg and the band had just put down a track in the studio and the guys came in to a playback. Reg wasn't with them so we guessed he must have gone to the loo or something and, after some time passed, we were becoming concerned about his absence, so we went to see where he was. He had gone.' Elton has left the building! To this day, nobody knows why.

One of the problems bedevilling Reg and Bernie's progress was management, or rather lack of it. With two singles and an album behind them, it was now clear to them that they needed a firm hand on the tiller of their careers. Even though Dick James had agreed to sell back the management agreement he had with them, the money that James was asking was still out of Reg and Bernie's price range. One solution they came up with was to call on Ray Williams, once again, to see if he could help. It seemed that he might.

'I remember they both came round to my apartment in Belgravia one evening, to ask me to manage them as Dick James had agreed to sell the management agreement, but I told them, I had no money to buy the agreement. They insisted that they wanted me to manage them, so I said I would try to raise the money to buy the contract. I had a very influential friend named Brian Morrison, over at NEMS – Brian Epstein's old company – who I thought might be interested in investing.'

Morrison was previously a music business agent, publisher and entrepreneur, who went on to build the Royal Berkshire Polo Club, and whose own agency included Pink Floyd as one of his main clients. His agency was eventually sold to NEMS whose managing director was Vic Lewis. Morrison's role with NEMS was to find new business. A meeting was arranged between Dick James, Morrison, Williams, Elton and Bernie, where it became clear that James and Morrison didn't hit it off. Morrison thought that James was asking for too much money. A further meeting took place with NEMS, which included Morrison, Williams, Elton, Bernie, Vic Lewis, the accountant for NEMS, and Tony Howard, who was an agent for NEMS.

The idea that emanated from the meeting was that NEMS would manage Elton and find the money to buy the management contract from Dick James. However, the arrangement stipulated that Elton must gross £75k of income over twelve months. 'Vic Lewis asked me if I was serious that Elton could gross this kind of money in a year,' recalls Williams. 'I said I was confident, but Vic Lewis was not convinced, and consequently the deal fell through. Morrison then contacted Dick James and told him that he was asking too much money and he couldn't afford to go ahead.

It was then that Dick James arranged to meet with Elton and Bernie to discuss what to do next, as it was clear that his two staff writers were less than happy with the arrangement. The compromise reached was that Williams would become an employee of DJM, in the role of managing Elton for a salary of £40 a week. Part of the deal was that James and Williams would split the management income on a 50/50 basis. 'I met with Elton and Dick and they put the offer to me as a good way forward and I agreed,' continues Williams. 'A contract was drawn up and witnessed by Geoffrey Ellis and both Dick and I signed it, giving me 50% of management income. The contract was to last until the end of 1970.'

But according to Ellis, he has no recollection of this agreement. As Stephen James explains, 'Ray started working for DJM and was the designated manager for Elton John, but at that time me and my father were Elton's managers, which is not what we wanted to do. It wasn't healthy, because we were also his publisher and owned the songs. The idea was that we would manage him in the early days but then hand him over to someone else.'

The appointment of Ray Williams as Reg and Bernie's manager, coincided with Caleb Quaye's departure from DJM. Although many were surprised when they heard the news, it was easy to understand why. He was leaving to pursue a career with Hookfoot, the band he had put together with Roger Pope just before recording the *Empty Sky* album. Not only that, but they were often seen jamming or recording with Reg during the period when he didn't have his own group of musicians to back him. 'Elton would often sit in on our gigs,' recalls Quaye. 'It's where we would flesh out some of the songs he was writing at the time that would end up on the next two consecutive albums, *Elton John* and *Tumbleweed Connection.*'

According to Quaye, songs like 'Take Me To the Pilot' and 'Ballad Of A Well Known Gun' were worked out at Hookfoot gigs. It is why, in some quarters, Hookfoot is still considered the most important and influential band to have worked with Elton during the early years of his career, and contributed in helping him discover what has been called The Elton John Sound.

'When we were recording *Tumbleweed*, most of the songs were completed in one take because we had been playing them live with Elton as a member of Hookfoot,' says Quaye. 'That is the reason why that album still sounds good today, because it was not only recorded live in the studio, but it was also rehearsed at live gigs. I remember Hookfoot and Elton playing a gig at the London School of Economics and the crowd loved it, something we repeated at other venues, like the Marquee in London. That's where we opened for Baldry one time, and blew him off the stage.'

Almost eighteen months before that album surfaced, Reg's third single as Elton John, and his first for the new DJM label was released in May 1969. 'It's Me That You Need' was again produced by Steve Brown, but instead of being recorded at DJM's own studio, it was taped at Olympic Studios in Barnes, London. Once again it featured Quaye and Pope, but on bass was engineer Clive Franks, who replaced Glover. It didn't trouble the charts, but Reg remained undaunted, and carried on gigging with Hookfoot, writing with Bernie, and working with his new found mentor Steve Brown.

Another eight months passed before Elton returned to Olympic to start work on tracks for his second album. He was joined by Hookfoot members, Quaye, Pope and Glover. 'The album was recorded in the spirit of a rock band album, but that's not how it turned out when it was released,' says Stuart Epps. And as far as Brown was concerned, it was not sufficiently different to *Empty Sky* to be the next album. Dick and Stephen James were also disillusioned with it. They were also concerned that they couldn't make a success with the songs Reg and Bernie were producing for publishing.

And making matters worse, was the fear that their investment in Reg, as Elton John, was showing very little return with the record buying public. 'DJM was now really concerned, and started thinking along the lines that their Elton John project was something of a loser,' explains Quaye, 'so they decided to bring in a new producer, and the position was very simple: if that didn't work, then they would cut Reg and the Elton project from the label.'

Most music critics would agree, that any second album by a new emerging artist is crucial, and Elton was no exception. Even though Hookfoot were being pretty successful in their own right, as well as with Elton, Quaye was now adamant, as were the rest of the band, that they couldn't be Reg's band for much longer. And that feeling was confirmed when Dee Murray and Nigel Olsson were asked to become Reg's backing musicians on all future gigs. Dee had already played with Elton on some of the early demos that Quaye had produced when he had been running the DJM studio. Another musician to emerge from those sessions was drummer Dave Hynes from the Mirage.

Back then, DJM was like a family, they all worked on each other's projects and socialised together. 'We all knew each other and we were all inter-connected through various recording projects,' remembers Quaye fondly. 'But when the time came for Elton to put a band together for the recording of "Your Song" and his second album, he naturally chose Nigel and Dee to help out because we were still into the Hookfoot thing. It was kind of ironic in a way because Nigel and Dee had been out in America making a last ditch attempt to be successful.'

Another one to desert the DJM ship around this time was Lionel Conway. He had gone to work with Chris Blackwell and Muff Winwood at Island Records and remembers:

> I had some early demos of Elton's that included 'Son Of Your Father', which would eventually turn up on his third album; so I played them to Muff, and he said Blackwell would love this stuff, so we arranged a meeting with him and Elton. But it didn't quite happen, because Chris had this vision of Elton John and when they first met it wasn't what he saw. He thought he was some blind guy from Alabama and in walked Elton with national health glasses and a Mickey Mouse T-shirt. So, he wasn't exactly the image Blackwell was looking for.

Dick found out that I had arranged this meeting behind his back, so he called me in with Muff and said that if we did it again he would sue us as he had a contract with Reg. He then said that, if we really loved this guy we could manage him. So, we decided to do a promotional gig with him as Elton John to gauge the interest to an invited audience only at the Speakeasy in Wardour Street, where his live set list was made up of the songs he had demoed at DJM. It was all a bit strange because it was his first gig as Elton and yet he wore the same Mickey Mouse T-shirt that he wore to the meeting, so he didn't really look the part. Nevertheless, we managed to encourage some representatives from NEMs and the Chrysalis Agency to come along to take a look at him, but they all turned him down. So rather than manage someone who really couldn't get any work, we decided to give him back his management contract.

Muff, however, has a different recollection of it all. 'When I left Spencer Davis to join Chris at Island, I had to move home from Birmingham to London, so I decided to buy a house in Pinner, because it had easy access to London on the Metropolitan Line and to Birmingham on the M1 motorway.

'I was travelling back to Pinner one evening, after work, when this guy came and sat down next to me on the train, and said he knew me from the Spencer Davis Group, and asked if I remembered him. He said he had been the piano player with a band called Bluesology, who had supported us a couple of times at the Marquee. I didn't recognise him, but we got talking and he said that he was now going by the name of Elton John and he had a deal with Dick James to write songs. He wanted to make an album but Dick James wouldn't let him.'

The two musicians got on well during the train journey to Pinner and, by the time they had arrived at their destination, they had arranged to meet at Winwood's house to talk more about the music business and Reg and Bernie's aspirations. 'The next night he and Bernie came round to the house and for the first time, they played me some of their songs. I thought they were really good, and I asked him why Dick James wouldn't let him record them and if he continued to refuse then Island would almost certainly want to record an Elton John album.' Feeling bucked at the prospect of having discovered a recording gem, Winwood went into Island the following day and discussed Elton John with Lionel Conway, who was responsible for the publishing arm of Island Records.

By coincidence, Conway was already aware of him through his time with DJM and agreed with Winwood that the guy was talented. However, Conway was also aware that Dick James wouldn't do anything with Elton or even release him from his contracts, but they both agreed that they should try and persuade James to release him to Island. 'We both went into see Dick and tried to negotiate to sign Elton for Island Records, but he was very much against it. We went to see him several times with different ideas for him to consider, and to try and persuade him, but he kept refusing saying that Elton was his artist and he wanted to keep him and not do any deals with anyone else. The last time we went into see him, we decided to tell him that we would do all the recording, promotion and selling for the album and Dick could have all the publishing. This meant that Lionel and I would do all the work and Dick would earn a lot of money with the publishing, without doing anything. But he still wouldn't have it.'

'Eventually,' continues Winwood, 'he became angry with both of us pestering him, and so on the fourth meeting, he said "if you think you guys are so bloody clever, you can look after him," he took out a wad of papers from his desk draw, and threw them at us. When we got outside, we realised that they were the contracts to be Elton's manager and agent. There was probably somewhere in the region of 30% of Elton's earnings in those contracts. We didn't want to manage him, or anyone else for that matter, because we had good jobs with Island, so I took the contracts to Elton at home that night and gave them to him and told him we couldn't manage him but he could have the contracts back so he could give his agency and management deals to anyone he wanted. He was so very grateful.'

The interest that Island Records showed in wanting to record Elton John, finally stirred Dick James into doing something. 'His staff, including Steve Brown, were telling him that if Island was so interested, then he must have something. So Island's interest, through me and Lionel, spurred DJM to record the *Elton John* album.'

Although Winwood and Conway had no direct interest in Elton John as an Island artist, they did take an interest in his early career and helped in other ways. 'We found him an agent and we helped to get him some gigs. He was so scared and weedy on stage though, he used to do all these goon impersonations to get away from his shyness. He had Caleb Quaye and Roger Pope with him on stage as his band and they sounded great together.' Through the early gigs and a lot of airplay, the new album started to get good reviews. 'Elton used to come round two or three times a week and play me and my wife all the stuff he was doing in the studio. He would ask for my advice on what should be released or be on the album. I was in the music business and so any tips I could give him, I did,' Winwood remembers.

Winwood became good friends with Reg and Bernie, meeting regularly to socialise at Winwood's home in Pinner and playing table football there. 'That was one of the things that cemented our friendship. I had one of the first bar football games in my home. The game table was hard to find at the time, but Jim Capaldi [Traffic's drummer and later a successful solo artist before his death in 2005] found one for me, and I refurbished it. Bernie and Elton were mad keen on the game, so they came round all the time to play it and that's how we became really good at it. Elton used to buy trophies and things like that, so we could play for them.'

In addition to table football, Winwood and Reg both loved tennis. 'We used to play regularly in Pinner, when he would tell me how he was doing in his career and ask for advice. I could talk with him freely as I was out of his career, so I could advise him and Bernie as friends. We used to discuss what he should release and we chose his singles together. I told him what I honestly believed and he appreciated that, as by the mid-seventies, he was surrounded by people who were yes men, all telling him how good he was. Not that I always got it right. I remember telling him how I thought one song he played me was crap, and that went on to be a great hit. He still teases me about it now.'

Despite Winwood's advice, there were a lot of record labels that turned Reg down, both in Britain and in the States. But, as Conway explains, 'Dick James stuck with him simply because he had invested around £6,000 to get him started which, for a new act in those days, was a lot of money.'

To a disinterested onlooker, the music business wrangles would seem pretty strange. At one point, Ray Williams had no idea that Winwood had returned the management contract back to Reg. If he was annoyed about it, it was understandable. He was, after all, supposed to be Reg's official manager, even though he was under contract with Dick James as an employee. Now that Reg had his management contract back, he could, theoretically, drop Williams like a hot potato at any point, so there was little in the way of security as far as Williams was concerned.

Certainly, Reg was approaching a turning point in his career that would indeed change everything, not only for Reg but the music industry in general. Steve Brown decided to find someone to produce the next album on the basis that he was not the right person to move Reg's record career in the right direction. 'Steve always wanted everything to be the best for Elton,' confirms Stuart Epps, 'even if it meant him sidestepping and letting someone else take over.'

Among those he approached was Denny Cordell, who was well-known for his work with Reg's idol Leon Russell amongst many others, but Cordell turned down the offer. Brown also considered George Martin, but he wanted too much control over the arrangements as well as the production so DJM declined, which was a brave move given Martin's reputation. Dick Rowe may have passed on the Beatles, but Dick James passed on the man who produced the Beatles.

As Brown continued the quest, he was introduced by Tony Hall to a young arranger named Paul Buckmaster. To many, Buckmaster had a very eccentric and charismatic personality, not that it mattered. The important thing was that Buckmaster was the ideal candidate to arrange the songs for the next album, as he explains:

I never really had to make a decision about becoming a musician. My mother was a concert pianist, and I was surrounded by fabulous classical music. My first memories of my mother were of her playing the piano, going to concerts and then taking piano lessons from her. She would take me to classical concerts whenever she could, including one specific concert in London, which was to be the defining moment for a career in music. We went to see this great master cellist at the Wigmore Hall who was playing the complete Bach unaccompanied suites, and I fell in love with the instrument, so my parents bought me a quarter sized cello and, at just 4 years of age, I started playing it. There was no question that I was going to be a musician, and after hearing me play, my parents wanted me to be a solo cellist. I had private lessons from various teachers in London and then, at the age of 10, I was auditioned at the Naples Conservatoire for two months, they assessed me and then, having returned to London, I received a letter confirming that I had been accepted.

I had an Italian State Scholarship, that paid for my tuition and my parents paid for my travel and student lodgings. I attended the Conservatoire for four years as well as completing my general school studies for my general educational qualifications. My parents couldn't afford to send me back to complete the course in Naples, and so I applied to the Royal Academy of Music in London and got a Scholarship for four years there.

As a student, Buckmaster continued playing in semi-professional groups and continued his auditions in his quest to find his place in the world of music while earning a living working in a department store. His first break came when his cello teacher contacted him and asked whether he wanted to go on tour as a cellist in a small backing orchestra for Paul Jones, the Scaffold and the Hollies. 'When the tour had finished, one of the violinists who did some contracting work gave me a call and asked me if I wanted to go on a Bee Gees tour as a member of their backing orchestra. I agreed and we toured Germany for three months, during which time I made friends and acquaintances with other members of the orchestra and, of course, the Bee Gees.'

When Buckmaster returned to Britain, he was invited to a recording session for Marsha Hunt, who had previously worked with Bluesology and was by then in the London stage musical of *Hair*. Her producer was Gus Dudgeon, and Tony Visconti was arranger. 'During a studio break, Gus asked me about my musical interests and generally took an interest in me, and asked me back to his office the following day. I took up his offer willingly, and when I turned up at his office, I also met his first manager, Tony Hall. Gus asked me if I had done any arranging and I said I hadn't, so he invited me to try it, and I agreed. A few days later, I received some tapes of Glen Campbell songs and an original song that was not very good, but he was trying me out to see how I coped with it. I went to the library and got a couple of books out on writing scores, so I could get the layout right, and I started writing the scores by hand and, without the proper score paper, I just figured it out for myself.'

Buckmaster remembers how he had to prepare everything himself: the rhythm section, the drums, the electric and acoustic guitars, percussion, piano, organ, small string section, small brass section, and so on. 'I had a small tape recorder and head phones and I stayed up all night playing the songs on the tape recorder through the headphones so I didn't wake my parents. I wrote the lot myself. I did the copies myself and although it was very untidy looking it turned out fine.' His work, despite Buckmaster's reservations, was enough to impress Dudgeon, which then led to more arranging work and a couple of minor hit songs.

Following his brief apprenticeship as an arranger, Buckmaster was contacted by Dudgeon to work on a project with him and a young artist called David Jones, who was soon to change his name to David Bowie. 'I got a call from Gus, telling me to go to his office at 10a.m. as he had a young artist for me to meet, who wanted an arranger. I was introduced to David, and we hit it off straight away. He played me the demo of a song he wanted to record and I agreed to arrange it for him, with Gus producing.' In no time at all, Buckmaster and Bowie had forged a close friendship, initially spending time in each other's houses discussing their respective musical tastes.

'I prepared the charts for a single that became "Space Oddity" and then we went into the studio at Trident and recorded and cut it in a day. We did almost all the track live, with the exception of a Bowie overdub on a Stylophone [a little synthesiser operated by pressing the keys with a special pen. Readers over the age of 45 may remember Rolf Harris fronted their advertising campaigns], and Rick Wakeman playing the Mellotron.' The track was released in July 1969 on the Philips label, and spent an amazing fourteen weeks in the British singles chart eventually reaching No. 5. In the States, the song was on RCA Records who wisely delayed it by one month due to the Apollo 11 Moon landing. To release a song about an astronaut in trouble, would have been seriously tempting fate.

In the same year as Bowie's hit, Buckmaster embarked on an instrumental record project of his own with Tim Mycroft, the Dorset-based keyboard player and musician, resulting in an album called *Sounds Nice*. Produced by Dudgeon, it was a project where the composers selected their own favourite tracks of all time and recorded them as instrumentals using their own individual style. The album, which included Buckmaster's own personal favourite, 'King Kong', originally recorded by Frank Zappa, produced a top twenty hit in Britain. More notoriously, it also produced a reworking of the previously banned 'Je T'aime' by Serge Gainsbourg and Jane Birkin, which Mycroft renamed 'Love At First Sight'. Other musicians who appeared on the album, such as Chris Spedding, Brian Odgers and Herbie Flowers, all went on to play, at one time or another, on the Elton John-Buckmaster recordings.

It was during the making of the album, that Buckmaster was introduced to his idol Miles Davis by Tony Hall, who had developed a friendship with the jazz god due to a mutual enthusiasm for designer clothes. In fact, Hall was one of the few people who Davis would socialise with when he came to London. When Davis played in London at the Hammersmith Odeon, Hall was able to get plum seats for himself and Buckmaster. 'I was very inspired by Miles Davis at the time, and one piece I composed in particular, was the Davis-inspired 'Summers End'. I remember we went to the show at the Odeon Hammersmith and the next day we took him around London, and then we went to see him play at Ronnie Scott's, followed by dinner at Tony's.'

At Hall's insistence, Buckmaster took along a tape of some music he was working on to share with Davis. 'I was composing a thirty minute exploration of this hypnotic rhythm that kept repeating but floating into other keys, it was very jazz/rock with a middle eastern flavour, so we played it to Miles and he was very taken with it and commented that he had been doing something similar, which later turned out to be *Bitches Brew,* and that they had been recording it during the Summer.' Davis was so impressed with what he had heard, he invited Buckmaster to collaborate on a project two years after they had met, which ended up as the *On The Corner* album.

It was during the Ronnie Scott's gig, that Buckmaster was introduced to a shy, bespectacled, well dressed young man going by the name of Elton John, who with the backing of his representative, Steve Brown, asked if he would like to listen to some tapes. 'I agreed, and listened to about four or five songs the next day and fell in love with the material immediately. I knew it was going to be a fantastic record immediately; even before we did it.'

At a second meeting with Brown, Buckmaster agreed to arrange the next Elton John album. Brown asked Buckmaster if he could recommend a producer. 'They came back to me and told me about the George Martin meeting and explained that they preferred the positions of arranger and producer to be separate, and could I recommend someone suitable? I had worked with about three or four producers in my brief time as an arranger, and Gus was the guy I got on with the best and was the person I felt I could collaborate with so, after recommending him, they asked me to take the tapes to Gus and play them to him.'

Dudgeon listened to the tapes and at first was a bit reticent about becoming involved. 'The vibe I got was that he liked what he heard, but it was not something he was interested in; it was a little sentimental for his liking, especially "Your Song", "The King Must Die" and "Sixty Years On". The songs on the tape were all in demo form, with Hookfoot as the rhythm section and no orchestration, so they sounded much different to the final versions that appear on the album. I said to Gus I can hear what I am going to do with these songs and this album, and it's going to be fantastic,' Buckmaster recalls.

When Dudgeon witnessed Buckmaster's enthusiasm, he decided on the spot that he would produce the album. When Brown finally got everyone together to introduce them all to each other, it was, apparently, one of those moments when you could just feel that something quite special was in the making. However the relationship started with some minor confusion.

According to Stuart Epps, 'Dudgeon thought Bernie was the singer on the songs, because he looked more like a rock star than Reg and, consequently, Reg couldn't understand why Gus was directing all the questions about the music to him. He was starting to get a bit pissed off, but the misunderstanding was soon rectified to everyone's satisfaction. Dudgeon was very quick to notice the potential in the songs, and you would have to be very musically illiterate not to have loved the demos.'

From the outset, Reg, strangely enough, wanted nothing to do with how it was going to be arranged. 'He told us that he trusted us implicitly and we could do whatever we wanted. If we didn't want him to play piano on some tracks then he accepted that,' says Buckmaster. 'We did agree later, that on some tracks, piano would not be the lead instrument and this was true of "Sixty Years On", on which Skaila Kanga took the lead on harp. I took the piano transcript with some minor amendments, but essentially that was how he played it on the piano but I arranged it for the harp.'

The songs that had been demoed at Olympic Studios by Clive Franks were slated for the next album. 'The new songs were almost classical and very different from anything on *Empty Sky*,' recalls Epps. 'To be honest, they were very different to any songs I had ever heard and I thought they were amazing.' Dudgeon recalled that the *Elton John* album wasn't really sold to him as being the launch of Reg as an artist in his own right but as a series of glamorous demos for other artists to cover, which was the traditional Tin Pan Alley way of writing and selling songs. However, James gave them a budget to do an album and off they went into the studios. And that, to all intent and purposes, was how the eponymously titled album was born.

# 14

# HOOKFOOT

By the time Caleb Quaye left DJM in 1968, he had met Roger Pope and Dave Glover of the Loot, and Ian Duck, all of whom ended up as DJM house musicians at one time or another, and became the backing musicians for some of Reg's earliest live performances. Quaye himself had played on quite a few of the Loot's A and B sides that were released over a three year period from 1966 onwards, as well as a couple of Page One unreleased demo singles for the Troggs, and the self-penned 'Try To Keep It A Secret' for the Loot.

Although the Loot failed to achieve the commercial impact that their collective talent suggested they should, they still recorded a number of strong tracks that, probably due to the considerable competition at the time, failed to achieve more than moderate success. But what was clear, is how Quaye and they appear to have got on like a house on fire in the recording studio, so perhaps it wasn't any surprise when they decided to form their own band together.

Like so many others who ended up working with Elton John, Roger Pope was another to hail from a musical background. His mother was a singer for numerous dance bands during the Second World War, and his father was an expert drummer who loved the music of Duke Ellington and Nat King Cole. And it was their records, Roger remembers which were always being played on the family gramophone during his childhood and teen years. 'I used to practice my drumming on balloons, until my mother took me to London when I was about 5 years old, and got me a little tin drum, and I can still recall following the guards outside Buckingham Palace playing it.'

Unlike the hero of Grasse's novel *The Tin Drum*, Pope finally gave up playing his tiny tin childhood drum by the time he reached his teens, and instead took up playing a full-size drum kit. 'My dad bought it for me for about twenty-five pounds, which back in those days was the equivalent of two weeks' wages. I started playing them straight away, but my mother still says that I didn't really practice properly, that I just used to play songs on it, but within a few months of messing around on the drums, and within a few months of turning 16, I joined my first band.'

Within three months, and after introductions made by his sister, Pope joined three other guys who had put a band together and needed a drummer. Armed with one amplifier and a little drum kit, they did gigs all over Southampton and surrounding areas and even went as far as Brighton which they got to in a battered old van that someone used to drive them around in. Much the same as Reg was doing with the Corvettes, and later with Bluesology.

The band was called the Countdowns and one of their early gigs, remembers Pope, was at Itchen Grammar School with another band called the Lonely Ones, who were a semi-professional group on the verge of making enough money to turn pro. They were carefully watching Pope's playing and liked what they saw, so, after the gig, they invited him to become a lonely one too.

'I was undecided for about three months, because the band I was with were now my mates, and I kept thinking that I can't let my mates down, but the band wasn't going anywhere and, on the advice of my father, who could see that the Lonely Ones were musicians and would stretch my abilities further, I decided to join them.' Within the space of one week, Pope had become a professional musician at the tender age of 16, and was touring all over Britain playing the club and university circuits.

It was when the Lonely Ones were playing at Southampton University, supporting Long John Baldry And The Hoochie Coochie Men, and their featured singer Rod Stewart – who did a 30 minute stint in front of the microphone – that Pope became excited about a new opportunity. 'I had never heard of Rod Stewart before, but when he came on, he was brilliant. I said to the guitarist that we should ask him to join us as our lead singer as he was only a little side man for Baldry.

They approached Stewart, who liked the band, especially as it had Don Shinn on organ, and he agreed to consider leaving Baldry to join them. 'He rang the next day and said that he would love to do it, but he wanted a third of the money,' remembers Pope. 'The rest of the guys in the band were not too keen, but I said with him in the band, we were going to instantly earn more money because he is a great singer and is going places, so let's do it and give him a third of the money.' Stewart joined up and, as Pope had predicted, they were an instant hit, even changing their name to Rod Stewart And The Soul Agents.

In no time at all, they were playing all the old Bluesology and Baldry haunts like residencies at the Marquee, which Stewart enjoyed most out of all the gigs they played. 'The Saturday night gigs were his favourite, because he could meet his mates and hit the town. If you thought Rod Stewart was bad, he was even worse when he got together with his mates.' Needless to say, the Rod Stewart connection was to be short-lived. Before anyone knew what had happened, Stewart had found the Faces, and was soon on his road to fame, fortune and various blondes.

It was the beginning of the end for the Soul Agents who, soon after, lost their charismatic organist Don Shinn to tuberculosis and hospitalisation. Pope, however, decided to put his professional career on hold until Shinn had recovered, as he could foresee that a future with him would be a successful one. While waiting for Shinn to get match fit, he took a job in a local Southampton casino, playing in the house band, and doing a few odd jobs during the day to get by for the next three months. When Shinn was finally released from hospital, they formed a duo playing the likes of the Waterfront Club in Southampton.

The Waterfront has another claim to fame too. The guitarist for a band called the High Numbers accidentally pushed his guitar through the low ceiling and the audience went ballistic. Thus began Pete Townshend's penchant for cruelty to dumb guitars, which continued when the High Numbers changed their name to the Who.

'I knew the High Numbers through my gigs with the Soul Agents,' Pope continues. 'I can still picture the day when their drummer, Keith Moon, said to me "I've got this new single Rog, you've got to hear this", and he played "I Can't Explain". I knew from the first few bars of the disc, that they were on the road to success, it was *that* amazing; very much like Keith was in real life. He was my best man when I first got married, and was an hour late. He had taken me out the day before, so I am still surprised he even made it at all after what we got up to.'

It was during a Pope and Shinn shindig at the Waterfront that Stan Phillips, who was managing the Troggs at the time, came to watch them play. 'I had already met him before as I had been asked to join the Troggs, but I did not like their music,' says Quaye, 'So Stan said he was putting a band together; he had a singer and a guitarist that he wanted to form a band around, and he asked me and Don to meet them in London, which ended up with us joining up. The singer appeared to be more interested in horse racing than anything else, and it was the only time I can honestly say I was musically whored out.'

Don Shinn was eventually released from his contract with Phillips, but Pope stayed on because he was offered good loot and was also having some success with the Loot, whose other band members included Dave Glover on bass, Dave Wright, and vocalist Chris Bates. The band toured the clubs in Britain and Scandinavia and supported touring artists like Gene Pitney. Apart from his work with the Loot, Dave Glover was another who was recruited to assist Reg with the making of his first album. He was at Page One's offices when he bumped into Caleb Quaye, who asked Glover if he wanted to help a budding musician called Reg Dwight to record an album. Quaye had already seen Glover and Pope play on *Ready Steady Go!* with the Soul Agents, and backing Buddy Guy, so he suggested to Glover that he bring Pope up to play drums as well.

'I had not done any sessions before for someone else, and so we went up there to the tiny studio at DJM, which had egg boxes on the walls, and met this guy Reg Dwight. I set up the gear and we talked first, because no-one really knew anyone, and we were all a bit nervous, but we just clicked, it was quite amazing. I think we did every number in about two takes. I had never heard the songs before; he would just play it through and off we went. And that's why I was only needed for about two days to complete my part on the album,' chuckles Pope. Let's hope he was on a flat fee and not an hourly rate.

It was during one of those sessions for *Empty Sky*, during a break, that Pope and Caleb started jamming together with Glover on bass. It was an instant rhythm jam that came together quite naturally and once Reg picked up on what was happening, he joined in as well. 'I said to Caleb that we ought to put a band together, as I was getting bored in Andover with the Loot and this had the makings of an exciting band.' Even though Quaye was initially reluctant, largely due to the amount of time he was putting in on session work, Pope still wanted to form a band with just Quaye and Glover. And that, to all intents and purposes, is how Hookfoot was formed, which really started from when Quaye worked with the Loot during the last throes of the band, and while he was working with Roger Pope and Dave Glover.

'We were doing our own material and I was writing a lot during that period,' recalls Quaye. 'I used to do a lot of studio work for Page One Records, so I got call saying they had a new group playing called the Loot but, at that time, I had not met Roger and Glover, but I knew who they were from when I had seen them in the Soul Agents in 1966 on *Ready Steady Go!* They were like an organ-based jazz trio, and I loved the way they played; so I started playing with them in the Loot. They were in and out of DJM, as they used the studio all the time.'

Although they did not have a band name at that stage, there were some promotional photographs taken under the name of the Loot, so Caleb became a member of the Loot before he was in Hookfoot. 'I let Stan know what was happening, and introduced him to Quaye. It was quite funny really, because I went up and collected Caleb from his home in Finchley, and I remember he was wearing his Afghan coat, and had a green suede bag with all beads on it and his guitar. When I walked in, Stan's face was a picture as I had forgotten to tell him that Caleb was half-caste [a common term at the time for people of mixed-race], but he was O.K., and he could see from my enthusiasm that something good was about to happen with the new band.

'We hired a little hall in a country village outside of Andover, which left Caleb speechless. He had hardly been in the countryside before, being a born and bred city boy, and this was as far into the countryside as you could get. There were cows looking through the window when we were rehearsing, and there was this fabulous little pub over the road that made us rolls at lunchtime, so we finished Elton's first album and backed him doing radio shows and clubs in London where invited guests, such as DJs, journalists and record company executives, would come to hear tracks from the album that we played live.'

Although Dick James was interested in signing the new band, their manager Stan Phillips, who had an inherent mistrust of James through his dealings with Page One, decided against it. They looked elsewhere for other recording deals and although Island and a few others showed a passing interest, nothing came of it. In the end, and ignoring the advice of Phillips, they signed a package deal with James that included a management contract, which meant they would have to kiss goodbye to Phillips.

There was still the small matter of what to call the band and even though several names were kicked around during rehearsals in Andover, they didn't come up with anything they liked until they were booked to do a couple of live gigs under the name of Cross Cut Saw, which Caleb had come up with. And it was soon after that, during a band rehearsal, that the hi-hat cymbal on Pope's kit kept slipping forward, and he had to keep hooking his foot around the stand and dragging it back. From that moment Caleb started to call him 'Hookfoot Pope' and everyone seemed to like it, so they cut out the Pope bit, and Hookfoot was born.

Quaye had the same musical background and knowledge as Pope and through his father's influence was raised on jazz and gospel music, and so the pair hit it off straight away. 'We both liked the same music, Art Blakey, Miles Davies and Jimi Hendrix, who we would go and watch every Sunday at the Charing Cross Road Theatre.' The idea for Pope's new band with Quaye, was to put something together that would best be described as Freeform Rock, almost like modern jazz rock with a lot of jamming.

'We decided that we needed a pianist or another guitarist as Quaye was doing both jobs, and as we had made a conscious decision not to include Reg at that point, we recruited Ian Duck, who could trade guitar licks with Quaye. I chose Ian because of the old days when I was in a band with him. But I don't remember anything ever being discussed about Reg joining us, even though he wanted us to back him, which we ended up doing every now and then. And when we did, we would rehearse with him at the village hall in Andover. We did a lot of promotional stuff for him as Elton John, TV things like *The Old Grey Whistle Test*, a few radio shows and some promotional gigs at places like the Revolution Club, to help him promote *Empty Sky*, but it wasn't very successful. Not only that, but we wanted to do other things rather than backing Elton all the time,' says Pope.

The other member of Hookfoot was Ian Duck, who unlike Pope and Glover, didn't hail from the Loot. He had been working in local bands in Gosport in Hampshire since the late 1950s, mostly with the Classics – whose main claim to fame had been supporting the original Manfred Mann whenever they went out on the road. 'I played in other bands, with people like Roger Pope and other musicians,' explains Duck. 'But then it all stopped, and I got into motorbikes.'

It was soon after Duck had been invited to rehearse with Hookfoot that their future *de facto* manager and all round organiser, Philip Greenfield, came into the picture. He recalls: 'I first became involved with them through Ian. We shared a keen interest in motorbike racing and went together to all the circuits, but I had no idea about Ian's life in music, until I was round at Ian's when he got a visit from Roger Pope asking him if he wanted to do this gig with this new band he had been rehearsing with. I was perplexed, as I didn't know what he was on about and also because my limitations with music stretched to watching Little Stevie Wonder on the Tamla Motown tour in Southampton at the Gaumont.'

One of the first things he was asked to help out with, was taking Duck to a gig in Andover in his Vauxhall Cresta. Duck had to ask Greenfield, because he only had a licence to drive a motorcycle, not a car, so without the lift he would have been stuck. As it turned out, the gig was staged on the back of a tractor trailer in the middle of a field in the grounds of an old mansion, having been organised by Hookfoot's then manager, Stan Phillips, who had put together an impromptu outdoor festival which saw the boys supporting the Herd.

All seemed to be going well, until an amplifier blew up. Greenfield, a dab hand at fixing things, went to the rescue, climbing up onto the trailer stage and fixed it. 'At the end of the gig, we went to the local pub and that is where I was asked if I would like to be part of the band as they needed a road manager.' They gave him a run down of what was happening with their gigs, recordings and the up and coming tour of North America that had been lined up, and did he want to be involved? He did!

By the time Greenfield had joined them, both Quaye and Pope were fast becoming two of the most prolific musicians working on the session circuit and had played on more albums than they care to remember for an impressive range of people. Artists like Long John Baldry, Cochise, Ray Fenwick, John Kongos, Al Kooper, Ralph McTell and Harry Nilsson, all featured Pope and Quaye on their albums. But it wasn't all work. There was the usual amount of partying to give them the breaks to wind down, and that's when they usually ended up sleeping over on Quaye's floor.

Although Reg was not officially a member of the band, he still came up with ideas for the Hookfoot sound as much as the others. And whenever there was a Hookfoot rehearsal going on for a gig, he would normally sit in, working on his own songs, and using the band as his vehicle. 'He just thought of us as a session band for him,' confirms Duck. 'We would go up to London and do a gig and get paid and come home again to Andover. We would also do some local gigs as Hookfoot, but then when we weren't, Roger, Gloves and Caleb went off to do sessions with Elton. And once that had happened, Elton started to come down more frequently to join in the sessions, and that was when I didn't play that much because Elton and me were both singers.' It was also around that time, that Hookfoot became the Elton John Band, just before he started to make a name for himself. According to Duck, they would often go through the numbers they had recorded for *Empty Sky*.

Before signing with DJM, Hookfoot were, strangely enough, signed to the Chicago Chess label who were best known for their blues, R&B, soul, gospel and occasional jazz releases, but not usually for the type of British music that Hookfoot were playing. Not to leave matters to chance, Marshall Chess personally flew from the East Coast to oversee the sessions at Pye Records in London to ensure that all went smoothly. It was, after all, the first time that a white band had been signed to the label and Chess didn't want to take any chances.

The Chess deal had came through music publisher Jeffrey Heath of Chappell Music who knew Stan Phillips, and had heard through the grapevine that Marshall Chess was looking for a British band to sign. And because Hookfoot were such huge fans of the Chess label and the whole blues scene in general, they thought, perhaps rather naively, that if they were signed to Chess they would end up with that famous blues sound that Chess was so well known for.

'After all,' says Quaye, 'we were a jazz blues band, not a pop band, so we thought, why not, and signed to them to make an album with us.' On meeting Marshall Chess for the first time, and playing him some of the material they recorded at Pye, Chess thought they sounded terrific, and told the boys that he would take the demo album back to the States and mix it in the Chess Studios, which was a dream come true for the band. But, when they heard the remastered version, it was a nightmare.

'We didn't like the album because when we heard it, it had been edited with pieces cut out. We were so disappointed we agreed to be bought out completely by DJM,' says Duck sadly.

The Chess deal, which promised much, delivered little 'I remember we went into the meeting at offices in the West End, in Berkeley Square,' says Greenfield, 'and sat down after greeting each other with hugs and compliments, and then Marshall said "We will play you the finished album." But when he started to play it, my immediate thought was how fantastic Ian's harmonica sounded, like very soulful, the type of thing that Sonny Boy Williamson or Brownie McGhee would do. But then all of a sudden, Caleb stood up and shouted "STOP!" The room completely froze, and he said "TURN IT OFF!" Marshall Chess wasn't sure what was wrong, so he asked Caleb what was up. "WHAT'S UP?!" screamed Caleb. "Who's playing that guitar lick, and where has the harmonica piece gone that we did, and what is that harmonica piece in there because it's not Ian?"

'What transpired was that when Chess had taken the album master back to Chicago, where everyone at Chess was said to have liked what they heard, they still decided to chop pieces out and put session musicians in from Chess, to add overdubs to the album. It was like someone had completely messed with what had been recorded. Caleb just blew up, there and then, and there was an out and out row, and Caleb told them to shove their label up their arse and we went out following Caleb. We all went back to his house and tried to calm him down,' Pope remembers.

Quaye convinced the rest of the band that they should terminate their deal with Chess and, with that in mind, Pope, Glover and Quaye called a meeting with Jeffrey Heath to tell him just that. But as they were already signed with a contract in place, it was not going to be easy to walk away. And it was only when Heath went out to another meeting that they came up with a wheeze to resolve it.

'We went back and told Heath's secretary that we had left something in his office, and left Dave Glover to sweet talk her while Roger and I went into Jeffrey's office to find the contract,' admits Quaye. 'We knew where he kept the contracts, so we went through the files and eventually came across the one we had signed. We stuffed it under a jacket and went out telling Heath's secretary that we had found what we were looking for. We ran out as quickly as possible and went back to Stan Phillips. It must have been around the same time that Elton had released *Empty Sky*, and it was really down to Steve Brown that we ended up with DJM, rather than any other label. We signed the contract, but had no idea what we were signing, it was all legal speak, and all we wanted to do was to make music and be in the studio.'

Prior to departing Chess, Hookfoot were slated to tour America to promote a new album, however, Ian Duck was about to put a spanner in the works. 'He went to the Isle of Wight Festival to see Hendrix. It was quite easy for him to get to, as he was literally living just across the water,' recalls Greenfield. 'He was into the whole love and peace thing, and said he was going to the Isle of Wight. So, without much warning off he went on the pilgrimage with his girlfriend, and the next thing I get is a telephone call at my parent's house, telling me that Ian was in Winchester Prison. He told me that he had been busted as soon as he got off the ferry. Back then it was like you had committed mass murder if you smoked dope or took pills, and he had his harmonicas with him that he carried around in a gas mask carrier from World War II, where the police found this ball of dope, and arrested him, there and then. We had a tour set to the States which was really hectic, and was to last for about three months, and Ian gets arrested, so it wasn't good.'

Greenfield was frantically trying to get everything organised for the tour with Chess, and so it was the last thing that Greenfield, or the band, needed. 'I called Caleb and the other band members and told them I was going to Winchester to see what I could do to get him out. Ian had already been to court and been found guilty and, in those days, having a criminal record for possession of drugs meant it was almost impossible for anyone to get an entry visa into America, so the tour looked to be dead in the water. Quaye suggested that the band get another singer in for the tour, and Ian agreed as he felt he had let the others down, so we started auditioning at DJM.'

Needless to say, the Chess tour didn't go ahead for Hookfoot, so instead, they concentrated on recording an album, and made plans to tour Britain. But by the time the album, *Good Times A' Comin*, came out in 1972, they too, were in America on tour.

▐▌▐▐▌

Soon after Reg's gig at the Troubadour as Elton John, the release of the *Elton John* album, and Hookfoot's jaunt around the States, they both became publicly linked to each other. To all intents and purposes, it appeared that Hookfoot was Elton John's studio band. Indeed, when the album was released and the album's lead single, 'Your Song', took off in the States, most of the songs that ended up on Elton's third album, *Tumbleweed Connection*, had already been written and recorded by Hookfoot and Reg – most of them before the *Elton John* album had been produced.

'In many ways,' says Quaye, '*Tumbleweed Connection* was more like a Hookfoot album than it was an Elton John one, simply because it was heavily influenced by the Hookfoot sound.' Prior to the *Elton John* album, Pope, Duck and Quaye found themselves in Olympic Studios recording an early demo version of 'Take Me To The Pilot', and even though this song was taken and arranged by Paul Buckmaster to appear on the *Elton John* album, many of the other tracks, recorded at the same time, would soon become the basis for *Tumbleweed*.

Ian Duck agrees. 'I didn't come across Reg until 1969 prior to the Hookfoot rehearsals in Andover. It was during the *Tumbleweed* sessions that I first met him when I did some sessions with him and Gus Dudgeon. I met him on the stairs of DJM of all places, but everyone met everyone on the stairs, because it was the only way in and out. I always felt a bit wary of Gus and his mates, though, as they all seemed very public school. I felt intimidated, but in the end it worked out fine.

'One of the first tracks I worked on was "Son Of Your Father", which was eventually included on the *Tumbleweed Connection* album. I was sent an acetate of the song and I rehearsed the harmonica part at home first, and then went to the studio. Dudgeon would run the track and we would do it in a couple of takes. We would just go in the studio, do our thing, and if Gus thought it was O.K., then he said you can go home. It was that simple. In those days we got about £30 a session, and if we had to do any overdubs, then we got a little more.'

Out of the studio it was quite different, especially when they were gigging prior to Reg's success in the States. Stuart Epps can still remember the gig at the Royal College of Art, where Elton John and Hookfoot played together. 'There were hippies all over the place, the smell of patchouli oil and moving psychedelic pictures on the walls and ceiling from the oil projectors. I witnessed all the very good musicianship of Hookfoot with Elton's music and songs and, although it was good, there was something not quite right about it, especially for Elton. He was playing away at his piano, playing songs from the newly-released *Empty Sky* album, with Caleb wailing away on his guitar, but there was no real focus.'

One of the problems was that Hookfoot were much more influential than Reg at DJM, and Caleb Quaye particularly so, due to his musicianship and knowledge of music production and sound. 'He had a big ego and you ended up doing what he said because he was so good,' continues Epps. 'And no doubt Reg felt the same. It couldn't really carry on like that with Elton, and it needed to be sorted out because Caleb was clear about his direction for Hookfoot, but it was less clear for Elton, so it had to come to a head. I know that he thought he was in Hookfoot's shadow, and who knows how much longer they could have lasted together?'

Amid rumours that Reg was going to join Hookfoot and tour the States, there was a lot of discussion behind the scenes between Ray Williams and Dick James about taking Elton John to the States on his own merits. In early 1970, Williams met Jeff Beck's manager John French to discuss one of the options for launching Elton John in America. 'We discussed the promotion of our respective stars. He said that Beck was a big star in the US and that it might be financially beneficial for Beck and Elton to tour together. A meeting was subsequently arranged and held at Dick's offices, which Dick, French, Beck, Elton and myself all attended to discuss terms, but we quickly became astonished when Beck said he would take ninety percent of the tour earnings, leaving Elton and his band with just ten percent, and that's when it became obvious that no deal could be concluded. Besides, we all knew, especially Dick, that within a few months, Elton would be a bigger star than Beck anyway,' says Williams.

And, of course, they were right. By that August, Reg was in Los Angeles playing the Troubadour followed by a mini promotional tour that took him to San Francisco, New York and Philadelphia and his star was definitely in the ascendency.

Making the decision that touring as a member of Hookfoot was no longer a viable option, Reg decided to put together a new band with Dee Murray and Nigel Olsson. 'What Reg was doing was controversial, as he didn't have a guitarist,' Epps explains. 'They were rehearsing at the DJM studios and I used to go up there, to lock up, and I used to listen to them rehearsing. Nigel had a great big drum kit, and Dee had a big bass guitar sound, and so the piano was miked up and what they produced was a great and unique sound, I thought, wow this is something else.'

Terry Carty agrees. 'When Elton first put together his own band with Nigel and Dee, the first gig they played was at the Roundhouse in London. I went with Steve Brown, Bernie Taupin, David Larkham and Stuart Epps on the tube to the gig and, by the time we arrived, Elton had just finished rehearsing. We met them at the bar in the Roundhouse, and we all asked Elton how it was going, and he said, it was O.K., but he was very nervous, and was passing a bottle of vodka round, obviously to calm his nerves. But when he went on, he was fantastic. I remember he walked on the stage wearing an overcoat, which he took off before he sat down at a grand piano and did what he did best, just played.'

It was probably quite difficult for Reg and the guys from Hookfoot to get used to the fact that they were destined not to play together again. According to Epps, on stage with Hookfoot, Elton was just someone who was singing and playing the piano. 'He was not at all charismatic and, in fact, we had to tell people to shut up and listen to him when the audience started talking. Inside Reg, there was this guy trying to get out that we didn't know about. It wasn't prevalent at the time as he was very quiet, shy and introverted on stage, and with no more flamboyance than the norm during the late sixties, although he did light up a room when he walked in.'

And on top of everything else, Elton John songs weren't really what Hookfoot were about. They were much more progressive but, in those days, it didn't matter as they just enjoyed playing live. Ray Williams organised as many sessions for Reg as he could, using Hookfoot as Elton John's band. 'Hookfoot were such great musicians,' raves Epps, 'but it was like a musicians' band, and the audiences, although enjoying what they heard, they were far from ecstatic about it. There was no real show at this time, just very much reproducing what was on the record as much as possible.'

'Besides,' adds Duck, 'Hookfoot had its own identity which was totally different to what Reg was doing. I'm sure Caleb, Roger and Glover were asked by James and Brown to be Elton's first band, but we wanted to be Hookfoot. We had our own ideas and our own way of playing and that was it.' It is probably why many, including fellow musicians, considered them a good live band which possibly came from the fact that Quaye was well-known for his session work with other musicians and had quite a reputation in the music business. 'We were friends with bands like Fairport Convention, and they often would come and watch us play live at the Marquee and the various other clubs we gigged at around London's West End at the time,' says Quaye. 'We just loved playing live.'

Greenfield, meantime, was becoming a dab hand at life on the road. He decided to fly out to the States with the Elton John Band, prior to the Hookfoot tour, to gain experience of touring in another country. 'I remember going to the States because Elton had gone out, and everything had taken off for him, and as he was on his second tour and starting to make headway. So, it was an ideal opportunity for me to learn the system.'

He hooked up with Elton's road manager, Bob Stacey, who was to become Greenfield's mentor. 'Bob was a fantastic guy and helped me enormously during the two weeks I went on the road with Elton. I remember we were in Minneapolis, St Paul, when I was told that the next day the Hookfoot guys were flying out and meeting me in New York for a one week residency with Elton in a club called the Gaslight and, by this time, I was feeling really comfortable with my role. It was, after all, the first tour in the US for the boys, and the excitement was at fever pitch.

'Having worked with Elton on his tour, really gave me an insight into what was going to happen when they arrived. There was only Bob Stacey working as a roadie for Elton at that time, and even though I was just a side man helping out, I would be at the side of the stage and if something happened to Dee or Nigel, I was there to help them, but I was also helping Bob as well, so it was all very rudimentary.' The first Hookfoot gigs in the States were a roaring success and the band played sell out shows and were asked back again.

Before they could do that, they needed to recruit a new bassist as Dave Glover had parted company with the band. They tried out quite a few bass players and eventually settled on Mick Grabham from Cochise, who agreed to stand in for a European tour. 'We toured with Grabham on bass for a while because we were between bass players, and as he had no other commitments, he came on board and played bass on a tour of Italy,' says Duck. 'We also invited Fred Gandy to join, who came along with a bit of dope, and so, that was it, he was in.'

As Gandy explains:

When Dave Glover left Hookfoot, Caleb called me and was straight to the point 'Fred man, we need a bassist do you want it?' There was no asking me twice, I just said yes, there and then. Everyone knew who Hookfoot were at the time, they were very popular, and so I was totally elated to be asked. It was ironic, but three months earlier I was living in a drugs rehabilitation unit, not because I needed to be rehabilitated, but because it was somewhere to live, and this German guy brought an album in by Hookfoot and we listened to it, and now I was in the band. It didn't get any better.

When I was first with Hookfoot, we went to rehearse somewhere outside of London for the album, *Communication,* and then when we went to Richard Branson's Manor studios in Oxfordshire to start recording, it was the title track that I remember laying down more so than any other. The control room was high up and you went down into the studio. We put the track down and it was great, and when we were walking back up to the control room, Ian suggested that we double up on the vocal, and Caleb came up with the idea of adding a guitar solo, and we agreed. Having worked with guitarists before, I thought a guitar solo would be perfect, and when we went back into the studio the next day, Caleb ran the track once, put the cans on, and played a great solo, and that was it, in one take.

Following the change in line up and with a new album to promote, the band set off on a three month tour of the States. Part of the tour was to provide support to their old friend Reg, who had now made himself a significant success with the *Elton John* album and had to promote the new one, *Tumbleweed Connection.* Hookfoot also had some dates on their own as well as supporting other bands. The first gig Hookfoot played without Elton was in Los Angeles at the Whisky A Go-Go nightclub in West Hollywood, before undertaking dates with San Francisco psychedelic rockers Jefferson Airplane, which kicked off in San Antonio, Texas. 'They were lunatics and frightening to be around,' remembers Greenfield. 'And they were heavyweights when it came to drugs.'

San Antonio was a happy hunting ground for the band. 'We did some stuff with Elton and we played San Antonio with him and we went off and did some stuff with Dr Hook and the Medicine Show in Kansas, so all in all, it was pretty good,' remembers Greenfield with affection.

Back on home soil, Hookfoot weren't really picking up that many decent gigs in Britain apart from a tour supporting Humble Pie. The lack of promotion for the band in the States by DJM was a further stumbling block. Suddenly, it seemed a struggle and it all seemed to happen overnight. 'I think the problem was,' says Quaye, 'that we were ahead of our time as a band, so we were not ready to conform to whatever was going on at DJM. Coming into 1974, after we had just finished a successful

American tour in 1973, the music scene was starting to change quite dramatically with the onslaught of 'Glam Rock' with artists like Gary Glitter dressing up in very flamboyant outfits and to us, and to me in particular, I just wanted nothing to do with it. The nearest we came to what was happening at that time was when got involved with Mr Bloe, which was something we ended up doing to simply survive, but it was music prostitution really.'

Although the Mr Bloe episode happened in the early days of the band's creation, in 1970, and before they became an act to be reckoned with in the US, it was a taste of things to come. Hookfoot, in hindsight, were still only seen as a house band at DJM, to be used whenever Dick needed their support. Elton was a classic example of this. Every time Dick had a successful single on his hands that needed promoting, he got Hookfoot to tour it and, as such, they were never going to enjoy enough support and promotion from DJM to be successful it their own right.

Roger Pope has some strong views on the subject:

No one gave a shit about the content or the quality of the music, all they wanted was money. Most of the people who were involved in Tin Pan Alley, such as Dick James, were from an era that concentrated on selling sheet music, so all they wanted you to do was bang out songs to convert into and sell sheet music to someone who wants to play it in a pub or at home.

We were like the house band at DJM and for *The Old Grey Whistle Test*. The title of *The Old Grey Whistle Test* was really derived from an old Tin Pan Alley phrase used years before, from when people would go into a music publisher and play some music, who in turn would play it to people they called the old greys, doormen in grey suits, and if those guys could remember the song and whistle it, having heard it just once or twice, then the publisher would buy the song, which meant you had passed the old grey whistle test. It was a typical Tin Pan Alley attitude that was still prevalent in some of the A&R people working at DJM.

Even when records replaced sheet music as the No. 1 seller it was still a con. When the Loot were not recording and touring, I used to drive around the country every week on behalf of the Troggs. I was given money and a list of shops that made the returns for the charts, and from Southampton I used to go to Birmingham, Manchester, Sheffield, Leeds, Glasgow, Edinburgh, and down to Hull, over the space of two days, every week, buying twelve copies of each record and ordering twelve more.

The shops didn't give a shit because they were selling records, but it would bump the record up the charts, and I used to get paid for doing that. As Hookfoot we were often called into work on a lot of albums for other artists and once, we even had to masquerade as Mr Bloe.

'Groovin' With Mr Bloe' gave Stephen James his first hit as a producer. Amazingly, it spent eighteen weeks on the singles chart and ended up at No. 2 in May 1970, and Hookfoot were called upon to go out on the road and play as Mr Bloe during their leaner periods to justify the retainer they were being paid. The song had come from an

American single B side and it typified the way Tin Pan Alley was now finding songs. 'I listened to it, and liked it, and we covered it in the studio,' recalls James. 'I was holding wires together because the equipment was falling apart and so we upgraded the studio after that.'

The song was recorded under the guidance of Zack Laurence who had been asked to do the arrangements, which would pave the way for Hookfoot, and Ian Duck on harmonica, to take the song on tour. The musicians who played on the record were a band of old Tin Pan Alley players put together by Laurence, and didn't include anyone from Hookfoot, but the success of the record meant that it needed to be toured, so Hookfoot got the job of being Mr Bloe 'In Person.'

The original song was played on an old chromatic harmonica and Duck had to learn it on a blues harp: 'I managed to do it, and it was released on DJM, and it started zooming up the charts, so Dick wanted a band to go out and promote it. He called Caleb, and asked him to tour Hookfoot as Mr Bloe. He said it was a harmonica-based song, so all we had to do was to play that song, and then we could play Hookfoot songs, and this, he said, would be an ideal launch pad for us. And on top of that, we were going to be paid one hundred pounds a night which was more money than we had ever seen in our lives, bearing in mind we were only on twelve pounds a week.'

Before Hookfoot went on tour as Mr Bloe, and because the single had taken off, they had to re-record it for *Top Of The Pops*. Zack Laurence, who had put the song together, was not about to do that, because he was a very straight schmaltzy piano player. 'We dressed up to hide ourselves when we did *TOTP*. I was a Red Indian and Caleb was a joker,' recalls Duck, 'when you did *TOTP* in those days, you had to record it the day before and we ended up doing *TOTP* three times, but we didn't really want to do it, as we considered Hookfoot was a serious band.'

Soon after the *TOTP* appearances, Hookfoot had to tour the tune. 'We had a major tour of seaside resorts as Mr Bloe, playing Blackpool Tower, Newquay and all those sort of cheesy holiday places. But when we did the gig at Blackpool, we were on a bill with people like Gerry Munroe, Mungo Jerry, Pickettywitch and all those kind of bands, and then there was us. It was amazing how abstract it all became. To start with it was a real buzz, because we were playing to packed houses with a couple of thousand people, so the adrenalin was running high, but then, in the end, Caleb just thought it was "a load of shit," and, of course, he was right. They were the wrong audience for Hookfoot – they were not going to buy our records. They were into candyfloss and all that,' says Duck.

'But,' as Greenfield says, 'the Mr Bloe set was one song, so we would go out and do the Mr Bloe song, which is what the audience wanted to hear and, afterwards, we would do our own Hookfoot set, which nobody wanted to hear.' Duck agrees. 'We opened in Blackpool and there was all the variety acts and Hookfoot. When the curtain went up, the front row were just old people who had come for the variety. We would do "Groovin" and it would go down a storm, and then when we did the Hookfoot set, we used to die a death.'

During one gig on the many Mr Bloe dates, the band had a revolt from the audience and Greenfield had to help the Front of House as people were demanding their money back, saying it was not Mr Bloe. The house manager was panicking and didn't know what to do, so he called Greenfield to calm it all down and asked him confirm to the audience that the band was indeed the real Mr Bloe. 'So I have gone out there and there were a bunch northern folk all shouting and swearing about it not being Mr Bloe, and I am saying what's the problem, we played "Groovin' With Mr Bloe"? But when the band did *TOTP* they went on in silly costumes, so they wanted to see the silly costumes.

'I am trying to convince them that it is Mr Bloe, and that they are the guys who they had seen on TV, but they just kept saying that they were not wearing the costumes so how could they be Mr Bloe? In the end, I had to feed them a story saying that the costumes had been stolen, and luckily I turned them around by saying, I will get them to play it again, and they all went back on stage again and played it again.'

By this time, of course, the band were fed up to the back teeth with the 'bloody song' and being Mr Bloe. Greenfield convinced the band that they should help the house manager out by playing the song again, and they did, but that was really the end of Mr Bloe as far as Hookfoot were concerned. They had done the circuit and had now had enough.

'Mr Bloe got gigs in Europe, Italy, Paris and all over Europe because Mr Bloe had started getting big out in those places, but Hookfoot refused to do it, and were replaced by the Claggers, who were the engineers at DJM: Clive Franks, Jeff Titmus, and Stuart Epps [and Kaplan Kaye], and they were told by Dick to be Mr Bloe and off they went,' laughs Duck. The Claggers went on to record one album, titled *Chumley's Laughing Gear*, which failed to sell and the band members went back to their day jobs.

**▌▌ ▌▌▌**

The catalyst for the band folding started when Quaye was approached to work on advertising jingles for television, a lucrative job. He resisted the temptation to move to America in favour of the draw of a third big American tour for Hookfoot, which he thought would be the making of the band.

The beginning of the end of the demise of Hookfoot started in, of all places, Caleb's mother's home in Finchley, which ever since the band had started was the regular location for meet-ups. It was while they were there that Quaye received a telephone call from a newly-found promoter in the US. He told Caleb that he had been kicked out of the New York office, and had been sacked by Dick James. Apparently, the New

York Office had taken offence to the promoter's demands on how they should promote Hookfoot, and had reported him to Dick, who immediately banned him from the American office and, with this news, came more.

Any support Hookfoot had hoped for from the US had now evaporated into thin air, along with the proposed third tour that promised to break Hookfoot in the States. 'It was a little bit of Tin Pan Alley creeping in, and they wanted to do it their way,' says Greenfield.

'When Caleb had come down off the ceiling the next day, or a couple of days later, the rest of us followed him into see Dick James. We marched up the staircase that I had carted equipment up and down many times before, and then we went into the reception and found Telly Savalas, TV's *Kojak*, standing there. He was the first person I spotted as I reached the top of the stairs and went onto the landing. All the girls were working away in there, and here we were, this group of angry young men, with an even angrier Quaye leading us into the reception next to James's office.

'The atmosphere was very intense, and the girls were probably feeling a little intimidated. At that point, we were like the Kings of the Castle, not in a negative or arrogant way, but in an angry way. I remember Caleb ripping the framed Hookfoot display off the wall as he sent it crashing to the floor. It was about 6' by 4' and had glass that went everywhere, and then he pushed Dick's office doors open, and we all followed him like the Pied Piper. He laid into James like you wouldn't believe, and was slamming his fist hard down on James's desk, so that each time he thumped it the desk shook. We just stood there all looking at each other, and then when Caleb had finished, we just said, "Let's have a drink", and off we went to the pub on the corner, and that was it.'

In the pub, Quaye was talking about going to the States and turning the Hookfoot tour into a make or break for the band. But then, out of the blue, he decided, no he wouldn't do any of that. Instead, he said he was going to call it a day. He told the rest of the band that he was going to go to Chicago. 'We were sat there, mortified, and even some days later during the calm after the storm, we just walked around in a daze, wondering what we should do next. Caleb had already gone to the airport, and was firing on all cylinders, and had moved on. They gave me the van and all the equipment inside it, and told me to go and set myself up and do something with it,' remembers Greenfield. And that's how Hookfoot came to its end. From that point on, they no longer existed as a band.

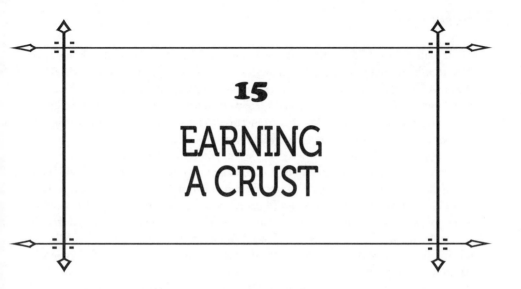

# 15

# EARNING
# A CRUST

For Reg, there was no place like Frome and the Prodigal Son returned to Frome Court in the aftermath of his breakup with Linda Woodrow. Not only did it mean that he was now back under the same roof as his mother and stepfather, it also meant that he was as close as he could get to his Aunty Win, who lived in the maisonette downstairs. His grandmother, Ivy Harris, was just around the corner, in the house where he was born. What could be better than having his nearest and dearest all within easy reach of each other?

According to Mick Inkpen, they quite naturally thought Reg was the bee's knees. 'They always followed his career, and they were always popping in and out; it was a very happy home. I remember when he bought an upright piano to practice with. To get it into the main living area of the flat, you had to go through the front door, turn right and up this very narrow flight of stairs but, somehow, we managed to get the piano up there, but it played havoc with the wall paper.

'We often met Sheila and Fred and they were always good humoured and welcoming,' remembers Inkpen. 'Cups of tea and biscuits would sometimes be offered, but mostly we were left alone to chat and listen to records.' Certainly, music was a favourite topic for discussion, as was politics. Reg was a Labour supporter and was by all accounts pretty impressive at sending up the politicians of the day from either side. He also loved word play and decided to turn Fred's name back to front and call him 'Derf' – a moniker that stuck.

Bernie, who was now sharing Reg's bedroom at Frome Court, was quite different: always quiet and thoughtful and never comfortable with expressing any strong views about anything much. 'Bernie's real love, after music, was books. He was really into Tolkien, *The Hobbit* and *The Lord Of The Rings* and so, I suppose, was Reg, although he was a bit of a sucker for book club collections. I remember him having the complete works of Dickens and other collections which were bought on a monthly basis,' continues Inkpen.

The other love of Reg's life was the Hillman Husky that his mother bought for him after he passed his driving test. It was a two-door estate, which had a wheelbase that was 9" longer than that of the average saloon car, but it was not a hatchback. It had a single side-hinged rear door, and there were individual seats in front and a bench seat in the rear which would fold flat to increase the load area. The trim material was leathercloth and both the heater and radio were optional extras.

'He used to drive it everywhere,' laughs Inkpen today. 'We came from a part of London where car ownership amongst the young was common, but it was still a big deal to have a car of your own at our age. He had only just passed his test so the driving was a bit tentative, but there were not so many cars on the road back then. I remember when we went to Ruislip Lido, one afternoon, to test out the new car. We had trouble finding a car park for some reason and found ourselves bouncing over a grass field. As our heads hit the roof lining for the third time, our driver exclaimed "Welcome On Safari with Elton John!"

It was during their time away from DJM and music, that Reg and Bernie could enjoy a reasonably normal way of life. 'My girlfriend and I went with Reg and Bernie to Pinner Fair,' says Inkpen. It was a traditional annual street fair, held in the centre of Pinner on the weekend after Whitsun, and to this day is protected by an ancient charter which allows it to run each and every year. It is something like 700 years old, and is equipped with movable street furniture for the purpose. Bernie was really into this and expected to see street jugglers, which was not the case. My girlfriend and I met up with Bernie and Reg and wandered the side shows. One pitch we stopped at was dedicated to the winning of goldfish by tossing ping pong balls into jam jars. Reg won two in short order. At the bottom of Bridge Street we came across a Big Wheel. I was not too keen, but my girlfriend wanted to go on, so Reg accompanied her while Bernie and I watched from below.'

Music, however, was never far away. 'While we were at Frome Court, I remember Reg getting a call from a band member of Three Dog Night who phoned to ask if it was O.K. to record a version of "Lady Samantha",' Inkpen explains. 'Was it O.K.? It certainly was! He was very proud that he had been personally asked, because it was a published song he didn't need to give permission for it to be used.'

Danny Hutton, the lead singer and founder of Three Dog Night, would eventually have an influence on Reg's success in America and, for a time, acted as his mentor, during what would become the preparations for his first gigs at the Troubadour in Los Angeles.

Reg's friendship with Danny Hutton had really started during one of Hutton's frequent visits to London. Rather than live in an impersonal hotel, he had taken a flat in posh Curzon Place in Park Lane, on the advice of friend Harry Nilsson who had rooms there, which appeared to be cursed. It was where Mama Cass died of a heart attack in 1974 and, in September 1978 in the very same apartment, Keith Moon would also be found dead from a pills overdose.

Hutton used his trips to London to find new songs, and part of his process for song hunting was to scour the record companies looking for new songwriters with unique songs for him or Three Dog Night. It was during one of those trips in 1969, which also included a Three Dog Night tour of Britain, that Hutton contacted DJM and asked if there were any songwriters who had songs that he might be interested in recording. After a positive reply from DJM, Reg, turned up at Hutton's apartment totally out of the blue. 'He had come from DJM to play me some songs,' says Hutton. 'He came into the room, and after exchanging pleasantries, he sat down and played me the demo acetate of "Bad Side Of The Moon". I was completely knocked out by what this guy could do.'

That was when Hutton invited Reg to a gig at the Revolution Club, but he got turned away, recalls Hutton. 'The bouncers wouldn't let him in because his name and Bernie's had been left off the guest list. He got a message to me and we met in the bar at the club, where he gave me a copy of *Empty Sky*. I really raved about his ability as a songwriter and performer, but he told me that he was just interested in writing and to have a career like Nilsson or Laura Nyro. I remember there was background music playing in the bar at the club, and Reg knew the songs and was singing along, and his voice was just great.

'He and I hung around a lot during that tour in Britain, and I recall that in order to get Reg into the Marquee gig he had to be our roadie, it was the easiest way for him to get access. He kept in touch with me, and frequently sent me demos of his songs on a regular basis. I ended up recording "Your Song" and "Lady Samantha" for two Three Dog Night albums.'

But, as Reg said when he was Elton John, the period between Elton becoming a household name and the Reg of Bluesology was a peculiar one. Due to the expansion of the Dick James Organisation and their partnership with George Martin's company, AIR, Reg was rubbing shoulders with some of the leading songwriters and artists of the day. This led to some impressive collaborative session work during his formative years with DJM and their other associated companies. Suddenly he found himself gigging for EMI Records with such names as the Hollies, the Barron Knights and the Scaffold.

If nothing else, it proved to be a very productive period for Reg. As well as mapping out his own musical niche as Elton John, he was also taking on session work, mainly for financial survival, but also to connect with others in the business. All the same, Reg was still not sure where his own music career was going, especially after the disappointment of *Empty Sky*. He was only too aware that Dick and Stephen James were becoming less confident in their Elton John investment. Was their gamble paying off? It seemed it wasn't. It is one of the reasons why, in the latter stages of 1969 and early1970, Reg was seeking other options to work as a songwriter and performer, and ended up significantly increasing his session work for other bands and artists.

Although James was still plugging the songs in the hope that persistence would pay off, and even though Tin Pan Alley still had a stranglehold on songwriters, success, so

Reg hoped, was waiting in the wings and even if no one else could see it, he could. 'As part of my job at DJM,' recalls Epps, 'I was responsible for trying to get covers of songs by the DJM writers who Dick had signed, and for me Reg's tunes were top of the list. I sent some to Ray Charles very early on, but they got turned down. Apparently he didn't think they were lyrically for him.'

During the same period that Hutton befriended Reg, there seemed to be a sea change in how Tin Pan Alley operated, and one of those changes was the emergence of the session singer. It was probably the late 1960s when they first started to make an impact on the industry. Suddenly the session guys were not only being used to demo songs to sell them for sheet music sales, but also, more importantly, to front 'one hit wonder' bands whilst still keeping their own anonymity.

One such person was Tony Burrows, who has had more hits than most people have had hot dinners, but many probably don't even know his name. He made his mark with the Kestrels, while Roger Greenaway was still a songwriter for Mills Music, and then, post-Mills, was a session singer with a significant number of hits as a session vocalist under a number of different names.

After the success with the Kestrels, Burrows returned to Bristol, where he ended up joining the Ivy League in 1966, as a replacement for founder member John Carter, who had quit that same year, having had enough of touring.

'I stayed with them for about a year. If truth be told, I wasn't enjoying the Ivy League by this time, and so when John Carter came along with a song called "Let's Go To San Francisco", and asked me to do the vocals on it, I agreed. But we needed a backing band, so we formed the Flowerpot Men and that is when and why I left the Ivy League.'

Burrows and Carter tried to persuade Jon Lord to come on board, but an offer to join a fledgling Deep Purple seemed a more promising option. Not even the fact that he was the Burrows' babysitter seemed to help win him over permanently to the Flowerpot Men, though he did tour with them. Following a massive amount of airplay from DJ Simon Dee on the BBC Light Programme [the forerunner to Radio 1, which was launched on 30 September 1967], the single inevitably became a hit, spent twelve weeks in the singles chart and reached No. 4 in the hot August summer of 1967. 'He [Dee] played the backside off it,' says Burrows. 'It charted and was quite successful but, by 1969, I'd had enough of touring so I decided to go back to London.'

Luckily for Burrows, session work was a lucrative way of earning a living for most musicians at that time, and Burrows, like so many, found that he was as much in demand as anyone. It was the same for Reg Dwight. It helped, of course, that the Tin Pan Alley songwriters had now identified another way of selling songs, and that was by getting known session musicians to record their work to release either as a solo artist or for forming a band, just for the sake of the song. Burrows recounts how:

There were about ten big songwriters back then, like Mike Leander, Bill Martin, Barry Mason, Tony Macaulay, Cook and Greenaway, Peter Callender and Mitch Murray, and I got to know them all, because they would come along and say they couldn't find anyone to record the demo of a song, so they would ask me to do it. I always agreed, because I would get a royalty for it, but the only drawback was that the songs were recorded under different names, so my name remained hidden behind a host of hit songs by some very short-lived bands. We used to do most of these demos at Regent Sound in Denmark Street because we had to do it on the cheap, but there were so many other studios as well. You didn't sample sounds, you had to record them, and you also had to play it like a live performance. In a lot of the big studios, like Decca, Pye and Philips, you had to lay down the tracks all together as if it was a live recording.

The Flowerpot Men were one of those session bands put together for the sake of promoting a song, and Burrows, it seemed, was at the centre of it. Although they split up, songwriters such as Roger Greenaway and Roger Cook were still writing songs for the band but, due to its demise, there were many songs in the can not destined to be used. 'Dick Rowe, at Decca Records, came to me and asked me if I wanted to release any of the songs. I couldn't see the point as the band had broken up, so I gave him permission to release some of them,' reflects Burrows. 'He wanted to release "My Baby Loves Lovin'" and I said he could if he could come up with a name for a band and I received a royalty; so he came up with the White Plains and I agreed to sing the lead vocal.'

After that, Burrows only did one more session with the White Plains but not as the lead singer as he was committed to other session projects, which were producing hit singles in Britain. 'I had other things going with groups like Brotherhood Of Man and the Pipkins, the latter of which was just me and Roger Greenaway. We recorded a song slated for a record for Freddie And The Dreamers who were recording a children's album about *Oliver In The Overworld*. It was the only song that Freddie Garrity wasn't featured on because it was organised as a filler for the album that John Burgess was putting together.

'I remember he came to us, and said he didn't know what to do with a song written by Albert Hammond and Lee Hazlewood, who had written a song for the album that was basically a conversation between a pianola and a metronome, and was originally titled "Gimme That Click". We thought it didn't sound right, so we renamed it "Gimme Dat Ding". Roger and I did it in one take, but I had quite a sore throat at the time so Roger did the high pitched stuff and I did the talking, so I was probably the first rap artist in history. It was released and became a big hit, reaching No.6 in Britain and No. 9 in the US, although it was banned in Italy, because the title was considered rude.'

Brotherhood Of Man, on the other hand, was a band put together by Tony Hiller from Mills Music in 1969, who had signed Roger Cook and Roger Greenaway as songwriters, following the demise of the Kestrels. The two songwriters were struggling to get hits in their own right, so they turned to session work to subsidise their writing. 'I will never forget the Giaconda café, because all of the music publishers, who would be on either side of Denmark Street, would go in there. We used to go in there every morning when we were still looking for work, and try and sit over one cup of coffee for six hours, until the big ballad guys used to come in looking for songs, or trying to find musicians to sing demos. I was often met by a panicked songwriter, who needed to get his song put down in the studio, and I was whisked off to Regent Sound to sing it for a fee.'

'United We Stand', was another song Hiller had written with Johnny Goodison, which was subsequently a big hit for what was originally a session band for Mills Music comprising Greenaway, Burrows, Sue Glover and Sunny Leslie. 'Goodison was writing with Tony, but Tony didn't really have a lot to do with that song,' says Burrows, 'so we put a group together to record the song and because Roger and I were doing everything together we decided to do it as a group. We went into Decca Studio No. 2, recorded it and it soon became a worldwide hit. And although Sue, Sunny and Johnny continued with Russell Stone, and continued working in cabaret as Brotherhood Of Man, Roger and I left to pursue other musical avenues and opportunities.'

One such project was with songwriters Barry Mason and Tony Macaulay. 'Tony knew exactly what he wanted and, as always, it turned out to be great. A guy named Lou Warburton was arranging the session, and it was during a break in between songs when I was discussing the session with him, he asked me if I could sing solo on a track that I particularly liked, so I did. When I'd finished, Tony asked me if I would like to do the vocals on a song called "Love Grows (Where My Rosemary Goes)". I agreed and recorded it in about two takes and thought no more about it. It was after Tony had taken it to another studio and tarted it up, that I asked him if we could release it. He agreed, providing it was released under the name of a group, but I wasn't keen on that idea, as I didn't want it to be a group record, just me as a solo artist.'

Macaulay was not keen, so Burrows presented him with an ultimatum that he either let him release it as a solo artist or Macaulay would have to remove Burrows vocal unless he was paid an undisclosed sum of money. An agreement was eventually reached, in which Burrows agreed to promote the song for television promotion only.

'I agreed, as long as I was paid and the record sold well within two weeks of its release but, in many ways, that was my downfall as a solo artist. *Top Of The Pops* came in, and said they desperately wanted to have it on the show, but we didn't have a band. But, as promised, I would sing it live with the BBC studio band, conducted by Johnny Pearson. But then, Tony found a band called Greenfield Hammer from Slough to mime the instruments. And they became Edison Lighthouse, but I refused to be involved with it any further. By doing the song on *Top Of The Pops* it created a problem for me with the production team and led to me being banned from the programme.'

At the time, Burrows was engaged in a number of sessions and was most popular among the Tin Pan Alley songwriters, who would call him in every time they wanted one of their songs recorded with a vocal. 'This happened over a period of six to nine months,' says Burrows. 'And all of these songs were sold at the same time, released at the same time and became hits at the same time: so I had a strange situation of being on *Top Of The Pops* with three different bands on the same show. I was changing clothes on the side of the set and going to the next band which really was quite bizarre.

'The producer came to me after the show, and said that the word has come down from above that you are not to be used again. The powers that be thought it was a bit of a con. I told him that *Top Of The Pops* had asked me to appear because the band had a successful record. At the time, the show was not a means to plug records but a form of entertainment for the kids, who wanted to see and hear the bands play a hit single, but you had to be seen to do well. I was banned for two years, which crossed over Edison Lighthouse and me making solo records with Tony Macaulay. We made three or four records together which, because of the ban, didn't get played very much.'

Reg was also becoming involved in session work, as a solo vocalist, piano player or as part of a band. It helped that he had got on well with the management team at AIR studios, especially Ron Richards during the time when he was signed to Gralto. Richards was one of the owners, and also the manager of some of its artists, and it was only a matter of time before he introduced Reg to Tony King, who was working with the Beatles during the Apple years, and also with George Martin at AIR. In fact, it was Richards who had produced 'Love Me Do', the first single for the Beatles, so the connection was simple to understand.

King first met Reg at DJM, before he became Elton John. 'He knew that I worked at AIR with George Martin and Ron Richards, and he also knew that I had worked with the Stones and Andrew Loog Oldham for a couple of years,' says King. Reg was very impressed with King, because he knew the Stones and the Beatles, and, at that time, he too was trying to follow in their footsteps in becoming a successful songwriter. He was also hugely intrigued with the entire music scene.

'I realised that Reg was a record fan like me,' remembers King. 'I used to get a lot of American records at the time. We would get an American record in, and then make a decision as to whether we could cover it with a British artist. "I'm Into Something Good" and "Tell Him" were good examples of how to turn American originals into British hits for Herman's Hermits and Billie Davis.

'Reg had seen my American record collection, and would ask, whenever he saw me, "Have you got any new American records in this week?" I got short with him one day when he asked, and I started acting like a school kid trying to stop him looking over my shoulder to copy my homework. I said something to him that was a bit of a rebuke, and he still laughs about it today. I liked him from the word go, because he was so interested in what was happening, and was an obvious music fan. His wit and his quickness were great and he had a good brain, and could hold a good conversation.'

And if that wasn't enough, King also liked Reg's musical ability. 'I always thought he was a good piano player, but not a great vocalist. I introduced him to people like Ron Richards and Peter Sullivan at AIR and they helped him a great deal. I told them he was a great keyboard player, so when Richards was looking for a pianist for, say, a Barron Knights or a Hollies recording, he would call in Reg to do some sessions, usually the same afternoon. In many cases, it was desperation on Ron's part as it was usually a case of the original pianist wasn't able to make it, or had cancelled out. I remember one time, I had to call Reg to ask if he could do a session at very short notice, and his mother answered. I asked her if Reg could do a session at Abbey Road for £9 an hour for three hours, and she said "I don't know, he's out cleaning the car at the moment, I'll give him a message."

'Not long after, I got a call from Reg saying he would be there, and he came up to the studio and did the session. The next day, I asked Ron how the session went with Reg, and he said "Great, it was really good, Reg gets it and he's fast." I remember he worked on quite a few sessions for the Barron Knights and the Hollies during that time.'

One of the highlights for Reg, during the Barron Knights session at Abbey Road in 1968 (where the group had gone to record their next single 'An Olympic Record'), was when Peter Langford, founder member of the band, introduced him to Paul McCartney, who was in the next studio recording 'Hey Jude'. 'We must have been some of the first to hear the song,' says Langford.

'I remember Reg was simply thrilled about it. We had about twenty minutes recording time left of our three-hour session, when Paul came in and said he had just written a new song and would we like to hear it. We agreed, but told him we were in a hurry, because we hadn't got much studio time left. He played "Hey Jude" and asked us what we thought. Obviously, we all thought it was brilliant. We introduced Reg as our session piano player to Paul, and you could see how thrilled Reg was about meeting one of the Beatles. I don't think he has ever forgotten that moment,' smiles Langford.

One month after 'Hey Jude' had become the twentieth consecutive hit for the Beatles, the new Barron Knights single, with Reg's distinctive piano playing, was released. It ended up spending four weeks in the charts, during which time it reached its highest position of No. 35 in October 1968.

At the same time that both the Beatles and the Barron Knights were enjoying their run in the singles charts, the Hollies were on the look-out for a song they could turn into their next single. Tony Hicks, the band's lead guitarist, was the one who would usually scour the music publishers to find a song, like in the old days of Tin Pan Alley, considering it the best way to find a potential hit. 'He would get in his car or on the tube and go round all the music publishers listening to stuff,' recalls the band's bass player Bernie Calvert, 'then he would take this stuff and give it to Ron Richards to consider.'

One of the songs Hicks found during his trip around Denmark Street was 'He Ain't Heavy, He's My Brother'. When he first heard the song, he was simply blown away with the very basic piano backing and soulful solo vocal. He immediately spotted the potential for a hit and even though there was no rhythm section on the demo, he still recommended the song to Richards. He agreed with Hicks that it should be the next Hollies single, but wanted to retain the piano piece.

Calvert had played a lot of keyboards on the Hollies recordings but, according to Hollies drummer Bobby Elliott, Calvert was not exactly a world class piano player so they needed someone who could really play. Calvert owned up and said, 'Of course, I am not world class, I just do what I can do.' That was when Reg was brought in to play on the session. 'I assume that through AIR, Tony King recommended Reg,' Calvert continues. 'He came in and we created the backing track in a very quick session, which was basically bass, drums and Reg on piano, and that was it, it was that simple.'

When Allan Clarke, the Hollies lead singer, came in to add his vocals to it, he had laryngitis, but that helped with the overall feel of the song, simply because he sounded croaky. 'It really put some emotional edge on it, he was finding it really hard to sing, but he did it.

'When Reg came in as a session player, we all listened to the song,' says Calvert. 'We didn't know whether Ron had given him the demo beforehand, but he certainly knew it when he came in. We all sat around the piano, and I got my bass part organised with Reg, and Bob Elliott, who was in the little drum booth laying down his drum part. It was "Take One" and off it went. We only did a few takes of it, because Reg was such a good keyboard player, we didn't need much practice.'

The backing track was produced in a day and then the rest, vocals and orchestration, came together over a period of weeks. 'It takes some organising because you don't book the orchestra until you have the backing track, and Ron Richards was superb at that as he could spot a winner.' It was released in October 1969, sold six million copies and became a top three single.

When it was released in America, it didn't pick up enough airplay to turn it into a hit, so Ron Richards got on a plane and went over there. 'He went into every radio station and persuaded as many as he could to start playing it, and he did indeed get it onto most airplay lists, which in the end helped it reach No. 5 in the American charts.' Basking in the success of 'He Ain't Heavy', the Hollies found another piano-based song, 'I Can't Tell The Bottom From The Top', which ensured that Reg was invited back to play on the record.

'But this,' says Calvert, 'was a totally different type of session. The introduction had a very classical approach to it, and was heavily influenced by the way Herbie Flowers played bass on the original recording and, as such, I was trying a lot of the stuff that he was alluding to at that time.' On both sessions, and even though the songs were massive chart hits, Reg, like most session musicians, would simply go and do the session, take his fee and then think no more of it.'

Reg was, of course, taking on a lot of piano session work during this period, particularly for AIR. It was not until he did a session for Jerry Lordon, who had written 'Apache' for the Shadows, that he finally got a chance to try to be a session vocalist as well. 'We were recording a demo song for Jerry, when Reg was asked to come in and play just piano on it,' says King. 'Jerry, even though it was his song, couldn't reach the high notes, so Reg said "Let me have a go." Not knowing Reg as a singer, I thought to myself, "I'm not really sure about this," but he sang it and it was really great. I played the demo to the office later on, and they all said how good it was, and asked who did it, and when I told them it was Reg, they were very impressed with how accomplished he sounded.'

What King probably wasn't aware of, was that Reg had already made his singing impact on the movie soundtrack for the Michael Winner directed film called *The Games* about four marathon runners (an Englishman, a Czech, an American and an Australian Aborigine) preparing to run in the Olympic Games. The film follows each one and shows what their motivations are for competing. It starred Michael Crawford, Charles Aznavour, Ryan O'Neil and Stanley Baker.

Francis Lai composed the soundtrack and he remembers that 'Reg Dwight was a chorister at this time and unknown. We had used the choir in the studio, and when we needed a solo singer for this song, Hal Shaper, the lyrics writer, and the choir-master, Barbara Moore suggested we use this young man.

The arranger, Christian Gaubert, took him in a corner to teach him the song, and he learned it very fast, Christian said that he was very talented. When he started singing, all those in the recording cabin who were listening, including Michael Winner, were utterly surprised to hear this amazing, original voice. Hal Shaper later said, that he regretted not to have signed a contract with him then and there.'

But, according to Moore, it purely through circumstance that he got the gig:

I was doing a film session at Olympic Studios, in Barnes London. The morning session had gone quite well, and we had broken for lunch to go and get smashed at the Barnes Common pub just down the road from the studio. I was meticulous as a worker and I was putting all the parts up for the afternoon session before going to meet the rest of the musicians at the pub.

After I had done that, I left the studio and passed the half open door of Studio 2 when I heard a song being played on the piano with a squeaky little voice over the top of it. I pushed open the door and with that he stopped. I said 'No, no please don't stop it's lovely', and I went over to the piano and sat next to him on the piano stool. He had curly hair and specs, and had an earnest expression and we introduced ourselves. He said his name was Reg. I told him what he was playing was lovely and asked him what he was doing at the studio. He said he had come to the studio to audition to get a recording contract with Cliff Adams. He had a briefcase next to him and he said he had about 40 songs in it that he had written with his friend Bernie that he wanted to them to listen to. I told him it was a *fait accompli* and anyone who didn't take him on would be foolish.

After that, I went over to the pub with the rest of the production team and musicians from the film. As we were going back to the studio there was an ambulance coming out, so I rushed in to see what the ambulance doing there, and they said it was Jimmy, the tenor, who had got flu or something and had been rushed to Hammersmith Hospital. My first thought was that I was now short of a singer for the afternoon session, but I suddenly thought of Reg, so I rushed back to the studio, and there was this dejected little figure standing outside the door. I said 'Listen I need a singer, can you come do the afternoon session?'. At first, he said no, and so I told him he could earn £9 doing the session, and I asked him what had happened at his audition. He said that they only played two or three of the songs, looked me in the eye and said they didn't have any commercial possibilities. I said, 'Look come and do this for me', he agreed, so I took him through the parts. He did a great job and we gave him a £9 cheque and we said our goodbyes.

A few weeks later I got a call from an excited Reg. He said he had got a recording contract with Dick James and they loved the song that I heard him playing, which was called 'Border Song'. There and then, he asked me if I would get him a choir and do the arrangement for the song. He said I could get as many singers as I wanted, and so I agreed and booked 30 singers for the session including Roger Cook, Roger Greenaway and Madeline Bell, and then he told me his new name was Elton John. After the success of that, Elton asked me if I would become his musical director for his touring band but because I had small children at the time, I couldn't afford to be away for as long as the job required me to be so I had to turn him down.

By now, King had decided that he should try his hand at producing, alongside Chris Thomas, another emergent producer working at AIR. Thomas was learning his craft as a trainee under the guidance of George Martin but, unlike Thomas, King remarks, 'I wasn't training to be a producer but thought I'd have a bash at it all the same.'

One of the areas which King was keen to explore was to assemble some of the best session musicians and make a 'mad' album of instrumentals. 'So I called on Reg, Bernie Calvert, Roger Pope, Caleb Quaye, Liza Strike and her husband, who had done some vocals on Donovan's 1967 hit, "Mellow Yellow", and two Jamaican percussionist who were introduced to the sessions by Liza when we did some sessions over at Abbey Road. We had such a laugh doing them, and afterwards at the local pub,' smiles King.

The unofficial name of the session group was The Bread And Beer Band and, although the sessions were not supposed to lead to anything significant, they did produce a single. 'The Bread And Beer Band was something else that Reg was involved in during those early years of his career,' confirms Quaye. 'And they were really good sessions too. We had no money, which is why we called ourselves The Bread And Beer Band. And all of it was down to Tony King, who instigated the whole thing. It was really just a one-off recording project that was never intended to be anything more than what it was, a lot of fun and an opportunity to make some money.'

According to King, nothing ever became of the songs or the album, but during the course of the sessions, his relationship with Reg, he says, was certainly cemented. Although Reg was in charge of the sessions, it was Chris Thomas who was overseeing the production, and King was taking care of social matters in keeping everyone happy. 'Caleb was always up for a laugh, and so was Roger. Bernie [Calvert] was subdued but a great bass player, so there was a lot of freewheeling, but the sessions were very inventive musically, and it was a lot of fun; especially the experimental side of things on some of the tracks.'

Calvert had been bought into the sessions because of his reputation as Hollies bassist and an all-round session musician for Ron Richards and AIR. Indeed, it was King who approached Richards with the idea of pinching Calvert for the Bread And Beer Band recordings, providing it didn't interrupt any scheduled sessions with the Hollies. 'At the time,' explains Calvert, 'I was considered a hot session musician, and I had played with other artists such as Simon Dupree And The Big Sound, and on many other sessions done at AIR.'

Calvert had joined the Hollies in 1966, as a stand in for Eric Haydock during a concert tour of Scandinavia that May. 'It lasted three weeks with two shows a night, six nights a week so it was an amazing baptism of fire,' he says. After the tour, Calvert went back to his day job working in a factory in his home town of Burnley. One month after, it seemed Haydock wouldn't be returning to the Hollies at all, so Calvert got another call, four weeks after he had gone back to work, asking him if he wanted to join the band permanently. He, of course, jumped at the chance to leave the factory again and join the Hollies, and, let's be honest, who wouldn't?

Despite his success with the Hollies, Calvert still wanted to be part of the Bread And Beer sessions, simply because he was keen to be involved in everything that was going on in the music business and to play with other musicians. 'We clicked very quickly,' confirms Calvert. King brought in two percussionists, who had already played with the Hollies on 'Carrie Anne' in 1967, so Calvert was already familiar with them.

'They were super cool Jamaicans, who on one of the songs, "Mellow Yellow", were trying to get a reggae feel going, and of course, these guys were experts in that style of music, but I didn't play reggae. They were telling me what to do, which I was a bit edgy about, and didn't like it very much, but I think we made a compromise in the end, and I met them halfway. I just couldn't feel it the way they did, I just couldn't pick up on what they were trying to do. That was the only tense moment I can remember in the sessions, but the rest went swimmingly. Roger Pope was, of course, superb and Caleb Quaye, already regarded something of a guitar legend, was a mean player, just pure dynamite,' remembers Calvert fondly.

With no rehearsals, or meetings, they went straight into Abbey Road and recorded it. 'I had a flat in London at the time, and had a girlfriend who had moved in with her sister, it was a basement flat in Kensington, and I was now O.K. about being located in the centre of London, and not moving back up North when the Hollies were not working. I had the time to do it, so I just treated it like I did any sessions I had done with the Hollies.' They started the session with 'Last Night' a twelve bar blues song and picked up on the vibe that started to develop. As the musicians all seemed to gel with one another, the album seemed to come together pretty quickly and take on a life of its own.

'We were probably averaging two or three tracks during the afternoon and evening sessions,' says Calvert. 'And when we analyse what was currently laid down, it was only backing tracks and not the finished product. You can hardly hear the melody on "If I Were A Carpenter", for instance, but Reg just tinkled away at the piano in the background, it was amazing. And on "Mellow Yellow", well, if it wasn't for the backing vocals, then you wouldn't have recognised it at all, so in many ways, I was surprised it all sounded so good when it was completed.'

It was during the sessions that Calvert says he was very self conscious, because he hadn't worked with such amazing musicians before, and he felt very exposed. 'When you sit down and there is a microphone on your amplifier, and they can cut everything out in the control room, as they are behind three quarter inch glass, you don't know what they are saying, so I was thinking, I hope this is O.K., but for the most part, yes, I think it was.'

King remembers that although it didn't turn out to be an earth-shatteringly good set of songs, he still enjoys listening to the album today, which was never officially released 'I like the version of "The Letter" and "Mellow Yellow" with Liza Strike's vocals, she had a wonderful voice. And there were a lot of laughs during the making of it, but it was also quite serious, because everyone enjoyed the fact that it was experimental. We were taking well known songs and doing them in a completely different style. "Mellow Yellow" for instance was turned into an up-tempo rock song, with some good R&B thrown in for good measure.'

King was no stranger to Abbey Road either, as he had attended some of the sessions that the Beatles were doing for *Sergeant Pepper* and the *White Album* between 1966 and 1968. 'The Beatles would come in and decorate the studio with lights and have incense burning and bits of fabric everywhere to break up the cold studio.' On the grounds that if it was good enough for the Beatles it was good enough for the Bread And Beer Band, King set out to recreate the same vibe. 'It was what everyone was doing at the time, even in their homes, with bits of fabric over lampshades, and sofas, anything to make something look less conventional or not conventional at all. So it was my idea to put coloured lights and things in the studio to create a better atmosphere. The studio where the sessions were held was pretty stark and lacked any kind of bright atmosphere.'

Bernie Calvert agrees: 'I can remember John Lennon having a bed in Studio 2 to get his head down if he felt he needed a rest.' It was at a time when the studios were beginning to appreciate the importance of creating an ambience for musicians to record in, to create a mood that represented the style of record that was being made. 'You have all these lights in the studio that could be adjusted and if you wanted to create something, you needed the right mood, and the other studios, such as the Manor, at the time were getting into the mood thing with coloured lights.'

It probably got started by the stories that had been circulating since 1960, that claimed Elvis Presley turned out all the lights in RCA's Nashville Studio B when he recorded 'Are You Lonesome Tonight?' And there were also rumours doing the rounds that Abbey Road was trying to capture a mood in the same sort of way, not only like Presley, but also like the other studios. 'It was all a bit Heath Robinson if you like,' laughs King. 'Even the engineers started trying it out in the control room, but it didn't really work, because they couldn't see what they were doing.'

The Bread And Beer Band sessions lasted three weeks and although a number of tracks were completed, the album wasn't. There was, however, a single that came out of the sessions. 'The Dick Barton Theme (Devil's Galop [sic])' was released in February 1969, with 'Breakdown Blues', an instrumental track on the flipside, but it only achieved minor success, and completely missed the charts altogether.

'"Breakdown Blues" came about because the band were getting ready to do the final track, when the red light went off in the studio, and King's voice came over the intercom to say they had a technical problem with one of the machines,' explains Calvert. 'We just carried on playing this twelve bar blues thing, and the red light didn't come back on, so we finished playing the jam session. And afterwards, Tony's voice came over the intercom shouting, quite excitedly, "Come on in boys and have a listen." We went into the control room, and Tony told us that the machine had been repaired and he'd been recording the jam session; we were impressed with the song and called it "Breakdown Blues" for the obvious reason.'

'The Dick Barton Theme', on the other hand, was recorded in isolation from the rest of the album because, unlike the rest of the tracks recorded for the ill-fated album, it took a lot more rehearsal and recording. 'I was given the original song, recorded from the radio and told it was going to be the Bread And Beer Band single,' continues Calvert. 'I brought it back up North on a cassette tape, and when I met up with Reg in the studio, he played it as he had heard it on the record, but it was in need of some arranging and mixing.'

There was a lot of work put into it to get to a finished master, even though it was probably recorded and released more as a novelty record to see if it was worth releasing the album. Instrumentals were not very popular at the time, and it was difficult to market the single and, of course, Reg wasn't famous enough to give it some weight, even though he had already started working with Bernie Taupin and had some demos under his belt with Quaye at DJM.

'Lady Samantha' had already been released, but had failed to register in the charts, so Reg was not really earning a crust, and was hoping that alongside everyone else involved with the sessions, he could make a success of the Bread And Beer Band project.

Despite the album never seeing the light of day, and the single not achieving quite the success that Reg and the others had hoped for, Reg returned to take on other session work in the aftermath of the Bread And Beer Band project, only to discover he was more in demand than before. In between his song writing exploits with Bernie and Quaye, he also discovered that he had two new mentors on his side. Roger Cook and Roger Greenaway started to book him on a regular basis as a session pianist and backing vocalist alongside Brian Keith, Greenaway and Tony Burrows. They ended up playing on a number of budget albums that featured cover versions of current hits for a number of different record labels that included Deacon, Avenue and Pickwick.

In a very short space of time, Reg had joined a small group of session musicians who became an elite club, producing faithful covers, often in one take, with a maximum of three days notice of what they would be recording next. The most popular was Pickwick's *Top Of The Pops* series that derived its title from the then un-trademarked BBC television show, with no direct connection to the pop show, but still enjoyed considerable success and buoyant sales.

They were even accepted into the main British album charts for a few months towards the end of 1971, during which time four *Top Of The Pops* albums charted, and two of them made No.1. But at the start of the following year, they were disqualified since their budget selling price of one pound or less was perceived as giving them an unfair advantage over the full price albums by established recording artists and their record labels. The albums continued to be released at regular intervals throughout the 1970s.

Men of a certain age reading this passage will, no doubt, retreat into a happy reverie when thinking about the cover art, which always featured scantily-clad females decked out in skimpy mini-skirts, hot pants or bikinis. This winning formula remained largely unchanged throughout.

These albums may not have been high art and the covers certainly weren't politically correct (but then neither were the 1960s) but they provided Reg and his colleagues with plenty of session work. For Reg, of course, it was ideal, not only from the earning potential but also for the opportunity to hone his vocal skills as well, as the singer needed to be something of an impressionist. Funnily enough, he found himself back inside Regent Sound Studios in Denmark Street recording cover versions of such hits as 'I Can't Tell the Bottom From The Top' for Embassy Records, another of the budget album labels.

Reg also covered some songs written by his mentors Cook and Greenaway, the most notable being 'My Baby Loves Lovin'' and 'Good Morning Freedom'. 'It was like a factory, but more fun. You went in and did your thing, got paid and then moved on to the next session,' says Greenaway. 'The covers were done at several studios including Pye Records at Cumberland Place, where Reg made an album of piano covers for John Bridges, one of the owners of AIR Studios, who sold it back to Dick James for double the session fees, as Dick didn't want to risk it being released, because Elton John was now looking like being a success.'

Like Reg, Tony Burrows also did a fair amount of budget albums as well. 'I was doing a lot of these sessions during the period from 1969 to 1971 and so was Reg because he could play and read music, and also had a really good voice,' recalls Burrows. 'I remember we were doing a big Decca session with six male and six female singers and Reg had a "bag of laughs" in his pocket. We are doing a live recording, and occasionally people would go to him and hit his pocket, and for about thirty seconds, this hysterical laughing started, and recording had to be stopped with Reg apologising profusely. It ended up with everyone in hysterics and the session disintegrated.

'The albums were put together quickly, with six titles produced on a session with two sessions in all. The sessions were from 10a.m. to 1p.m. with an hour break and it was likely that we had other sessions to do across the road in Tin Pan Alley during the break. If not, we would all go for a drink in Soho, and then back to the studio from 2p.m. till 5p.m., followed by a two hour break for either more sessions or more drinks, and then back in the studio from 7p.m. till 10p.m. We sang everything live, having been given the songs to learn first, before we got to the studio. In most cases because the songs had been hits, we knew them anyway, but we all read music and we just got on and did it, normally in a rush,' Burrows recollects.

Burrows, as mentioned earlier, had been having hits in the charts under different names for some time, and many had been featured tracks on the budget albums he was now recording with Reg, such as 'My Baby Loves Lovin' and 'United We Stand'. 'I couldn't sing on them, obviously, so they asked Reg to do them, and I remember he was asked to do "United We Stand" with Kay Garner as it was a duet. I wasn't actually asked to do it, as the producer would have known I was under contract for the hit recording, but I believe I did parts of it though.'

Indeed, Burrows regularly sang with Reg in the studios and he remembered the experience was a good laugh. 'We got the job done but we enjoyed it at the same time. We were singing for nine hours a day on these albums, and then we would get asked to do television and radio jingles on top of the record sessions, and this would mean, more often than not, we would be on the go for seven days a week. We were too busy earning money to stop and earn a fortune.'

Not that it worried Reg. On top of all his session work, he had also plunged himself into a busy schedule at DJM writing and recording his own compositions. 'I remember during the sessions, Reg would always want to play his own songs and he would ask us to listen to them and get our opinion. He wanted to play all the time. He was earning a lot of money and needed to, because he hadn't had any success with his own writing for DJM,' recalls Burrows.

Reg, however, didn't forget Burrows when his career started to take off as Elton John. When it came to using session singers on his first few successful albums, Burrows, along with the other Brotherhood Of Man singers, were called on to help. 'I remember I did *Madman Across The Water* for him at Trident,' confirms Burrows. 'We worked through the night starting at midnight. He used to work hard on his albums and take a lot of time, unlike what we used to do on the budget albums. He had a lot of success by then, and although we were booked to work we wouldn't do anything for two or three hours. He was an extremely talented man.'

When Reg was not writing or recording his own compositions, or working on the budget albums, he would fill his time working as a session musician for DJM. One of the most memorable in August 1969 was for Scottish band, My Dear Watson. That was when the band's manager, Albert Bonici, arranged a last ditch attempt for some kind of success by organising a recording session at DJM for the following year. Although John Stewart, the lead vocalist, guitarist and songwriter for the band had recently left for domestic reasons, he was still actively involved with writing material for recording and performing. For the session at DJM, he had composed twelve songs from which, it was hoped, a potential hit single would emerge. If so, then an album would be released.

Robin Geoffrey Cable was the main sound engineer at the time, and the tape machine operator and general assistant was Kaplan Kaye. The band and engineers worked in the studio for ten days until 4 February 1970, creating the single and an ill-fated unreleased album. At the time, Reg had recorded and released the 'Lady Samantha' single under the name of Elton John, and was picking up a fair amount of airplay on Radio 1. 'We thought it was good,' says Watson's bass player Bill Cameron. 'We had played the Cavern Club in Liverpool in January 1966, and just before we played, Bluesology had done their set. They were just another band on the bill alongside many other bands that were touring and playing the clubs at the time.'

'Basically', continues Cameron, 'My Dear Watson was a guitar, bass and drum outfit, and during the first week of recording, someone at DJM asked whether we would like to use a keyboard player. We were not told who the keyboard player was, so I asked "Is he any good?" and was told 'We believe he is pretty good, yes." And he was. We felt our songs needed some colour added, so we agreed to use the unknown piano player to see how it worked out; we were the kind of band to try anything once. So, in came this small guy, who had short hair and was clean shaven, who was introduced to us as Elton. The guitarist was already in the studio doing some overdubs, and that's when Elton asked me, what chords was he playing?'

Once Cameron and Elton had planted themselves on the sofa at the back of the control room, Elton took out his notebook to note down all the chords that were being used in the song. Soon after that, Cameron remembers, 'We set up the microphones and a grand piano, and played Elton the backing tracks that had been recorded earlier. He listened intently, and then told us to give him five minutes to go over it, and five minutes after that he was telling the band that he was ready to do the take. We switched on the mics and started the backing tracks and Elton started playing the piano to our backing tracks. The sound that came from the piano was stunning, we all looked at each and said "God, this boy is good!"

'For the next three days we recorded with Elton in the same way for each song. We put down the backing tracks, he noted the chords in his notebook, disappeared for five minutes and then he played over the backing tracks. He played grand piano, organ and electric piano. When he finished, he would come in to see us on a regular basis to see how it was going, he would mess about on the piano and do some jamming sessions with us. And, on one occasion, Bernie Taupin came in and sat on the sofa just to hear and see what we were doing.'

After the sessions, the band went back to Scotland where John Stewart had written a song that was a strong candidate for the successful single that they were desperately looking for. The title was 'Have You Seen Your Saviour?', and the eventual B side was 'White Line Road'. They went back down to DJM to record the song, and Elton was, once again on hand to play the piano exactly as before.

The following month, on 12 March 1970, My Dear Watson went into Trident Studios to record the vocals for the single and the B side. 'Elton came with us, and we all agreed that we would do a vocal harmony for the B side which included Elton. His vocals were overwhelming, it made us realise how bad we were at singing. He sang with such power. He was about 6' away from the microphones and we were about 6" away and his voice still dominating.'

When the single was finally released on DJM, it didn't get any airplay so, quite naturally, nothing happened to make it work as even a minor success and the album was shelved, and the tapes returned to the vaults, where they still remain to this day. Although the single was played once on the radio, and the band played it live on Radio 1 on 13 June 1970 in Glasgow, it was not enough to get anyone excited, least of all the band. Soon after the debacle of the flopped single and abandoned album they decided to call it a day.

In the same year as the My Dear Watson sessions, Lionel Conway asked Reg if he would be available to do some session work for him. Although Conway had recently left DJM to join Chris Blackwell at Island Publishing, and was on the lookout for new talent to sign, during his last year with DJM he became fully aware of Reg's musical exploits and thought what a great idea it would be if he could arrange some BBC radio shows for him to showcase his talent.

He also persuaded Dick James to persevere with Reg, even though nothing seemed to be happening for his future success at that time. Conway thought the BBC sessions would help as would something else he had in the works. 'In 1970, while I was with Island Records, I signed Roger Hodgson to an exclusive song writing contract and, to promote his songs, I arranged for him to go into the studio to produce some masters.' recalls Conway. 'He came to me as a writer, and I liked his writing but I knew I would never get covers for his songs but I thought he was terrific. So, I called on Reg and his band to do some recordings for me. Although Roger came up with some names for a band, I didn't like many of them, apart from Argosy, which is the one I ended up going with.'

Hodgson was a fresh-faced school leaver of 19, who had never been in a recording studio before. 'And my first time in a studio,' he says, 'was a real eye opener and a thrilling experience.' He was another who wrote all his own material, and a song that he had composed called 'Mr Boyd', later released as a single with 'Imagine' on the B side was a fine example of his work. He was down to play the piano on the recording, but when Reg came in, there was no need for Roger to worry. 'I wrote "Mr Boyd" on piano, but Reg played the piano in the studio, and I didn't play anything, I just sang.'

The session to make the record was literally completed in two days. The first day was taken up with rehearsals and recording with the band, and the second, rehearsals and recording with an orchestra. When the recordings were completed, Conway went to Dick James and placed the master with him. At one time, there were plans for Argosy to do some more work together but it never materialised. Instead the single. which was put out by DJM in Britain and Congress in America, became a 'Hit Pick' on Radio Luxembourg, but even that was not enough to turn it into a chart hit.

Soon after the single had been released in 1969, and the planned follow-up single for Argosy had been abandoned, another strange turn of events would change Hodgson's future for ever. He met keyboardist Rick Davies at an audition, as a result of an advert Davies had placed in the *Melody Maker*, and, as soon as they met, they hit it off. The idea of the audition was to start a band, and so, with Roger in tow and two other musicians, guitarist Richard Palmer and percussionist Keith Baker, he formed Daddy. The advert had been placed because Davies had been given an opportunity to form his own band by a Dutch millionaire named Stanley 'Sam' August Miesegaes, who had just dumped another band he had been financially supporting, but in whom he had lost interest.

'The timing was perfect,' says Lionel Conway. 'I got a call from Miesegaes, who wanted to buy Roger's contract, and I couldn't keep him as Miesegaes wanted all the rights to publishing and recording, and, as Roger was happy to sign, I couldn't really keep him, so I let him go.' That new band became Supertramp, who went on to become one of the first groups to be signed to the British arm of American recording giants A&M Records.

|| |||

Another to have a radically different background that also played a role in Reg's development was Joe Boyd, the accomplished folk and rock producer who was best known for introducing the electric side of Bob Dylan to an unsuspecting audience at the 1965 Newport Folk Festival. He has also been credited for contributing to the successes of Lovin' Spoonful, Fairport Convention and the Incredible String Band. And at the time of meeting Reg, he had just discovered a young singer called Nick Drake, who he wanted to use to produce a publishing demo for his own publishing company Warlock Music.

'The idea was to do some straightforward versions of our most coverable songs so we could push them into the hands of other producers,' says Boyd. 'I invited some session musicians to take part in the project and amongst them was Reg Dwight, who had been recommended to me by DJM. The sessions were done at Sound Techniques in London during the summer of 1970.'

The idea of choosing Sound Techniques was a good call. It was one of the earliest independent sound recording studios to be established (during the winter of 1964 by Geoff Frost and John Wood) and had been converted from an old cow shed in Old Church Street in Chelsea 'The songs were all recorded in the old fashioned way of everyone playing in the same room, with Reg singing from his piano bench, and Linda Thompson singing from a sound booth'.

The album, however, was never intended for general release, but a number of copies – probably about a hundred – were pressed to be handed out to other producers for demonstration purposes. Years later, when Reg had become Elton John, he was asked about the sessions. As far as he could remember, it was one of those peculiar projects where he had to try to make Nick Drake songs sound more commercial. 'An impossible task, really. I needed the money, so I did it.'

It was during the Drake sessions that Reg would meet arranger Derek 'Del' Newman for the first time, but who would be called upon, some years later, to help arrange *Goodbye Yellow Brick Road.* For the time being though, for the Drake album, 'Joe Boyd, who I had not met before, called because he heard that I was interested in arranging,' remembers Newman. 'I wrote all the stuff. There were eleven songs in all, and the original plan was for Reg to play and sing seven and Linda was going to do four.' Newman had not met Reg before, but already knew Linda Thompson – the then wife of Richard Thompson.

'We all met in the studio, which had a little glass control room in the corner where all the equipment was located, and the rest of the place was the studio,' says Newman. 'They were all well-known session musicians but I didn't know any of them, apart from Linda. I was into films at the time and not up on who was who in the music business.' It was while Newman was handing out sheet music, he met with the drummer and handed him the score that he had painstakingly prepared. 'He asked me what I was giving him and when I told him that it was his music, he said he didn't read music so I took it back.'

Afterwards, continues Newman, 'Joe asked me whether I knew who the drummer was, but I didn't, and then he told me that it was Jim Capaldi, the drummer for Traffic. I was none the wiser but, yes, he was an excellent drummer even without the dots.' The sessions started at 5p.m. and wrapped up by 11p.m. It also helped that the backing vocalists had been given their words before coming into the studio and had learned all their parts. 'We put a guide vocal down, and the backing track by the band, and then Reg and Linda just spent the last hour singing their songs in more perfect pitch and harmony. Joe was a gentleman all the way through and, at the end, he told us all it was a job well done. When he had the acetate made later, he kindly gave me one to keep.'

To pursue his goal of leaving the wilderness of session playing and moving into the green fields of a more stable musical environment, Reg would try any means to get

*Left:* Home for a young Reg but where some classic Elton John songs were written - Frome Court. © Keith Hayward

*Below:* The Prefab huts at Pinner Grammar School where Elton studied. © Keith Hayward

*Bottom:* The inspiration for 'Saturday Night's Alright (For Fighting)'? © Keith Hayward

*Top:* Reg proudly playing his Vox Continental, known as the 'Connie'. © Len Crawley

*Above:* Helen Piena's piano where a young Reg Dwight practised. © Keith Hayward

*Left:* Reg's friends and colleagues in the Kestrels, supporting the Beatles. © Keith Hayward

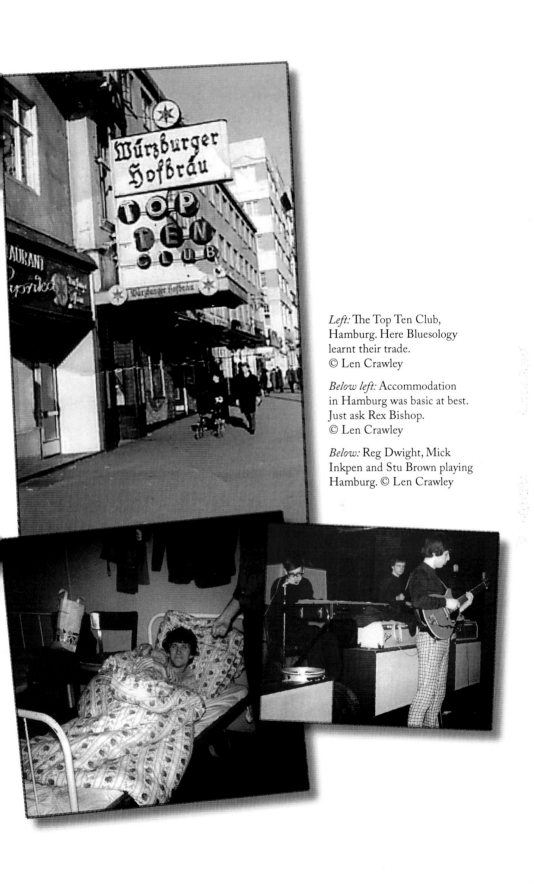

*Left:* The Top Ten Club, Hamburg. Here Bluesology learnt their trade.
© Len Crawley

*Below left:* Accommodation in Hamburg was basic at best. Just ask Rex Bishop.
© Len Crawley

*Below:* Reg Dwight, Mick Inkpen and Stu Brown playing Hamburg. © Len Crawley

*Opposite:* Round glasses were popular circa 1968 as Bernie and Elton prove. © David Larkham

*Above:* Elton's first single 'I've Been Loving You'. © Keith Hayward

*Top:* The entrance to the Furlong Road flat share where Elton, Bernie and Linda Woodrow lived. © Keith Hayward

*Above:* Hookfoot fooling around in 1970. © Roger Pope

*Left:* Elton with Simon Dupree drummer Tony Ransley and their roadies, Brian and Fred West, 1967. © Peter O'Flaherty

*Top:* The Krumlin festival may not be Woodstock size, but it mattered to Elton.
© John Wharton

*Above:* Programme and ticket for the Krumlin Festival 1970. £2-10 admission for the weekend!
© Keith Hayward

*Left:* The launch of a career - Advertisement in the LA Free Press.
© Keith Hayward

*Below:* After the gigs here, things could never be the same again.
© Keith Hayward

a foothold in the business. If his career as a solo artist was not going to happen, then he was going to try and make it by working in a band. And that is when he decided to jump at the opportunity of working with Simon Dupree And The Big Sound, and joined them on the road for a tour of Scotland.

'It was 1967, and Eric Hine, our keyboard player and good friend of the leader of the band Derek Shulman, had fallen ill with glandular fever and was unable to play for several weeks,' recalls Dupree's bass guitarist Pete O'Flaherty. 'The illness happened suddenly and the band had contractual commitments to keep, so the promoter, Arthur Howes, contacted another agency that had a database of session musicians. They asked Reg if he wanted to work with us and he agreed for twenty-five pounds a week. They didn't have time to audition anyone to replace Hine, so the first time we met Reg was in the small recording studio in London where we were running through some rehearsals. We didn't know Reg before the tour and he was sent to us through an agency. We had a rehearsal for a few hours with him, during which we went through our set list for the up and coming tour, he made some notes, and that was it. He knew our whole programme. The following day we collected him from Frome Court and headed off to Scotland to start the tour,' recalls the bassist.

According to O'Flaherty, Reg was very easy to rub along with. 'We all travelled to Scotland in a large Jaguar MK9, with Reg taking turns with the driving duties. His driving was a little less than perfect, especially when he saw his favourite car, the Reliant Regal, a three wheeled fibreglass vehicle that was slow to say the least. He would love to speed up behind one, and then with a screech of the wheels would overtake it as quickly as possible nearly knocking the poor car and occupants off the road.'

On reaching Edinburgh, their first stop on the tour, the boys found their way to the appointed guest house, which turned out to be one Reg absolutely adored. Once settled, he turned his attention to the out of tune piano. 'He played for us what were to become the songs from his first two albums, including "Your Song" as well as songs from *Empty Sky*. We thought they were very good and so very different for their time,' says O'Flaherty.

In true Tin Pan Alley fashion, Reg asked the boys, whether they wanted to record any of the songs but they didn't. Derek and Phil Shulman turned down the offer, saying they had enough material to be going on with. It was during the tour that Reg announced to the rest of the band that he intended to change his name. 'We laughed when he said he was thinking about using the stage name of Elton John. It didn't really seem to be a very fitting name for a rock star.'

It was also during the tour of Scotland that the band stayed in a small hotel in Lamlash, near Brodick. It was here during the day that they would play knock-about tennis and kick a football on the run-down tennis court. On other occasions, they would hire a rowing boat and go hand fishing with a few lines that caught them some fish. 'We took these fish back to the hotel and asked if they could be cooked for our dinner,' remembers O'Flaherty. 'And when it was time for Reg to leave the band at the end of the tour, when Eric Hine had returned, he asked the band's manager if he could stay on. We had all become good friends with Reg, so we would have preferred it if he had stayed, but our manager said we had to take Eric back.'

Hine was a school mate of Derek Shulman at Portsmouth Grammar School, and Derek felt it would be wrong to replace him with Reg. In the end though, Reg and Bernie did write 'I'm Going Home' for the band, which was never released (though is available on the 2008 deluxe edition of the *Elton John* album). Reg also played on a few other tracks that included 'Laughing Boy From Nowhere' and 'Give It All Back' which can be heard on the Simon Dupree anthology *Part Of My Past*.

When Simon Dupree And The Big Sound finally broke up in 1969, Reg kept in touch with the Shulman brothers, particularly Ray, who regularly went to visit Reg and Bernie at Frome Court and in the studio when they were recording the *Elton John* album. It was clear, despite the amount of work Reg was doing in the studio with his peers, that he was still feeling somewhat insecure about his own future.

So much so, in fact, that he apparently made overtures to Shulman about joining his new band Gentle Giant, as the keyboard player. But Shulman politely declined the offer as Reg's style of playing didn't really suit what the new band was going to do.

It was also during this period that King Crimson were short of a vocalist when Greg Lake decided to leave to form supergroup Emerson, Lake and Palmer. The Crimson King himself, guitarist Robert Fripp, had to find a suitable replacement for Lake, so Reg was booked to do the vocals for Crimson's second album *In The Wake Of Poseidon*, in March 1970. Fripp recalls: 'King Crimson's management company, EG, gave me a copy of the first Elton John album, *Empty Sky*. I listened to it, and although it was a respectable effort, Reg was clearly not the voice for King Crimson, and so I cancelled the session.' As with Gentle Giant, Reg had another narrow escape from being incarcerated in a prog rock band!

Reg was also to return to his old haunt and former boss Tony Hiller at Mills Music , when he was asked to work as a session musician for child star Tina Charles. He recorded an obscure but pleasant duet, given the relative inexperience of the two budding stars, called 'Good to Be Alive' in 1969. Tina remembers Reg showing off his crocodile shoes when he went into the studio to record with her.

At the turn of the decade, Reg was still working to find his way in the difficult world of Tin Pan Alley and the music business. The ups and downs almost persuaded Reg to call it a day and give up on his dream to be a singer-songwriter, despite the discussions that were going on for him to join the newly-formed Jeff Beck Band. 'He came into the office and said he wanted to join the Jeff Beck Group,' recalls Sue Ayton. 'Dick always made time for Reg whenever he wanted to discuss anything. It seemed as if there was a great deal of mutual respect. In one such meeting, they discussed him joining Jeff Beck and, from what I recall, Reg was quite animated about why he wanted to join the band, but Dick was equally animated about why he should stay and persevere with his own songwriting and recording career. In the end Dick's view prevailed, and Elton decided to stay put.'

# 16

# FINALLY ON OUR WAY

In May 1968, Dick James struck a deal with Bell Records label boss Larry Uttal while the latter was on a promotional visit to London. The idea was to release songs published by Northern Songs, as well as distributing DJM material in the States. The first song Uttal took on was 'Step Inside Love', which had been recorded by Cilla Black and released in Britain on Parlophone. Uttal was also in London to launch the British arm of Bell Records and to work more closely with EMI, who had been releasing all of the Bell products in Britain up to this time. It was because of the new distribution deal with Bell that Dick James found an opportunity to release Elton's 'Lady Samantha' to the American record buying public, not that it made much of an impact; well, no more than it had in Britain.

By the time 'Lady Samantha' had been distributed to the American record stores, Elton John was starting to take on a whole new personality of his own. As far as Reg was concerned, it was no longer just a project – it was now much more than that. It was to become everything in Reg's life. After the poor sales of *Empty Sky*, and having been heavily influenced by Steve Brown, his new found mentor, colleague and friend, Reg decided that changes were needed. The *Elton John* album would not only introduce those changes, but also morph Reg into Elton permanently.

With the album already in progress, Reg's idea was to make it significantly different to his first album. Even though the demo songs had already been produced by Reg and Hookfoot, not even Reg was sure if they were what he wanted. It was something that had already been mentioned in his conversations with Danny Hutton: 'Reg said that he wanted it to be a heavy rock album, but after meeting Paul Buckmaster and Gus Dudgeon, and handing them both the musical control of the album's production on a plate, it was now pretty obvious that it was about to become a much more orchestrated affair.'

The pre-production planning of the new album took place, in part, on Reg's bedroom floor at Frome Court, and was to prove crucial to the final recording and production. 'My girlfriend and I had arranged to visit Frome Court one evening,' recalls Mick Inkpen. 'Reg told me that, because time was short, some of the planning of the new album was still under way, and would we mind if he and some people who were working on the new disc completed what they were doing? We said we didn't mind. We got to meet Gus Dudgeon and Paul Buckmaster, and I seem to remember that Gus and Paul were spread on Reg's bedroom floor with notes strewn about everywhere. They had virtually finished things off by the time we arrived.'

Although the songs had been written and demoed by Hookfoot, it was now time to consider the instrumentation, arrangements and the musicians who would play on the final product. As it was no longer to be a rock album, it was decided to move away from Hookfoot, even though everyone knew they had produced stalwart work in the past. Buckmaster himself was a cellist and, being as accomplished as he was, it was no surprise that he would play on the album sessions, as well as constructing the orchestra and writing the music charts.

With time being of the essence, Dudgeon and Buckmaster spent hours discussing the song sections and construction of the music charts for the orchestra and band. It was a tall order to combine an orchestra with a rock'n'roll rhythm section, without losing the best of both worlds, and then to add the piano on top to make Elton sound his best. Dudgeon's idea was to try and persuade Buckmaster to write more cello parts for the album. Buckmaster resisted at first but in the end he did play the cello on some of the songs. 'He played beautiful solo cello on "The Greatest Discovery" and on "Take Me To The Pilot",' recalls Stuart Epps. 'Instead of the standard rock track that was demoed by Hookfoot, and produced by Brown at Olympic, it now featured some ten cellos coming in on the bridge and chorus; very unusual and very dynamic.'

Certainly Buckmaster was not the type of musician to be frightened to try new things and with the musical talents of his girlfriend, Diana Lewis, they introduced the sound of the Moog synthesiser, which was a relatively new instrument at the time. 'It was a big modular analogue Moog with four large boxes and a small keyboard with a ribbon on it where you could do the slides,' Buckmaster explains. 'We had to hire it in from AIR studios along with the guy who could set it up. Diana played an improvised part on "First Episode At Hienton", which is a very gentle, wistful, love song into which she added a beautiful crescendo which sounded very much like a soprano. She did that when I was out of the studio having a lunch break. She stayed behind and created it with the engineer and the operator, who set it up. I came back and listened to it and it was wonderful. She also played on my written part for the bridge of "The Cage". This was originally going to be a brass piece, having been demoed as a piano piece by Elton and Hookfoot, but I changed my mind and chose the synthesiser. The idea came about having heard the brass on "The Magical Mystery Tour" by the Beatles.'

The arrangements for the *Elton John* album were written at Buckmaster's home, which was a small apartment, no more than a single room. 'I didn't have a piano or any keyboard. I just had a tape recorder, headphones and my score sheets, and everything was written head to paper,' says Buckmaster looking back on it today. 'I was responsible for the rhythm section as well as the orchestra.' Indeed, the rhythm section was recorded mainly live, and the strings were recorded separately, although on one or two songs, they were recorded live.

'For "Take Me To The Pilot", the cellos were out in the studio, and the piano was played live. 'We had twelve cellos on "Take Me". What I wanted to create was a muscular, masculine, trucking, driving, funky machine. The piano lid was closed because the studio was anechoic [non-echoing]. If you shut the doors of the studio, there was total sound absorption and everything was created by the plate and the chamber, there were no reverbs, it was all done by the chamber, the plate and tape delay. The piano was covered by heavy duty leather, lined with heavy felt that took two people to pick up, so the piano was very isolated but Elton could hear it in his headphones as could we all. The rhythm section musicians took their place in a booth underneath the control room and, they too, were isolated. The only thing that was overdubbed was the congas and the background vocals, all of the rest was played live, and 'Sixty Years On' was recorded entirely live including the vocals.'

Because the musical parts had been written by Buckmaster, who could read music, the musicians had to read music too, even the drum parts were written out, including the drum fills, so there was no opportunity for the band to busk it. There was one rehearsal or possibly two to iron out any mistakes in the charts or to take account of any suggestions from Dudgeon, and then it was straight into the recording. The team only had a limited time and budget to record the album – and time was money. This was no place for the faint-hearted.

Roger Pope, who was Elton's regular drummer at the time, could play the drums by ear, but it was likely to take longer to create the sound Buckmaster wanted alongside the rest of the musicians so, with the exception of Caleb Quaye, Hookfoot was replaced by session musicians who could read charts. Robin Geoffrey Cable was chosen as the engineer alongside Dudgeon, who, himself, was a consummate engineer too. 'Geoffrey knew exactly how to saturate the tape, the needles were just touching the red all the time; we had the best sound created by a very competent team even though, at the time, we were only 23 years of age.'

The album was recorded over twelve consecutive days, with two songs being completed at every three hour session. 'There was no metronome in the studio to keep the beat, it was all played by talented musicians who knew how to play in time,' says Buckmaster proudly. 'Each song was regarded as an entity in itself. We programmed each song and agreed how it would sound and which instruments would come in at different times, the arrangement was designed to fit the song.'

Buckmaster arrived at the studio with all the parts for the musicians for each song so they were all ready to go as soon as he handed the charts out. It wasn't all scripted work though, as was demonstrated with the improvisations from Diana Lewis, so the musicians had some freedom to express themselves within the confines of the charts.

However, an unscripted and impromptu session did get slipped into the final mix, unbeknown to Buckmaster.

'The cellos at the start of "Sixty Years On" were a Gus afterthought and weren't programmed as part of the arrangement. The song started with the harp in the original arrangement, but the demo started with the piano. During the recording of the piece, the 8-track machine we were using broke down and had to have technical attention, so there was some down time. As a bit of fun, and after a break, we all agreed to play a note and with me cueing each cellist in at a different time, and them using a slow vibrato smearing around the note. By this time they had repaired the machine, and Gus was hearing what we were doing and told the engineer to record it,' recalls Buckmaster. Dudgeon added the impromptu result as the introduction to the song after the mastering without telling Buckmaster, who only heard it after the song was finished.

Skaila Kanga, who Reg knew from their Royal Academy of Music days, was hired to play lead harp on two tracks, as well as part of Buckmaster's orchestral arrangements on others. Most notably it included the tracks 'Sixty Years On' and 'I Need You To Turn To' with Reg on harpsichord and Kanga on harp, combining to make a very unique sound for the time.

Kanga had left the Royal Academy in 1966 after doing two years in the senior classes. 'I had a job in a ballet company for a while and then I went freelance,' recalls Kanga. 'I met a contractor or fixer who my father worked for, as he was a session violinist, and he fixed things like the Bee Gees tours, and so, by 1968, I went on European and UK tours with them.' After going out on tour with the Bee Gees, David Katz, the album's orchestra contractor, called Kanga and asked her to go to Trident Studios in Soho. It is where she met her old friend Paul Buckmaster, who used to play the cello in the Saturday morning school at the Academy, and another session musician, pianist Pete Robinson, another friend from the Academy.

'Paul came in with this whole pile of music, which was a string overdub really and we were told to play it,' remembers Kanga. There weren't any headphones and so Kanga and the rest of the orchestra had little speakers next to them, through which the rhythm track and vocals was played, and the orchestra had to play along with the track. 'When he brought in this massive pile of music and said it was for Elton John, I looked at it and I thought "God". He said just play what you think, so my instinct for improvisation kicked in and I picked the bones out of the music.'

Kanga played entirely improvised solos on songs like 'Your Song' and 'Sixty Years On'. 'The concept was in the sheet music but the final product was essentially improvised. I remember recording "Your Song" and the music was so black it looked as if it needed some sorting out, and so what you hear from me is some improvising on what Buckmaster had written.

'I remember that the control room was upstairs and the studio was in the basement, and after one session this guy came down stairs and said to me, "Do you remember me, Skaila?" and I politely said "Yes", not really knowing who he was, and he said he had been in the harmony class at the Academy. He had changed his name and appearance to become Elton John. In the harmony class there had been a lot of tremendously bright people who had done good classical stuff, and now here was Reg, who was doing what he really wanted to do.'

Whereas *Empty Sky* was recorded quickly, the *Elton John* album was more organised and professionally produced and arranged. However, like *Empty Sky*, the cost of the album was becoming a factor because Dudgeon and Buckmaster were used to big budget albums. 'I remember Steve Brown being worried about the costs of the album,' recalled David Larkham, 'because the costs for orchestras and the backing vocalists that Dudgeon and Buckmaster had asked for would be pretty prohibitive for a then-unknown artist.'

He was also probably concerned about the album cover, but Larkham had some pretty original ideas for it when asked if he could do the artwork. 'Because the music was dark, and very melodramatic, I immediately thought of Rembrandt paintings and in particular those that were lit with a lantern from one side with a dark background and that was my vision of Elton for the cover of the album. The back cover was two shots joined together which was easy because of the black background.' Although, Larkham didn't take the shots, he directed the photo shoot, with an ideal freelance photographer that Brown had found. His name was David Bailey!

Although the concept for the cover was Larkham's idea, he had to get the agreement of Brown and Elton. This was painless though as Elton would accept most things that Brown suggested and so Elton didn't have that much involvement with it.

It was clear from the planning stages of the album that it was all going to be quite costly, especially as Dudgeon had abandoned any ideas he may have had about returning to Olympic Studios. His preference was to go to the more expensive, top of the range, Trident Studios in London's Soho. At the time, Trident was probably one of the most professionally advanced studios, or it was when compared to the studios at DJM. Trident were already using 24-track machines, and even though the control room could never be described as spacious, the advantage was the four huge playback monitors they had, instead of the usual two which most other studios were then using. There were no tape machines in the room, they were placed on the floor above, and Robin Geoffrey Cable spoke to the tape operator via an intercom.

Despite the projected cost, Brown somehow managed to persuade Dick James that a miracle was about to happen and secured the necessary £5,000 budget required to produce the album, which in those days was a large amount to spend on an unproven artist. The fact that James agreed shows he was still keeping faith with his young star in the making.

'I remember them coming back to us and playing us seven tracks,' recalls Stephen James, 'but we were expecting ten tracks. We thought it was really good, but he had run out of money to complete the album after only doing seven tracks, so we gave him some more money, and told him he had to complete the three other tracks and the album with that.'

Stuart Epps was tasked with getting the best session musicians who could read music and work with classical musicians, which included bringing in Barry Morgan on drums to replace Roger Pope. Like Pope, Morgan was also another accomplished drummer, but the advantage Morgan had over other drummers was that he could make his tom-tom drum sound more like an orchestral timpani, which was exactly the sound Dudgeon was looking for.

Although Morgan was reading the music chart given to him by Buckmaster, he mistakenly jumped a line and played a drum fill in the wrong place. Morgan knew what had happened but played on and was horrified when he later went to the control room to hear the track played back, but Dudgeon was not disappointed. In fact, he congratulated Morgan on a stroke of genius and refused any pleas from Morgan to re-do the take. As Dudgeon remarked at the time, it was this type of accident that can enhance a track. It was like breaking all the rules, but by doing so created something quite unique and original. Everything from Spanish guitar to harp to huge orchestral strings, was exactly as Dudgeon had imagined it and, in some places, far exceeded his expectations.

Although Brown was involved with production meetings, it was his assistant Epps who was responsible for booking musicians, studio time, backing vocalists, and instruments. 'Gus wanted big sounding backing vocals, so I just rang all of the best male and female singers, which included Roger Cook and Madeline Bell from Blue Mink. And on "Border Song", which was released as the lead single from the album, there was also a choir.'

Even if working with a choir was a new experience for Reg, working with Blue Mink wasn't. Over the years he had stepped in to help out on gigs and sessions whenever the band's keyboard player Keith Coulam wasn't available. Blue Mink had seven chart hits, mostly written by Cook and Greenaway, sometimes with co-writers such as Herbie Flowers or Hazlewood and Hammond. But it wasn't just Bell and Cook who would work on Reg's projects. The other Blue Minkers, drummer Barry Morgan and bassist Herbie Flowers would both go on to contribute to some of the early Elton albums, most notably on *Madman Across The Water*. More importantly, it was during his sessions with Blue Mink that Reg came across Ray Cooper, the band's drummer from 1972 onwards, who would later, more famously, become the percussionist for the Elton John Band from 1974 to 1976, and then again for the Single Man tour in 1978

The final recording session for the album took place in January 1970, and it was then time for mixing down. Buckmaster was present at all the mixing sessions, which were completed manually by Dudgeon, Cable and himself using phasers. 'The cellos on "Take Me To The Pilot" are flanged which was something I did myself by putting my thumbnail against one of the reels,' says Buckmaster. 'There is one little guitar phrase in "Your Song" that Gus loved so much that he pushed it up and I told him he was pushing it too far, but Gus replied that he thought it was a nice piece, and should stand out.'

Both the recording and mixing sometimes took all night, especially if there was a mistake; so it was long hours with lots of tea. 'The two guys who were apprentice engineers made the tea as well. We nicknamed them "Flood" and "Deluge" because of the amounts of tea they were making,' smiles Buckmaster. Dudgeon also liked to have the volume at ear-shattering level, which must have made the sound even more amazing. He was a complete perfectionist and the mixing sessions, although quick by later standards, took longer than any album the team had worked on before. The album, when finished, was cut in Trident's cutting room to the very highest standard, making sure that the volume cut into the vinyl was as loud as it could be without distortion or making the record jump.

Test pressings were meticulously checked over and over before they were passed for pressing. And Larkham was tasked to find the best quality card and print to use for the sleeve. He ended up choosing a grained effect card, similar to that used on Crosby, Stills & Nash's first self-titled album. Of course, like everything else on the album, it came at a price, which made it one of the most expensive sleeves at the time to produce.

One of the jobs that Epps was responsible for, he says, 'was to go through all the lyrics that would be reproduced on the inner sleeve, checking them against the recordings, as it was always possible that Reg wouldn't sing exactly what was written. It was quite a task, but one I simply saw as a pure labour of love.'

'When the album was finished,' says Buckmaster, 'everyone was knocked out with it and we were all asking each other "Did we really do that?"' And it wasn't only friends, acquaintances and those behind-the-scenes of the album who rated it. Dick James, too, was thrilled for his rising star. According to Sue Ayton, he arranged a launch party for Reg's 23rd birthday on 25 March. Reg played extracts from the new album to those invited from the press and then James presented him with a birthday present.

As with any new album, the promotion was one of the most important factors in making or breaking it. For Elton's new release, the idea was to spread the word as far and wide as possible. It was to include television advertising, and a sticker and poster campaign exclaiming 'ELTON WHO?' for the London Underground and buses. Point-of-sale displays were taken in all the major West End record shops, even though the album had not yet charted. In those days, as now, record stores were reluctant to stock anything other than chart stuff. So to help get the album into the shops, DJM staff were instructed to order as many copies of the album as they could, to improve the album's sales potential.

Although the album received a generally positive response from the British music press, sales were less than enthusiastic. 'When the *Elton John* album came out, I remember it had wonderful reviews,' confirms Ray Williams. 'We promoted the album excessively, and I even managed to get overseas TV interested, which, of course, got it released all over Europe, and we started to get shows in Scandinavia and Berlin. We filmed "Border Song" in Berlin for a TV show and we did another in

Belgium for a festival because the director loved the music of Elton and wanted to do a full programme on him. The programme was entered for an award and it won. Most of the promotion for the album was subliminal but it certainly set the ground work to build upon.'

Although 'Border Song' was the lead single from the album prior to its release in March 1970, 'Your Song' was, of course, the breakthrough hit. Strangely enough, it wasn't considered commercial enough to be the first single; 'Border Song' was always considered the stronger of the two. 'We all liked its soulful content,' recalled Epps, 'You could imagine Aretha Franklin singing it, or Ray Charles, and because these were Reg's favourite singers, it seemed a good choice.'

It also helped the general feeling that the right choice had been made when *Top Of The Pops* asked Reg, now Elton, to come onto the programme and perform it. 'Obviously everyone, including Reg, was over the moon,' continues Epps. 'The sales of the single hadn't been great to that point so this, we were all convinced, would surely send it soaring up the charts. And with the album already scheduled to follow, it seemed perfect.' Epps booked the band and backing singers and, with some newly-bought stage gear from Carnaby Street, everything was set to roll.

'In those days you sometimes had to record the track again at the BBC studio instead of using a backing track, and I think that is what happened. Whatever the *Top Of The Pops* broadcast was like, I can't remember, but the fact is there was no or very little change in the sales figures in the days that followed, so it was all very disappointing.'

Long before the single or album had been released, Elton and Hookfoot were back in Trident recording the next album, *Tumbleweed Connection*. Once again, the sessions would bring Buckmaster back into the fold to take care of the arrangements, which when combined with Elton and Hookfoot's raw and improvised tracks were, according to *Rolling Stone's* Jon Landau, exceptionally good. Certainly Buckmaster was responsible for creating the effective atmosphere on 'Burn Down The Mission' by using the same formula as he had used for the previous album, while other songs like 'Ballad Of A Well Known Gun' and 'My Father's Gun' were basically live studio tracks that featured just Elton and Hookfoot.

In a way, it marked a return to the sound of the *Empty Sky* album; more rock, less orchestral. Glover recalls:

> Reg was at DJM in the same part of the building that Hookfoot were working in, and that's where we met him. He would be wandering into the studio to see what was happening and heard us. He was quite busy by then, but the first time I really recall meeting him was at Trident Studios where we rehearsed the numbers after he had written them. He would come in with his songs then write down the chords for us, and we just rehearsed then and there in the studio. He would then play the piano and we would listen. I preferred to write down the chords and then just play with him. We only recorded when he was happy with everything. It all seemed very easy and relaxed. Gus

Dudgeon was a confident producer; he never changed anything that I know of, but most of his skill was in the sound he produced through engineering. The sessions took over three days of afternoons and evenings, and the final recording would normally be the second or third take.

We used to go into the studio and then go off to The Ship pub with Elton and have a few beers and then go back. He was a funny guy, friendly and a good laugh. We all got on very well, and it did not feel like we were recording or rehearsing in a studio, it was more like a rehearsal in a rehearsal room. Caleb had recorded with Elton before me but *Tumbleweed* was the first recording session I did with Elton. At Trident we did about half the tracks on *Tumbleweed* and then we played these at BBC sessions to promote the album. Bernie was always in the background but he was very quiet and skulked around.

David Larkham agrees. 'They had lots of songs ready, which were based much more on Bernie Taupin's sepia-tinged view of the American West. The album happened much quicker than the previous one, because the professional team was together by then. And by the time it came for me to do the album sleeve, I had struck up a bond with Bernie, so really my idea for the cover, was a vision I got from something he said about *Tumbleweed Connection,* and it made me immediately think of a run-down American West railway station, so I managed to find the ideal place to do a photo shoot. It was a small railway line in Sussex, somewhere on the Bluebell Railway.'

Once again, Steve Brown managed to persuade Dick James to cough up a budget to cover the cost of the special packaging that Larkham had in mind. At the time, single album covers were the norm, usually printed on card and laminated in a clarifoil finish, but Larkham had other ideas. 'I wanted a grained card that kind of had an Old West sort of look, and I wanted to produce it as a gatefold sleeve, with a booklet and lyrics, which back then, for a still emergent recording artist was pretty much unheard of, and especially one who yet had to gain the exposure to warrant such elaborate packaging. And remember, all this, the songs, the recording, the sleeve and all the associated artwork, was all done before the *Elton John* album was even released, and before the Troubadour trip that would establish Reg as a fully fledged rock star, so it was a pretty big deal to get DJM to agree to it.'

Indeed, two months after the release of *Elton John*, and following the ill-fated 'Border Song' single, another single was put out under the title of 'Rock And Roll Madonna'. 'It really didn't do very much at all, commercially, but it did show yet another side to Elton's versatility in writing,' says Epps. 'It was also Gus having a bit of fun.' The track was made to sound as if it had been recorded live in front of an audience, but the audience was actually 'borrowed' from a recording that came from a Jimi Hendrix gig at the Royal Albert Hall. Subliminally, it reminded record buyers that Elton John was a live performance artist as much as a studio one.

Although the *Elton John* album struggled to make much of an impact on the British album chart, despite the hard work of DJM's staff with promotion, it did end up with some reasonable reviews in the popular music press and, despite a poor sales performance, Dick James was still prepared to put his hand in his pocket. Many artists faced with the disappointment of poor album and singles sales might have gone into despair, but as Stuart Epps says: 'He is probably the most determined person I have ever met. His energy for succeeding in whatever he attempts to do is very high, and it was quite easy to spot how he used his energy to good effect, whether he was on stage in front of a difficult audience, or playing a bad game of table tennis.'

Not even the poor sales, however, seemed to deter Dick, NEMs or Vic Lewis in their interest for him, explains Ray Williams. 'He was getting good reviews for the *Elton John* album; there had been good press all across Europe, and he was picking up gigs in Britain, so it was far from bad news.' And even more intriguing was how Vic Lewis seemed to change his outlook on Elton. He suddenly went from being sceptical about the whole thing to become much more interested. And if that wasn't enough to convince Reg that he was finally making headway, then perhaps the agency agreement that Lewis set up with DJM and NEMs would be.

**II III**

Although the *Elton John* album didn't score well in the British charts, in America it was about to get an unexpected boost courtesy of Uni Records, part of the massive MCA group. This was actually down to luck more than judgment, which is often the way things pan out in the haywire world of the record business. Or, maybe it was less luck and more a case of 'it's not what you know, it's who you know'.

Elton stalwart Roger Greenaway was a regular visitor to the States and whilst on a trip there met with Lennie Hodes, DJM's US representative, in New York. They were both going to LA so took the same flight and the pair booked in at rock'n'roll central – the Hyatt House hotel. In a place like that you never know who you are going to bump into, and they hit pay dirt, as far as an unsuspecting Elton was concerned, when they bumped into Russ Regan, head of Uni Records.

The problem that Hodes, and by proxy Greenaway, faced was that Bell Records was DJM's distributor in the States and Bell boss Larry Uttal had politely passed on *Empty Sky* (it wasn't released in America until 1975 when Elton was a superstar), so was unlikely to take a punt on the next album. With no distribution deal in America, they pitched Regan the idea of distributing Elton John. Here, in full, is his account:

> Roger Greenaway and I were at the Hyatt House hotel in Los Angeles, where we used to have breakfast, when Roger was in town. Lennie Hodes from DJM came over and told me he had something for me. He rushed upstairs to his room and brought me a brown manila envelope with some records and tapes and stuff in it, and said 'You're gonna love this guy, he's great, he sounds a bit like José Feliciano, and

you're gonna get it.' Hodes went on to explain that Bell Records had just released Elton John from his contract with them, and Hodes was looking for somewhere else to place him.

I asked him what his name was and he said Elton John. Roger Greenaway then said Elton John was going to be a star, which coming from Roger must have meant something. By this time, Reg had been turned down by five record companies. I said, 'Lennie, why are you giving me this?' and he repeated again that 'You are going to get it, Russ', so I took the package back to my office and I left it there. At about 5.30p.m. when the telephone stopped ringing, I decided I was going to listen to this stuff; it had 'Empty Sky', 'Lady Samantha' and some other tapes like 'Border Song' in it, and so I played them, and I thought, what is wrong here? This is good.

I called Lennie at the Hyatt and asked him what the deal was on this guy, because I liked what I heard. Hodes was excited, and said 'I knew you'd like him.' I repeated, 'What's the deal with DJM?' and he said 'Russ, if you like him, you can have him for nothing.' So, to my surprise I got Elton John for no money.

He was signed to Universal for three years on the subsidiary Congress label. Now Regan had Neil Diamond on Uni and Elton John on Congress. Dick James then arranged a deal with Uni in the USA through Regan and Mike Maitland, who was head of Uni. 'I got him a deal with MCA in America,' raved Stephen James. 'And, as we were keen to break him in the States, Russ came up with the idea of bringing him over as a support act at the Troubadour in Los Angeles.'

'We put out "Lady Samantha", and it made a minor impact, so we then released "Border Song" and that was a small hit in Memphis, Tennessee, and across the South,' continues Regan. After only having a minor impact on the American charts, Regan decided to close Congress and put Elton with Neil Diamond on the Uni label. At the same time, DJM sent Regan the next Elton John album release after *Empty Sky*.

'I got an album in the post called *Elton John*, and I listened to it, and thought "Oh My God, thank you, thank you!" I closed the record company down for about an hour and a half and got everyone in to listen to it; it was just a brilliant piece of work.' Excited by the prospect of the new album, Regan dreamed up the idea to bring Elton over to America for a promotional tour.

Regan wasn't just any old run of the mill American music mogul. This is the man who suggested a small group from California called the Pendletones change their name to the Beach Boys. He was also responsible for assisting the careers of Barry White and Neil Diamond, amongst others, so he knew his onions and if he was raving about Elton John, it is fair to assume there was something worth raving about.

With a new American recording deal in place, it was now more important than ever that Elton be heard by fans in the States. Regan arranged for him to play at the Troubadour Club in Los Angeles but, before that happened, Ray Williams felt it was equally important to grab Elton some exposure in Britain and for him to become familiar with a new band, instead of Hookfoot. It was also important that Elton play only his own material.

'Due to my association with NEMs, through Tony Howard and Neil Warnock we started trying to get some gigs for Elton,' recalled Williams. 'Elton needed a band so we engaged Nigel Olsson and Dee Murray to join him and got some gigs in the UK. Elton started rehearsing for the UK tour put together by Williams to promote the *Elton John* album. The rehearsals were to become the catalyst for the early Elton John Band and were held at DJM Studios. Elton had chosen musicians he knew in Olsson on drums and Murray on bass.

It was clear that Reg was upset that he couldn't team up with Hookfoot for his first tour and he expressed that disappointment to Danny Hutton. Hutton received a letter and a package on 29 November 1969 from Reg that contained a lot of demos. (He later sent him another package containing the demo of 'Bad Side Of The Moon' that he had played to Hutton in London). 'The letter accompanying the package said that he [Elton] was planning to come to the US for a promotion tour,' recalled Hutton.'I really liked the demos and I played them to a good friend of mine, Doug Weston, who owned a club called the Troubadour. At the time, the Troubadour was the premiere showcase club and the first Los Angeles folk club to go electric. All of the hot new musical people who were arriving in town would hang out at the bar and it was where many famous acts were conceived. Doug was equally impressed and I suggested that he should get Elton to play his club.'

Of the songs Reg sent to Hutton, Three Dog Night recorded two. The first was 'Lady Samantha' for their second album *Suitable For Framing* and 'Your Song' for the third album *It Ain't Easy*. 'Reg was disappointed that the band he was working with [Hookfoot] had now signed to Chess Records, and that he had wasted seven months, so he was having to rethink his musical aims. He wanted to concentrate on writing and producing more demos of his own compositions, which was proving difficult, but he was determined not to sell out and write crap. He also went on to say that 'Lady Samantha' had earned him enough money to cancel out his royalty advance,' says Hutton.

The Congress label signed Elton in early May of 1970 and promptly re-released 'Lady Samantha' in the States before he embarked on his promotional tour of the UK. 'Lady Samantha' didn't do any better than the DJM release and so the label put out 'Border Song' from the *Elton John* album. Unfortunately this song also sank without trace having had a few airplays but little else. Regan had a great deal of faith in his new signing and, through his sales force, arranged for a series of promotional opportunities with the local radio stations to drum up support for Elton, giving DJs DJM copies of the *Elton John* album prior to its release in the USA on Uni in July 1970. The DJM album sparked a considerable interest in Elton John and 'Border Song' was reissued on Uni and got positive reviews thus paving the way for Elton's US tour.

Whilst Elton was on his UK promotional tour culminating in his appearance at the Krumlin Festival, Russ Regan and his colleagues at MCA were putting together a series of coast to coast promo appearances for Elton in the USA, which comprised of luncheon and dinner events for a selected audience from the press, radio and television. The strategy was to give Elton John and other selected artists the opportunity to break into the difficult playlist schedules of the Top 40 radio and television stations across the US.

The opening live appearance would be in Los Angeles at the Troubadour Club with Elton's hero David Ackles on the bill followed by an appearance at the Playboy Club in New York. Journalists from all over the North East would be invited to the latter including representatives of *The Ed Sullivan Show*, *The Tonight Show*, *The David Frost Show* and *The Griffin Show*: in other words, some heavy hitters. Local college media students were also invited to encourage the college scene to buy the records.

On the Playboy bill, in New York, with Elton were the McKendree Spring and Ken Lyons. All the attendees were given a copy of the *Elton John* album and the feedback was positive with promises that the album would be played on the relevant stations. The next stop was San Francisco, to another of Doug Weston's Troubadour Clubs, with the finale at the Electric Factory in Philadelphia on 11 September 1970 where the promotional effort was primarily focussed on the college market.

## ▌▌▐▐

At the time of agreeing to fund the *Elton John* album, DJM had made it clear to Reg that his career was on a knife edge. James was not going to continue to bankroll albums, singles and tours with very little return financially. Reg continued his heavy schedule of session work while being continually on the lookout for other avenues in the music business. He was also amenable to joining a band, even though he was about to embark on a tour as Elton John. 'Reg came down to Andover to rehearse with Hookfoot,' recalled Phil Greenfield. 'and then he got the call to go to the States and that was it.

'At that point in time we were just rehearsing and he was considering working with Hookfoot. He felt that he wouldn't be in charge of his own destiny if he teamed up with Caleb as Caleb was a strong character, I knew there were a lot of discussions going on at the time about Elton playing keyboards in Hookfoot, but I didn't really listen in on those sorts of things, and I just carried on doing what I was asked to do'

Although Caleb was one of the first people to recognise Elton's talent, they were both strong personalities and any further working together would probably have led to clashes. Also Hookfoot had a record deal and Caleb wasn't keen on them getting known as Elton's backing band. He had his own dream to follow and so their split, at least gigging wise, was inevitable.

However, the formation of the very unique sounding trio of Elton, Murray and Olsson with, unusually, no guitar, would actually help take Elton to the very top of the rock tree.

'I can very vividly remember walking into the studio when they were rehearsing,' recalled Epps, ' and at first being a bit disappointed there was no Caleb and his roaring guitar and no Popey [Roger Pope] on drums. This was quickly forgotten when I heard the new trio playing something like "Sixty Years On" from the *Elton John* album.

'Dee Murray was the bass player with the Mirage and was known for playing amazing bass chords, I had never seen this before on a bass and it created a huge sound,' enthused Epps. 'Nigel Olsson had been playing in the pop band Plastic Penny and had a massive drum kit, soon to get bigger. He was playing brilliant solid rock.' It wasn't easy in the early days to amplify a grand piano or even to make sure a good one was available at the gig. Elton's style and technique though sounded amazing with this line up and, without guitar, had plenty of space to come through. 'It was great to hear the orchestral tracks from the album turned into these huge rock tracks,' Epps recalls fondly.

The first gig that the trio played was at the Revolution Club at the end of March 1970. This started out like a fairly normal gig, not too dissimilar to what Epps had seen during rehearsals. The audience were receptive to what Elton and the band were doing and towards the end of the gig, Elton was playing a new song 'Burn Down The Mission' and then went into a rock'n'roll medley. 'He suddenly stood up from the piano stool and stopped playing, got a tambourine and was whacking it on his bum,' laughs Epps, 'I was feeling very uncomfortable now and a bit embarrassed to be honest, I thought, what *is* he doing, he's going to blow it!'

As Epps looked round at the audience he could see they were getting into it and the atmosphere was changing. Elton had lifted the crowd to another level and he had them eating out of his hand. He was getting them to clap along and this bit of showmanship was really working. 'When he went back to the piano to join the band, the concert was at another pitch atmosphere wise, roaring in fact,' says Epps.

'Between the three of them they could make the show quite dramatic,' agrees David Larkham. 'Elton had this other side to him; he always told his mother he was going to be a star and she would constantly ask Caleb to calm him down.' In reality, Reg was a shy, almost introvert person and he knew that if he was seen as a bashful musician then his career would inevitably suffer. 'He had a whole different personality inside of him and that's what came out in the trio when they played live,' stresses Larkham. 'He could rock with the best of them and was very Leon Russell-based in his piano playing style. The kicking of the piano stool to one side and standing up was evidence of this emerging personality on stage, which evolved into handstands on the piano as he played and as his confidence grew.'

The fifteen date UK Elton John tour took him to venues like the famous Roundhouse in London's Chalk Farm, which had its own resident DJ, Jeff Dexter – a regular feature at DJM where he cut acetates. Jeff went on to manage the band America. They also played the Marquee, the Country Club, the Lyceum, the Speakeasy and more, but wherever they went, Elton wanted the audience on their feet at the end of the gig, not just clapping politely in their seats.

'It's hard to expect an audience to go berserk over songs they've never heard before,' reasons Epps, 'and up to this point Elton hadn't really written many rock songs where you could get this sort of audience participation. So, adding a few classic rock covers was the way to do it.' Elton knew this was risky and that he could fall flat on his face if it didn't work, but it was a gamble he was prepared to take. 'He was willing to take the risk to make the show great, not average,' insists Epps. 'In my opinion that was what separated Elton from the folk rock artists of the time like James Taylor, Cat Stevens, Jackson Browne, or Neil Young.

The Speakeasy in London was owned by the notorious Kray Twins, but managed by Laurie O'Leary, who was very down to earth. 'I asked him whether he could get a concert tuned piano for Elton's gig as at most places the pianos were almost always out of tune and had been badly treated,' recalled Ray Williams. 'Laurie said "You must be fucking joking". However I was very friendly with Laurie and we got along well and when Elton turned up for the gig, he had this multi-coloured concert tuned piano. My energy levels were at a high back then and I covered a lot of ground getting people to do things that were helpful to Elton's career; after all if he was successful then so was I.'

One of the last gigs that Elton played in the UK before going to the USA was the ill-fated and much maligned Krumlin Festival in Yorkshire. The gig was in a field in a dip and wasn't a particularly well organised affair. For instance, Pink Floyd were advertised as the headliners, but they didn't appear and some suggested that they were never booked in the first place. The Move were not on the bill but they turned up in their van anyway, only to get stuck in the mud bath as a result of the torrents of rain hitting the small narrow lane leading to the stage – so they didn't move, or play. Manfred Mann suffered the same fate as the Move.

The show was due to start on Friday at 3p.m. but was delayed until 7.45p.m. because of disagreements over the billing and the weather. All in all it was not a pleasant time for the 2,000 strong audience; it was cold, wet and basically miserable for bands and punters alike.

Elton John, Olsson and Murray appeared early evening at about 8p.m. to a torrent of rain and a cold and wet audience. After about three numbers, Elton realised that he couldn't do slow stuff because of the weather, which was affecting the morale of the audience; he needed to do fast songs to rock the place out and he did. 'He was doing one or two Rolling Stones numbers, as he realised he needed to keep the crowd warm,' recalled Chris Charlesworth, then a journalist for *Melody Maker*. 'Towards the end of the show he got some bottles of brandy and plastic cups and said, "If you're cold come and have some brandy". This went down really well and I was really taken with him; this guy was really trying hard under difficult conditions to cheer everyone up.'

At the start of the festival Elton John was largely unknown to the audience. By the end he was hailed as one of the highlights. 'After his set I went backstage,' recalled Charlesworth. 'I didn't know what his songs were called; I knew one was called "Border Song" and another was "Lady Samantha" and he probably played "Your Song" but

I didn't know them at the time. He was in a caravan getting changed and relaxing, because he was energetic on stage. I knocked on the door and someone answered and I told them I was from *Melody Maker* and asked to speak with Elton. Elton overheard and said if it was really someone from *Melody Maker* then let them in. I told him that it was a real cracker of a show and asked him about his songs; "Take Me To The Pilot", "Your Song", and the others and so he clued me in on the songs. I remember Sandy Denny, from Fairport Convention, was in the caravan and we all chatted.'

The next day Charlesworth drove back to London and wrote his piece on the Krumlin Festival and reported that the shining light was a newcomer called Elton John, a keyboard player, who was making his festival debut. 'I said I think we are going to be hearing a lot of this man in the near future, he was fantastic,' Charlesworth remembers. The article came out and the following week, Elton's publicist Helen Walters called Charlesworth and thanked him for the article and told him that Elton was really thrilled.

Walters asked if Charlesworth wanted to meet him again; he agreed and did an interview. 'Suddenly, and within the next two months, it all started happening for Elton John so I had just caught him before all that.' In fact, Charlesworth's advocacy for Elton played a part too, of course, as *Melody Maker* was a very influential publication.

The later press statements about the Krumlin Festival recalled that Elton John was the star of Friday night. 'He went through his songs with the professionalism of a veteran.' Both Nigel Olsson and Dee Murray worked extremely hard, with Nigel breaking at least a dozen sticks and Dee playing chords on his bass guitar.'

One journalist commented that 'A man next to me said he thought Elton was a "White Aretha Franklin", playing songs like 'Border Song', (the man thought it was called 'Holy Moses'), and 'Sixty Years On'. Both songs had the whole field clapping and cheering for more and more, especially when he played the Rolling Stones, "Honky Tonk Women".' Elton cheekily shouted to the crowd when he finished the set, 'I hope this dispels the myth that I am Radio 1 Club and the Tony Blackburn Show' before returning to do a much-deserved encore. When he finally left the stage it was to cheers echoing across the freezing cold and rainy Yorkshire Moors.

The festival was a washout after the Friday and so none of the bands appeared on Sunday because rain stopped play. This was probably of no concern to the young Reg Dwight; he had played a storming gig and made a name for himself. Now he was bound for warmer climes and bigger things.

# 17

# GOING TO CALIFORNIA

The pressure was on to get Elton some gigs in the USA, so Vic Lewis, who was now a believer, used his influence with Chartwell Artists in the USA, (owned by Jerry Perenchio) to get gigs for Elton. 'The New York agent offered a gig in New York for $50 and I remember talking with him by telex and saying "you must be joking",' laughs Ray Williams. At the instigation of Danny Hutton, Jerry Heller then called from Los Angeles and offered a gig at the Troubadour for $175 which increased to $200 after some negotiations with the venue's owner Doug Weston.

'We went back to Dick James and said we now needed the money to go out on the road and do the Troubadour,' says Williams. 'I had already been to Dick for money for the UK tour and he had given me £1200 for all the equipment we used, so I was not too sure how Dick would take to being asked for considerably more to take Elton to Los Angeles. However he agreed to everything.' This was possibly because of Vic Lewis' interest and James trusted him.

'It was about this time when I started to see a change in Elton's temperament,' Williams believes. 'I remember us sitting with him talking about him doing a radio programme that would give him more exposure in the UK. We asked him to do it and he just shouted "I'm not doing it, I'm not fucking doing it!" and walked out and slammed the door. It came as a shock to us all but we put it down to the pressure he was now under.'

After the success (and rain) of the Krumlin Festival, the Elton John Band along with Ray Williams went off to sunny Los Angeles on the newly-developed plane, the Boeing 747. The band was now confident after some impressive reviews following the short UK tour. In an interview with the press at the time Elton stated that: 'It's a real band now, and the boys have helped me a lot. It's so tight now, but in a year's time it'll be unbelievable, and I don't even have to tell them what to do, because we all know what we're doing. There are some songs with very broken rhythms, but they just play them without having it explained to them.'

'When we arrived at LA airport we were greeted by a public relations guy called Norman 'Norm' Winter from Uni, (wearing a ten gallon hat), and his assistant Barbara,' recalled Williams. 'We couldn't believe it but he had arranged for a red London bus to pick us up at the airport.' On the side of the bus in great big letters it said something like, 'Elton Arrives In LA.' So they drove from LAX airport to the hotel in a London bus, which was not ideal after a long journey from the UK when everyone was tired. David Larkham remembers it all very well:

> It was very exciting. To me it was a novelty to go to America and be part of the entourage that was to play at the Troubadour. The others had jobs to do but to me it was a holiday and so I had taken my camera. Nigel and Dee had been part of Plastic Penny and Spencer Davis and they had been to the States before, and so had Ray Williams, but for Elton, Bernie and me it was the first time. Elton would have preferred to have been picked up by a limousine; to come from London to be met by a London bus was a bit of a letdown to him. The atmosphere on the bus for Bernie and I was fantastic; being fascinated by America we were looking at the cars and the sights, taking everything in like normal tourists.
>
> For the business people, they got down to organising what was going to happen straight away; access to the venue, sound checks, DJ interviews, etc. It was a double decker [bus] with different conversations going on the different levels. My memory is that Bernie remained very quiet during the LA trip. He was a convivial bloke with a sense of humour but like us all he loved music. Me and Bernie shared this American fascination. All along the route from LA airport to the Hotel, Bernie and I were commenting on the size of the cars, the outrageous architecture and I remember seeing a doughnut stand whose roof was a 40' doughnut; for fans of Americana we had arrived at the right place.

'We stayed in a hotel on Sunset Boulevard called the Hyatt House and we took a few days off to recover from the journey. The gig was due to start the following week, so we had a weekend to spare,' Williams recounts.

'During check in at the Hyatt House Elton decided to use the name William A Bong, such was his sense of humour. In fact throughout the brief stay at the Hyatt he would regularly play games on the hotel staff. On one occasion when he was in the foyer he went over to the person at the reception desk and a little while later there was an announcement paging "Mike Hunt" [Hopefully, I don't need to explain this juvenile reference!],' Larkham chortles.

When they had all checked in and unpacked, Williams realised that someone needed a hairdryer so he called an old girlfriend and got her younger sister, Janice. She brought the hairdryer over to the hotel with her friend, Maxine Feibelman. The next day Ray Williams suggested that the entourage, including Elton, go out for the day and relax in Palm Springs. The two young girls, who had been introduced to the boys the previous day, were invited along by Williams.

'I went back to the hotel to tell the others that we were going to Palm Springs to have some fun and they were all up for it. This is when the dynamic between

Elton and me started to change. I always considered Elton more as a friend than a business interest. I told Elton that we were going to Palm Springs and he said he didn't want to go. He was probably getting nervous about the gig. So I said we'd go without him and we did. We had a fabulous time and the result was that Bernie met and eventually married Maxine, and Janice met and eventually married David Larkham.'

'We all went out for the day,' Larkham recollects. 'We drove to Palm Springs in the morning, had a few beers. We were taken to the edge of the desert and then we drove back to LA. From this first brief introduction there was an attraction between Maxine and Bernie, which added to Bernie's attraction for the States,' Larkham remembers. 'It wasn't obvious at first but it became so very soon after.' According to Larkham, in 1970 California girls were a new concept to innocent boys from the UK. 'Janice and Maxine acted like they were your mates and went along to Palm Springs without any problem. They were more natural and were happy to have a few beers with the boys, which the average English lady in 1969/1970 would not do; it was more of a free and easy lifestyle and attitude.'

Not so easy was what awaited them on their return. 'When we got back to LA from Palm Springs, Elton was in a bad mood and basically he had become homesick when we were away,' Williams admits. 'He was shouting at Ray and not very happy at all that we had left him,' shudders Larkham.

At breakfast the next morning he told me he was not doing the gig and he was going home, so we had a big row and he stormed off. Later I went to the swimming pool at the Hyatt and Elton and I made up and it was cemented by him pushing me into the swimming pool. We agreed that Elton would stay in LA, the band would rehearse and we would start doing the gigs at the Troubadour.'

Roger Greenaway saw the situation a little differently to Ray Williams. 'I went back to LA with Reg and Bernie and we stayed just around the corner from the offices of Universal, at the Hyatt House Hotel which was owned by Roy Rogers at the time. Ray Williams made himself scarce after the second day, which Elton got angry with him about because he wanted Ray to be there all the time.'

It is easy to understand how Elton must have felt. He was a long way from home, had a possibly career-defining set of gigs lined up and was looking for support from those around him. After all, this was a business trip not a vacation and, as we have seen, Elton took work very seriously.

According to Greenaway, Elton was very relaxed during the lead up to the Troubadour gig and used to hang out and eat with Greenaway at the hotel restaurant. The rehearsals went well and Elton was in good spirits, even interrupting once to ask Greenaway if he had any requests to which Greenaway replied 'Yes. "Gimme Dat Ding".'

On August 26, Elton and the band played the first of a week of now legendary concerts at the Troubadour Club in West Hollywood working with David Ackles, which was a bonus in itself for Elton.

'The opening night at the Troubadour was a brilliant occasion for Elton and the rest of us,' recalled Williams. 'Russ Regan and Norm Winter did a marvellous job getting so many prominent people to turn up'. During the gigs at the Troubadour, and in spite of the wealth of talent in the audience, Elton appeared to have iced water flowing in his veins: he must have been nervous but it didn't show. 'On stage he was totally in command; even at the beginning he knew what he was doing and was a great performer,' says Greenaway. 'The stars respected his music and he had a style of piano playing which was unheard of in America at the time.'

'Elton's favourite musician Leon Russell turned up,' Williams remembers, 'and so did Quincy Jones and his family and so many others.' On Leon Russell's visit to see him play, Elton told the press the following day that, 'He's my idol as far as piano playing is concerned, and there he was sitting in the front row. My legs turned to jelly ... I mean, to compare my playing with him is sacrilege. He'd eat me for breakfast.'

It was also an exciting time for Bernie in more ways than one. Not only was he going to have his words sung to an audience of stars and his musical peers, but he had met his future wife Maxine. 'Maxine and Janice were invited to the gigs at the Troubadour and this was the grounding for the romance between Bernie and Maxine,' Larkham intimates.

Elton came on, having been introduced by his Uni stable mate Neil Diamond, who had enjoyed the new *Elton John* album. The stage, with just piano, drums and bass guitar, must have looked a little sparse to an audience who may have been expecting a larger band and a formal show from a reserved English folk singer. Elton came on sporting a beard, dressed in jeans and a T-shirt and did his show, and what the audience got was something completely different from the sedate folk singer they probably expected.

Hutton was there with Brian Wilson and they were both joined later by Randy Newman. The atmosphere was electric and there was an air of expectation. Everyone knew that something special was going to happen. Elton was already well prepared for the gig having played some dates with his new band of Nigel Olsson and Dee Murray in the UK. For the next one and a half hours, expectations were realised and Elton's performance and songs went down a storm.

'There was a newness about his music,' recalled Hutton. 'He had a bluesy voice but it was English, it was classical but with rock'n'roll. Along with Bernie he had the full package; the song writing, the playing, the vocal ability and the performance.'

'After the first couple of nights at the Troubadour you knew something was happening,' affirms Larkham. 'People were beginning to talk about him and his records were being played on the radio and his showmanship really won them over.'

MCA Records took the entourage out during a rest day to Disneyland. 'We didn't have to queue up and even then the people who were there were saying "That's Elton

John" such was the immediacy of the buzz around his performance,' Larkham says. 'I was at the front of the stage taking photographs at most of the gigs and there was definitely an excited buzz about the place. It was only a small stage and it was near the end of the set when Elton would kick away his piano stool and I remember it almost hitting me. By this time he was also doing his handstands on the piano and the atmosphere was electric; people were on their feet applauding before he had even finished his final song. You don't get that sort of reception from a showbiz audience, as they are famous for being cynical. If he had been a dud, there would have been a bit of clapping and murmuring and some sidling to the bar and that sort of thing, but there wasn't.'

After the gig the showbiz luminaries were going in and out of the dressing room backstage wanting to shake hands with a new star. 'Neil Diamond was backstage anyway as he was asked to introduce Elton to the audience,' Larkham states, 'But I do remember Quincy Jones coming backstage and Elton introducing Bernie to him, and Bernie saying a brief hello before sidling off somewhere quickly. I remember Elton taking Bernie aside afterwards and saying "Look that was Quincy Jones you just met; if we are going to make it you need to make an effort here."'

Bernie was barely out of his teenage years and Elton had been on the periphery of the music business for most of his life, but he knew he was always going to be a star, therefore he knew what he had to do

The net result was that the *LA Times* said of the Troubadour shows: 'A Star Has Been Born'. Robert Hilburn, the respected critic from the paper, produced an ecstatic review exclaiming that Elton was the future and was a star. There was a real music business buzz and the album sales picked up. Uni wised up that they had a star on their hands and that was it: Elton John was on his way.

'After the success of the Troubadour I was on my way to LAX airport when I heard the local rock station DJ in LA say that there was a new Messiah in town; his name is Elton John,' enthuses Greenaway. 'I almost fell out of the car and then he played some tracks from the *Elton John* album and I thought "He's cracked it". By the time I had got back to London they were in New York and by then the word had filtered down from LA that a star had been born and he went down a storm. He was right for America but at the time he was never going to make it in the UK,'

The gigs at the Troubadour were such a success that a Los Angeles radio station took a full-page ad in the *LA Free Press* to thank him for coming over. The reviews and the reaction from the press and audience alike was that Elton John was an original in that he had a diverse array of styles that could be delivered and executed with considerable power. The headlines made the British music audience sit up and take notice of this British artist who had been such a hit in the USA.

'I remember asking him how his trip to LA and the Troubadour went when he came back,' Inkpen reminisces. 'He said it was "Amazing and terrific and I got to meet Mae West, it was wonderful, and Jimmy Durante, and I got a signed photograph". No mention of the Troubadour gig, he was just fascinated by the celebrity. He sent me a card and it said something like: "Did the Troubadour, it went down a storm, best wishes, Reg".'

On the Friday night, the last night of the Troubadour gigs, Williams was asked to meet Doug Weston, who owned the club. Weston was a tall, gregarious man with a booming voice. He was full of life and enjoyed holding court in his upstairs lair at the club, especially after midnight and usually until dawn.

'Doug asked me to go to his office which was upstairs at the club to attend a meeting,' Williams recounts. The upstairs area was Weston's own private club which was decorated in sixties hippie chic by a carpenter called Freedom. On any given night you could meet anyone from the author Ray Bradbury to Miles Davis. 'All week I had been asked to sign the agreement that Doug had prepared, but I was concerned that it didn't resemble the agreement we had discussed with Chartwell, so I refused to sign it,' Williams says defiantly.

In Weston's contract was a clause that meant Elton would have to return to the Troubadour for other dates. 'In the end though, we agreed a deal which meant Elton would return the clause monies but he would do one return gig later.' Years later, Elton would return with his new band in a charity gig that he dubbed '5 Years Of Fun'. Such was Elton's success at that point that tickets could only be bought if the lucky fans succeeded in a ballot to buy them.

The following week Elton played at the San Francisco Troubadour and this was not such a positive experience, not at all like the LA gigs according to Williams. It was a Doug Weston show but it was more of a showcase for a few chosen people; early fans, DJs and opinion makers. 'By this time there was a buzz going round about Elton, but San Francisco was less of a big impact: it was more of an invited audience of journalists, DJs and MCA local people and friends and possibly some people from the street, invited by a radio station – so it didn't have the same opening night atmosphere as the LA Troubadour... but by the end of the show he still had them on their feet.'

The entourage then moved on to New York. 'We stayed in a Japanese style hotel,' remembers Larkham, 'and Maxine was there with Bernie. Elton did a showcase show and then we all went down to Philadelphia where Elton did a couple of shows in really well-known big venues. By Philadelphia it was people from the streets coming to watch and there was a buzz both on the East and West Coasts about Elton John and he was regularly on the radio. It was a genuine crowd who acted very honestly to a brilliant show; Philadelphia was very successful.'

'After the Troubadour gigs I went on the road with Elton and after LA we went to San Francisco and he did his thing at the Troubadour there; we then went to New York and to the Playboy Club,' Russ Regan relates. By this time, news of Elton's success had reached the DJM offices in the UK and Dick James decided to take a flight to New York and catch Elton's performance and congratulate him in person, such was his new found enthusiasm.

'The Playboy was a terrible place to put him and he was upset and I was upset.' recalled Regan. 'He just didn't do very well; we then took the train to Philadelphia because we were going to do the Electric Factory the next night.' Until this point Elton was mainly playing to music industry people and the press. In LA he was hailed a star but in San Francisco and New York he went down less well and especially in New York where he was not happy with the venue.

'We were at the hotel in Philadelphia and I had a suite and Elton was next door and we were having people coming over all the time,' Regan remembers. 'I used to order turkey club sandwiches, because you could cut them up and use them as finger food, and I'm ordering them at twenty at a time. I got a phone call from my office asking me what the hell was I doing, as someone had told them I was spending a lot of money.'

Having told the person at the office that he was on the road with Elton John and was going to make him a star, Regan recalled the now amusing response: 'He replied, "You know Russ, I hate to tell you this but do you know what they are calling you and your Brit? They're calling him fuckin' 'Regan's Folly'". I exploded, as I had a temper in those days, and called him every name in the book.' Regan went to Elton's room next door and told him what had happened. 'He looked at me and said "Russ, don't worry about it, tonight we are going to burn the city of Philadelphia down, (after 'Burn Down The Mission')", so I said "OK, fine" and so we went to the Electric Factory, that held about 2,000 kids, and Elton came on, and what a night,' enthuses Regan. 'The last song he did was "Burn Down The Mission": for 20 minutes; he was under the piano, on top of the piano, he was out in the audience. Nigel had a solo and it was electrifying. He got a standing ovation.'

Regan got to bed about 4.30a.m. and was awakened at 11a.m. by the MCA distributor for Uni Records. He said, 'Russ, I hate to wake you up but I had to call you, we have just had an order for 5,000 copies of the *Elton John* album, something's gone crazy here and the record stores are calling to get the album,' says a triumphant Regan. 'He asked me what happened the previous night at the gig and I told him about the Electric Factory, and he replied that whatever he did it was working. "We're getting calls from record shops like crazy."'

Regan hung up, satisfied that his perseverance with Elton had paid off, and went back to sleep only to be woken again at 1p.m. 'He woke me up again and said "I hate to do this to you again but I have to order another 5,000 albums,"' recalled Regan. Needless to say, the album went on to be a hit and to launch Elton's career across America. 'Everyone thinks he, (Elton), made it at the Troubadour in LA but he broke open properly in Philadelphia,' asserts Regan. 'Prior to that gig he was only playing to an industry crowd, it wasn't the public. In Philadelphia, it was the public and when the public likes you, the greatest thing that can happen to you is word of mouth, and it was incredible and it spread like wild fire.'

The US gigs were, as we have seen, the culmination of years of hard slog, touring around Europe, working on different numerous projects and having to deal with disappointment and frustration on the way. Now, however, the stage was set for the rise of Elton John.

# AFTERWORD

Nothing is forever and change is inevitable. Music publishing has not been immune to these truisms and the process is ongoing.

The mid-Sixties witnessed the beginning of major change in this sector, prompted by various economic pressures and an increasing interest in the music business and the value of copyrights from the City and the investment world. Affiliated Music Publishers, alluded to in the Preface of this book, was a combination of formerly independent companies such as Francis Day & Hunter, Robbins and Feldman, which EMI acquired in 1973.

This purchase greatly expanded EMI's hitherto modest involvement in music publishing, which began with Ardmore & Beechwood – headed by the gentlemanly Syd Coleman – to which was added the Keith Prowse and Central Songs catalogues in 1969. Now it is part of Sony/ATV Music while EMI Records has been swallowed up by Universal.

Independent publishers found it increasingly hard to exist as their world became more corporate in nature, rather than the family atmosphere which had largely characterised Denmark Street in the first half and middle of the 20th century. There had always been keen rivalry but mostly of a friendly kind. The amalgamation of companies into larger groups proved a painful experience for many of the individuals involved. Songwriters who often regarded their publishers as personal friends as well as business associates found themselves dealing with total strangers, usually of a younger generation, who knew little or nothing of their work and achievements and frequently made little effort to disguise their indifference and lack of interest.

Employees of the companies before the mergers found, for the most part, that they were surplus to the requirements of the new owners and with their departure went a large amount of knowledge and expertise concerning the catalogues involved.

'Big is beautiful' became the catch phrase and big also described the cheque books and financial resources of the new groupings. Surviving independent publishers were unable to compete in offering advances to new songwriting talent and artists. Veteran songwriters, often with several major hits to their credit in the past, felt uncomfortable at their new corporate homes and began to suspect, often with justification, that their songs were being ignored for continuing promotion and exploitation in favour of the new kids on the block.

Another growing problem, and shortcoming, as corporate catalogues swelled in size and numbers was the impossibility of exploiting individual songs which were not brand new. There have even been some instances of an oldie being revived for recording or use in a commercial by artists or advertising agencies without any prompting by the publisher, becoming successful again sometimes many years after its initial impact, and the current conglomerate publisher top management not noticing the documentation for its use until it appeared in the charts.

With the continuing decline in CD sales and the consequent slump in mechanical royalty income, synchronisation has become the name of the game for the music publishing fraternity. The major conglomerates and the surviving independents have departments devoted to licensing songs in advertising campaigns, feature movies or the thriving video games market. This is a means of ensuring useful additional exposure and sales success for new material or a renewed lease of profitable life for older repertoire.

A partial solution for the problem of these departments, being unaware of the full extent of the song repertoire at their fingertips, is the existence of several agencies specialising in sourcing suitable repertoire for specific projects staffed by people with extensive knowledge and familiarity with the various genres and able to trace the various copyright owners for sync permission.

Sampling is another activity which can generate significant revenue for publishers. It describes the process whereby artists and songwriters utilise several bars from someone else's song to incorporate in their own work, often to provide a memorable hook. It is a practice not universally applauded and there is a considerable school of thought that regards it as lifting from someone else's creativity to compensate for the inadequacy of one's own. However, if permission for the sampling is sought from the songwriter and publisher of the original and a deal is reached for a share of any resulting royalties, then no harm seems to be done.

John Fogarty and his team at Minder Music are particularly astute at detecting any sampling of their copyrights and have pursued unauthorised use as far as the courts on several successful occasions, including an action against Dr Dre for which they were awarded $1.5 million in damages.

Minder is one of several independent music publishers of various sizes successfully surviving in today's climate and continuing to fight the good fight. It was founded by Fogarty and his partner Beth Clough in 1985 and publishes what it terms as 'an eclectic mix' of copyrights ranging from an old 1920s music hall favourite, 'The Laughing Policeman' (still frequently used in commercials), through R&B classics to standards from the Fifties and Sixties from the Schroeder catalogue, recorded by Frank Sinatra, Gene Pitney, Bobby Vee, Elvis Presley and others. Minder has offices in South Africa, Australia, Italy, Scandinavia, Israel and Los Angeles.

Another independent family affair is Hornall Brothers Music, founded in 1996 by Stuart Hornall, his wife Janie and daughter Zoe, with a songwriting roster including Mark Knopfler, Graham Lyle, Paul Brady, Garth Brooks, Paul Overstreet and Joan Armatrading. Hornall worked for many years at Rondor Music, the UK arm of the Herb Alpert-Jerry Moss Almo Music enterprise, and is a prime example of a highly popular publisher often preferred to larger conglomerates because of his personal touch and involvement with his writers.

Andy Heath is an independent music publisher who has specialised in the alternative music field for most of his career and is noted for his long-term commitment to developing new talent and the adoption of new business initiatives. The younger son of the late Jack Heath, my original mentor in music publishing, he now runs 4AD Music within the Beggars [Banquet] Group of which he has been a director since 1991. He headed the Group's Momentum Music from 1987 until it was sold to Universal in 2001 and is co-founder and director of UK Music, the lobbying and educational organisation, as well as a past president of the Music Publishers Association.

Bucks Music Group is led by managing director Simon Platz, son of the late David Platz, who headed Essex Music at 4 Denmark Street and founded Bucks in 1967. He inherited his father's ear for musical talent and Bucks has continued the Essex tradition of signing and nurturing the best of new talent as well as maintaining momentum for its established songwriters and artists. Among the former are Professor Green, Blood Red Shoes and Amanda Ghost and among the latter are David Bowie, Carly Simon and Mick Jagger. Its roster of distinguished film and TV composers includes David Arnold and Nigel Hess.

Kobalt Music Group was founded in 2000 by Willard Ahrdritz with the emphasis on modern online global copyright administration, creative and synch/licensing services, digital collections, neighbouring rights management and pipeline advances to artists, writers, publishers, labels and other rights holders. It collects from 37 territories worldwide, administering more than 250,000 copyrights with offices in London, New York, Nashville, Los Angeles, Berlin, Sydney and Stockholm and agents in 20 territories. It offers a reduction in royalty collection time of up to 50% and more effective collection and transparency.

The Music Sales Group, headed by American-born Bob Wise, provides services in five main areas: music copyrights, printed music, music book publishing, music retail and digital publishing. Its copyrights span classical (Novello & Co, Chester Music, J Curwen & Sons, G Schirmer, Edition Wilhelm Hansen, United Musical Ediciones and Bosworth); popular (song catalogues stretching from the 1920s to the present day and including Campbell Connelly, Noel Gay, Sparta Florida Music Group and Bosworth & Co) and administering copyrights for various international publishing companies.

In third party licensing, Music Sales represents the printed music interests of the two giants, Universal Music and Sony/ATV Music, and peermusic, Andrew Lloyd Webber's The Really Useful Group, Imagem and Chrysalis amongst others. It also operates one of the world's largest hire libraries of mainly classical and public domain music plus theatrical music by Lord Andrew Lloyd Webber and Alain Boublil of *Les Misérables* fame.

Imagem Music Group was launched in 2008 by a large Dutch pension fund, Stichting Pensioenfunds ABP, in conjunction with a Dutch independent publisher and media company called CP Masters BV. It got off to a flying start by purchasing some catalogues divested by Universal as a condition of the latter's acquisition of BMG Music Publishing, imposed by the European Union. Included in a deal worth 140 million euros were the catalogues of Rondor, Zomba, 19 Music and BBC.

In the year of its foundation, Imagem also acquired for £126 million Boosey & Hawkes, a leading classical music publisher including the works of Benjamin Britten, Rachmaninov, Prokofiev, Steve Reich, Peter Maxwell Davies, Aaron Copland and Stravinsky. Another important acquisition is the Rodgers & Hammerstein Organisation, bringing the duo's top musicals such as *Oklahoma!*, *Carousel*, *South Pacific*, *The King and I* and *The Sound of Music* under the Imagem roof, which also now encompasses classic standards by Irving Berlin such as 'White Christmas', 'Easter Parade', 'Always', 'Blue Skies', 'Cheek to Cheek' and 'Isn't This a Lovely Day?'.

Imagem's pop/rock catalogue includes writers such as Phil Collins, Vampire Weekend, The Temper Trap, Daft Punk and Genesis and it has offices in London, Berlin, Brussels, New York, Los Angeles and Hilversum

As can be seen from the foregoing, there is still a healthy, if considerably reduced, independent music publishing sector existing alongside the giants of Universal, Sony/ATV Music and Warner/Chappell Music. They all face the same problems from the internet and the belief that music should be free, coupled with related attempts to erode if not eliminate the law of copyright, and a lingering reluctance by internet service providers to co-operate in establishing an effective prevention of illegal downloading.

As for Tin Pan Alley, the dispersal of the song firms began in the late Sixties. They were either amalgamated with their new owners based elsewhere or disappeared altogether. The last major music publisher to depart from Denmark Street was peermusic in 1992, situated at No.8 in an interwar building of vaguely Art Deco style. It had been in the Alley since the Thirties, mostly under the name of Southern Music, and had included a small recording studio. Formed in America in 1928 by Ralph S Peer and now with 35 offices in 28 countries around the world, it has thrived as an independent founded on the foresight of Peer, whose early field recordings gave birth to country music with recordings by pioneer acts such as the Carter Family and Jimmie Rodgers; jazz, with artists like Fats Waller, Louis Armstrong and Jelly Roll Morton and a large Latin American repertoire of music from Mexico, Brazil, Argentina and Cuba also initiated by the enterprise of Peer.

It is now headed by his son, Ralph Peer II, under the identity of peermusic with its UK office based in leafy Richmond upon Thames led by Nigel Elderton, who is also European president.

The future of Denmark Street is as uncertain as ever and threats of its disappearance, never greater than at the time of the 1960s Centre Point redevelopment, are never far away. The latest proposal applying for planning permission comes from Consolidated Developments and is for a new shopping and leisure destination including an 800-seat underground auditorium, gallery, hotel, restaurants, bars and offices.

We can only hope that Tin Pan Alley continues to survive as the scene of a remarkable era in British popular music and will not be destroyed and replaced by another towering edifice to continue the disfigurement of the London skyline.

*Nigel Hunter*

# INDEX

# ABOUT THE AUTHOR

**Keith Hayward** is a human resources specialist whose previous writing credits include a number of volumes on work practices, recruitment, employment, negotiation, equality and diversity. He is also a renowned music collector, expert and historian, who has met Elton John on several occasions and recently became Roger Pope's manager. *Tin Pan Alley: The Rise of Elton John* is his first book. He lives in West Sussex, England, and has travelled the world in his quest to document Elton's early life and career. He is currently working on a multi-media project, tentatively titled *2020 Vision*, with arranger, conductor and composer Martyn Ford.